Dreamweaver MX: PHP Web Development

Gareth Downes-Powell

Tim Green

Bruno Mairlot

© 2002 glasshaus

Published by glasshaus Ltd,
Arden House,
1102 Warwick Road,
Acocks Green,
Birmingham,
B27 6BH, UK

Printed in the United States
ISBN 1-904151-11-6

Dreamweaver MX: PHP Web Development

All rights reserved. No part of this book may be reproduced, stored in a retrieval system, or transmitted in any form or by any means, without the prior written permission of the publisher, except in the case of brief quotations embodied in critical articles or reviews.

The authors and publisher have made every effort in the preparation of this book to ensure the accuracy of the information. However, the information contained in this book is sold without warranty, either express or implied. Neither the authors, glasshaus nor its dealers or distributors will be held liable for any damages caused or alleged to be caused either directly or indirectly by this book.

web professional to web professional

© 2002 glasshaus

Trademark Acknowledgements

glasshaus has endeavored to provide trademark information about all the companies and products mentioned in this book by the appropriate use of capitals. However, glasshaus cannot guarantee the accuracy of this information.

Credits

Authors
Gareth Downes-Powell
Tim Green
Bruno Mairlot

Technical Reviewers
Aaron Brown
Allan Kent
Martina Kosloff
Jason Lotito
Aaron Richmond
Wendy Robb
Murray Summers

Commissioning Editor
Simon Mackie

Technical Editors
Amanda Kay
Matt Machell
Simon Mackie
Dan Walker

Managing Editor
Liz Toy

Project Manager
Sophie Edwards

Production Coordinators
Rachel Taylor
Pip Wonson

Cover
Dawn Chellingworth

Indexer
Adrian Axinte

Proofreader
Agnes Wiggers

The cover image for this book was created by Don Synstelien of http://www.synfonts.com, co-author of the glasshaus book, "Usability: The Site Speaks For Itself". You can find more of Don's illustration work online at http://www.synstelien.com.

About the Authors

Gareth Downes-Powell

Gareth Downes-Powell has been working in the computer industry for the last twelve years, primarily building and repairing PCs, and writing custom databases. He branched out onto the Internet five years ago, and started creating web sites and custom web applications. This is now his main area of expertise, and he uses a variety of languages including ASP and PHP, with SQL Server or MySQL backend databases.

A partner in Buzz inet, *http://www.buzzinet.co.uk/*, an Internet company specializing in web design and hosting, he uses a wide range of Macromedia products, from Dreamweaver MX through to Flash and Director, for custom multimedia applications. Gareth maintains *http://ultradev.buzzinet.co.uk/* as a way of providing support for the whole Macromedia UltraDev and MX Community. There, he regularly adds new tutorials and custom-written extensions to this rapidly expanding site.

Gareth enjoys keeping up with the latest developments, and has been providing support to many users, to help them use UltraDev and Dreamweaver MX with ASP or PHP on both Linux and Windows servers. Rarely offline, Gareth can always be found in the Macromedia forums (news: *forums.macromedia.com*), where he helps to answer many users' questions on a daily basis.

Tim Green

Tim Green is a full-time IT Manager and an eBusiness/B2B Advisor based in the North West of England. Beginning his working life as a COBOL and Assembly Language programmer, he moved into web application development in 1996, after dabbling in numerous other careers, from acting to being a chef.

A contributing developer to PHAkT, an implementation of PHP for UltraDev 4, he was contracted by PHAkT's creators to work on their other PHP implementation, ImpAKT, and the NeXTensio toolkit, and became the first developer to release additional extensions for UltraDev PHP, including a shopping cart management system called IntelliCART.

Writing this book has both been an honor and a great experience, but it really wouldn't have been possible without the help and support of a number of key people. I would like to thank (in no particular order) Bruno Mairlot, Gareth Downes-Powell, Simon Mackie, Matt Machell, the whole of the glasshaus team, Massimo Foti, Jag Sidhu, Tom Muck, Waldo Smeets, George Petrov, the UDZone.com team, and the Dreamweaver Extension Development Community as a whole.

A very special thanks goes to my wife Becky. I don't know how I would have done it without her; she's my best friend and my rock. Thanks babe.

Bruno Mairlot

Bruno Mairlot works for a network security and Internet solutions company based in Luxembourg. He specialises in developing implementations of network and Internet protocols with PHP and MySQL. He began his working life as the founder of a web site development and network services company four years ago, then moved on to work with other companies, but always working mainly as a web site developer and security consultant for the Web.

Along with Tim and Gareth, Bruno is a contributor to the Dreamweaver and PHP community, and is part of the management team of the community site http://www.udzone.com. He is the author of a project that aims to give users a powerful MySQL administration console in Dreamweaver as an extension.

Writing this book has been a tremendous and exciting experience, but wouldn't have been possible without the help of many people. First and foremost I would like to thank is my friend Tim Green. His support and enthusiasm on this project has helped me more than I could say. Thanks Tim. Next, my thanks go to my soul mate, Pascale. I couldn't have written any of this book without her being at my side, encouraging me and supporting me. I would also like to thank Simon Mackie from glasshaus, who did a tremendously good management job.

Special thanks go to my colleague and friend, Con Dorgan, who helped me during my working hours and gave me a lot of suggestions for the book.

Table of Contents

Introduction 1
    Style Conventions 2
    Support/Feedback 3
    Web Support 3

Chapter 1: What Is PHP? 5
    What Is PHP and What Is It for? 5
    Introducing Dreamweaver MX 12
    Dreamweaver MX and PHP 20
    Installing and Configuring PHP 21
    Summary 28

Chapter 2: What Is MySQL? 31
    What Is MySQL? 31
    Installing and Configuring MySQL 33
    MySQL Basics 35
        The MySQL Console 35
        Introduction To Databases and SQL 35
        Selecting the Working Database 37
        Tables in MySQL 38
        Configuring MySQL 40
    Additional Tools for MySQL 46
        MyCC 46
        PHPMyAdmin 49
    Summary 53

Chapter 3: Getting Started with Dreamweaver MX 55
    The Essentials 55
    Creating a Site Definition 56
        Site Definition Wizard – A Step-By-Step Guide 56
        Advanced Site Definition – An Overview 65
        Creating a Database Connection 70
    Summary 72

Table of Contents

Chapter 4: Planning the Web Site — 75
- Architecture of a Dynamic Web Site — 76
- The Brief — 76
- Determining Site Features — 77
- Planning the Database Structure — 78
- Determining Site Functionality and Features — 80
- Summary — 88

Chapter 5: Beginning Site Development — 91
- Setting Up the Database — 91
  - The bookings Table — 91
  - The clients Table — 92
  - The room Table — 93
  - The users Table — 94
  - Creating the Tables — 94
- Using Templates To Standardize Layout — 102
- Summary — 115

Chapter 6: Manipulating the Database — 117
- Database Operations within Dreamweaver MX — 117
- The Hotel Booking System — 117
  - Making a Booking — 118
  - Changing a Booking — 119
  - Canceling a Booking — 120
- Building the Pages — 120
  - Creating the Bookings Pages — 121
  - Changing a Booking — 146
  - Canceling a Booking — 159
  - Editing the Template – Linking the Pages — 162
  - Suggestions for Expansion — 164
- Summary — 165

Chapter 7: Advanced SQL Usage — 167
- Creating an Advanced Recordset — 167
  - The SELECT Statement — 168
  - Using DISTINCT — 168
  - Choosing Columns — 169
  - Tables, Joining Tables, and Foreign Keys — 172
  - Filtering Rows — 178
  - Grouping — 182
  - Filtering Using HAVING — 187
  - Sorting the Recordset — 187
  - Limiting the Number of Rows — 188

Modifying the Structure of Existing Tables	190
The ALTER TABLE Syntax	190
Optimization	**191**
Summary	**195**

Chapter 8: Creating a Search System — 199

Search Engines	199
Designing the User Interface	**201**
Building Your Page	201
Retrieving the Value Entered By the User	203
Building the Query	**204**
The Base Query	205
Creating the Dynamic Query	206
Displaying the Results	**212**
Summary	**215**

Chapter 9: Hand Coding within Dreamweaver MX — 217

PHP Code Syntax	217
Statements	218
Variables	218
Control Structures	221
Functions	223
PHP Resources	223
Why Hand Code within Dreamweaver MX?	224
Coding Options in Dreamweaver MX	**224**
Code View and Code Inspector	224
Code Options in Preferences Window	225
New Hand Coding Features in MX	227
Good Hand Coding Practices	**240**
Code Options	241
Indenting Code	241
Commenting Your Code	242
Naming Variables	243
Balancing Braces	244
Practical Example – Login System for Dreamweaver Hotel	**246**
Overview of Our Login System	246
The Database Users Table	247
Create Users Page – The Layout	247
The PHP Include File	249
Create Users Page – Adding the Code	252
The Login Page	256
The Menu Page	260
Create Users Page – Security	261
Summary	**262**

Table of Contents

Chapter 10: The Server Behavior Builder — 265

What Is the Server Behavior Builder? — 265

When To Use the Server Behavior Builder — 268

How To Build a Server Behavior — 268
- Starting the Server Behavior Builder — 269
- The Code Blocks — 269
- Building an Interface for Our Server Behavior — 276
- Finishing the Server Behavior — 280
- How To Copy a Server Behavior — 281

Summary — 282

Chapter 11: Debugging Your Code — 285

Programming Errors — 285
- Syntax Errors — 286
- Run-time Errors — 288
- Logic Errors — 289
- Error Types in PHP — 290
- Custom Error Handling — 296
- Viewing Your Server Settings — 305

Debugging Techniques — 307
- Creating a Custom Debugging Function — 307
- Two Brains Are Better Than One — 314
- SQL Errors — 314
- Where To Seek Help — 314
- Macromedia Forums — 314
- Web Sites — 315
- Newsgroups — 315

Summary — 316

Index — 319

Table of Contents

Introduction

Macromedia Dreamweaver MX is a truly superb piece of software; it enables rapid and easy development of web applications. It is a great step forward from the previous incarnation of Dreamweaver, because it incorporates the server-side development tools previously found in Dreamweaver UltraDev, plus some new features, such as built-in support for PHP and better support for standards like XHTML and CSS.

PHP is a very popular server-side scripting language. It's fast, has plenty of hand built-in functionality, and, perhaps more importantly, is free. Most hosting companies offer PHP support, and there's a large community of PHP users on the Web ready to help out if you get stuck. The combination of Dreamweaver MX's visual interface and PHP's ease of use is a powerful one.

In this book we'll be looking at how to use Dreamweaver MX to produce PHP code. Throughout the book, we'll be building an example web application, a hotel booking system, which you can see in action at *http://www.phpdreamweavermx.co.uk/*.

We start off with some introductory chapters covering Dreamweaver MX and MySQL, the free database we'll be using for this book. We'll look at how databases work and cover a little SQL. We then move on to show how we designed the sample web application. The later chapters cover some more advanced topics, such as creating a search tool for your site, more advanced SQL, hand coding in Dreamweaver, and debugging your code. By the end of the book you should be skilled at using Dreamweaver MX to build PHP web sites.

This book doesn't aim to teach you in depth how to code PHP, but the hand-coding chapter has a small PHP syntax primer to get you up to speed.

> *For an in-depth look at the PHP language and syntax we recommend the Wrox books,* Beginning PHP 4 *by Chris Ullman et al (ISBN 1-861003-73-0) and* Professional PHP 4 Programming *by Luis Argerich et al (ISBN 1-861006-91-8)*.

Introduction

Who's This Book for?

This book is for web professionals who want to learn how to use Macromedia Dreamweaver MX to produce database-driven PHP web applications quickly and with the minimum of fuss.

This assumes that the reader has some knowledge of HTML and web design concepts. It doesn't assume any knowledge of PHP, SQL, or databases.

What Do I Need To Begin?

All you need to get going with this book is a copy of Macromedia Dreamweaver MX. A trial version can be downloaded from the Macromedia web site at *http://www.macromedia.com/*. We'll show you how to download and install any other software that you need as we go through the book.

Style Conventions

We've used a number of styles in the book to help you understand what's going on.

We've used the **important words** style to flag up new or important subjects.

Screen Text is used to indicate anything you'd see on the screen, including URLs.

New blocks of code are in this code foreground style:

```
<html>
<body>
<script language="JavaScript">

  var myCalc = 1 + 2;
  document.write("The calculated number is " + myCalc);

</script>
</body>
</html>
```

If we're amending a script, perhaps adding in a new line or making changes to an existing one, then we use the code background style for the code that you've already seen together with the foreground style to highlight the new code:

```
<html>
<body>
<script language="JavaScript">

  var userEnteredNumber = prompt("Please enter a number","");
  var myCalc = 1 + userEnteredNumber;
  var myResponse = "The number you entered + 1 = " + myCalc;
  document.write( myResponse );

</script>
</body>
</html>
```

Introduction

To talk about code within text we use this `code in text` style, which is also used for file names like `MyFirstPHP.php`

> Essential not–to–be–missed information is in boxes like this.

Asides to the current discussion are presented like this.

A Note About Code Formatting

We've tried to make the code as easy to read as possible. This does mean that there is sometimes whitespace in the scripts that would break the code if you used it exactly as it is printed. For example, this JavaScript code:

```
        output+="<a href=\""+getPageName(pages[i][j])+".html\" class=\"page\"
title=\""+pages[i][j]+"\">";
```

will look like this in the book:

```
        output+="<a href=\""+getPageName(pages[i][j])+".html\" class=\"page\"
              title=\""+pages[i][j]+"\">";
```

The code in the download is without the whitespace.

Support/Feedback

Although we aim for perfection, the sad fact of book publication is that a few errors will slip through. We would like to apologize for any errors that have reached this book despite our efforts. If you spot such an error, please let us know about it using the e-mail address `support@glasshaus.com`. If it's something that will help other readers then we'll put it up on the errata page at *http://www.glasshaus.com*.

This address can also be used to access our support network. If you have trouble running any of the code in this book, or have a related question that you feel the book didn't answer, please mail your problem to the above address quoting the title of the book, the last 4 digits of its ISBN (in this case, 1116), and the chapter and page number of your query.

Web Support

Feel free to go and visit our web site, at *http://www.glasshaus.com*. It features:

- **Code Downloads**: The example code for this, and every other glasshaus book, can be downloaded from our site.
- **Book Errata**: Any errors that have crept into the book are posted onto the web site.
- **Site Galleries**: Some glasshaus books have galleries of example code for you to use on your site.

We're adding new features all the time, so keep checking back.

1

- Overview of PHP
- Where to get PHP
- Installing and configuring PHP on your web server

Author: Tim Green

What Is PHP?

This chapter is a basic introduction to the workings of **PHP** and how it all began. We will briefly discover its origins as a programming language, looking at how it has evolved in earlier versions of Dreamweaver to its current implementation in Dreamweaver MX.

As an introductory guide, we will take you through your first steps in working with PHP. We'll look at where you can obtain it, and discuss the various installation options that are available to you. We'll also cover, in detail, the necessary steps to install and configure PHP to work with your preferred web server.

Summarizing this chapter we also include timely troubleshooting hints and tips should you encounter any problems or difficulties with your new PHP installation.

What Is PHP and What Is It for?

Put simply, PHP is a tool for creating dynamic web pages. Its presence is completely transparent to the end user. PHP is easy to learn, and most importantly, it's easy to implement.

PHP in the Real World

So, PHP creates dynamic web pages, but what exactly do we mean by **dynamic**?

Today's web sites come in all shapes and sizes. Some provide rich user experiences using Flash animations; others provide interactive page elements created with JavaScript, or a combination of both (or other) technologies. These types of web site can be described as being dynamic as some part of them changes as a result of either a manual or automatic stimulus. PHP is no different in this respect, as it too, reacts to a series of stimuli in a pre determined way. However, there is one primary difference between these two methods.

Dynamic pages created with JavaScript, or other similar technologies, rely on the ability of the web site visitor's own computer to manifest their effects. This is called **client-side scripting**, the web pages are sent via the web server to the visitor's web browser, and once loaded the scripts begin to work. Because the code that generates these interactions is sent directly to the browser it is open to public scrutiny, and is therefore not the best choice in all situations. A user authentication system, for example, becomes ineffective because the code that handles the login process is completely visible, and therefore insecure.

PHP, however, works in an entirely different way. A web page containing PHP code is "pre-processed" by the PHP engine, called an interpreter, and the results of this processing are passed back to the web server and on to the visitor's web browser. As only the results of the PHP processing are sent to the browser, the code that generated them remains hidden, and is therefore much more secure. This kind of pre-processing is called **server-side scripting**, and while it doesn't provide the same kind of dynamic effects as JavaScript, PHP pages can be called dynamic. Given the example above, of a user authentication system: one page of PHP code, can process a username and password, determine if these values are valid or invalid and based on this determination, send the user to a login failure page, or to a successful login page.

Dreamweaver MX allows us to harness the power of PHP in a visual way, without delving into the code itself, unless we want to. Because of this, Dreamweaver MX is perfectly suited to the rapid development of dynamic web sites. To better illustrate this throughout the book we will base all our examples around a single case study, which will allow you to work through each chapter and watch the whole process of dynamic web development evolve.

The case study chosen for this book is that of a hotel booking system. This is a good example to use as it allows you to view the process from the perspectives of both the hotel staff and the customer. Both parties will interact with the web site in totally different ways. The customer will see the web site only via its public interface, where they will be able to find out more about the hotel itself, and make room reservations. The hotel staff, however, will have additional access to a private administration area where they will be able to view the customer bookings and more.

The Hotel Booking System

Booking a hotel room is now a very common practice on the Internet. It is quick and easy. To book a hotel room, the customer visits the web site, enters the date of arrival, date of departure, and the type of room required. Using this information, the web site searches the reservations database to ensure that there is an appropriate room available for the dates specified. When the search is complete the customer's reservation is either denied (if no rooms are available), or confirmed in which case the customer then proceeds to enter their credit card details to secure the booking.

As you can see from the above example, this is a type of dynamic web site. The customer provides the stimulus (the dates of the stay, and the type of room required), and the web site dynamically determines whether those requirements can be met. This type of web site is more commonly known as a **database-enabled web site**, as all of the information that the web site needs is stored on a database. Through the magic of PHP this information is retrieved, searched, sorted, and evaluated to determine the appropriate response.

Throughout this book, we will return to this example, and explore elements of it in more detail. We will look at the development tasks required to develop just such a system. All of the principles used in the book are applicable, regardless of the type of project you are working on.

A Brief History of PHP

From its earliest beginnings PHP was designed for environment-independent development. Able to run on many different web servers and operating systems, it is an easy-to-learn and very flexible development tool.

Born from a series of Perl (or CGI – Common Gateway Interface) scripts written by Rasmus Lerdorf in 1995, PHP was initially two independent tools. Personal Home Page Tools was written purely to track the number of visits to the author's online resume. To increase performance and provide greater stability, these scripts were soon rewritten in C. The functionality they provided soon attracted the attention of other developers using the same web server. Rasmus allowed these developers access to his scripts, which proved to be so popular that he was soon receiving requests for additional features. Rasmus was also interested in the use of databases wherever possible, and had developed another series of Perl scripts called Form Interpreter (FI). These scripts processed requests to databases and routed the information back to a web page, to create interactive, dynamic forms.

Soon, both PHP and FI were merged into a single unified tool. This tool was called PHP/FI v2, and was the forerunner of PHP as we know it today.

In 1997, as the development of PHP/FI continued to escalate, it became apparent that the project was becoming larger than one man could handle and the development of PHP was opened up to a group of developers. Two members of this group, Zeev Suraski and Andi Gutmans were responsible for a complete rewrite of the core PHP code, which became known as the Zend engine, a name derived from both author's names. This engine set out the architecture and functionality for all future versions of PHP.

Along the way the meaning of PHP itself also changed; it became a recursive acronym, one where the acronym's meaning refers to itself. PHP now stood for "PHP: Hypertext Preprocessor".

The power and flexibility offered by PHP 3 grabbed the attention of the web professional, and PHP became a more mainstream development option. Due to this huge increase in popularity, the Zend Engine was rewritten once again, with further enhancements and functionality. This final rewrite forms the basis of the current PHP versions, version 4.

Before looking more closely at PHP, it really is only fair if we take a step back and look at the other options available. PHP is by no means unique in what it does, in fact there is a whole wealth of different technologies available, and like PHP, all have their strengths and weaknesses. Some of these technologies are open source, or free for developers to use in non-production environments, whilst others require you to purchase a license before you can begin to learn about them. In fact, there are so many different options that delving deeper into this subject will reveal quite a number of possibilities!

Rather than discuss all of these available options, we shall, for the purpose of this book, concentrate solely on the other scripting languages that are supported by Dreamweaver MX.

The Alternatives

With everything in life, no matter what you decide to do, there is always another way to achieve the same goal. Creating a database-enabled web site is no exception. All of the different technologies available achieve, ultimately the same thing, but they all do it slightly differently.

The main alternatives are Active Server Pages (ASP), Java Server Pages (JSP) and Cold Fusion Markup Language (CFML). There are, of course, others, but these four are the main contenders in terms of popularity (of course, all of these alternatives are also natively supported within Dreamweaver MX). All of these technologies have their own strengths and weaknesses, as does PHP.

Whilst the majority of alternatives are commercial in nature, some are more developer-friendly than others, providing free development-only versions, which are useful for testing and learning. However, in a production environment, there are usually costs associated with the installation of the relevant production-level server.

ASP, for example, requires that you purchase a version of Windows that comes with Internet Information Server (IIS). Windows NT Server, Windows 2000, and Windows XP Professional all come with a version of IIS, but it can prove to be an expensive option when installing a production server of your own. There are alternatives, however, so that ASP pages can be used on other web servers, such as Apache. Amongst these are ChilliSoft ASP, and iASP, both of which are fairly popular. Though still commercial in nature they do provide a cheaper alternative and do not commit you to the use of a Windows-based web server.

ASP has proven to be a popular choice amongst developers, as there are many relatively cheap hosting companies that provide ASP hosting via a shared server, where multiple users and web sites exist on the same machine. In such an instance, you are not required to buy any form of Windows, and ASP really does become a viable option.

ASP.NET is similar in nature to ASP, in that you must have an appropriate Windows-based operating system and web server to process ASP.NET pages. However, Halcyon Software, the developers of iASP, are currently working on a version of the .NET framework called iNET, for use on alternative web servers. This will ultimately lead to another commercial program, but does open up more possibilities for development. For more information on iNET see *http://www.halcyonsoft.com/products/iNET.asp*. As the popularity of ASP.NET grows, it will undoubtedly become just as viable an option as ASP. As more hosting companies provide ASP.NET support via a shared server, the price of ASP.NET hosting will reduce dramatically.

JSP is slightly different in that there are both commercial versions of JSP as well as open source versions. This is good as you can experiment with versions of JSP, to discover which one suits you best, and as you aren't tied to one particular operating system, as there are versions of JSP available for most forms of web server. Unfortunately, JSP pages haven't proved to be a popular option, not many hosting companies provide JSP support, and those that do usually charge a premium for the service.

CFML is a totally commercial server option. If you wish to install ColdFusion onto your production server, then you have to purchase the ColdFusion software, which is available in Professional and Enterprise versions depending on your requirements. Whilst there are flavors of ColdFusion that will work on a number of different web servers, it hasn't proven to be a popular option amongst host providers either, as even in a shared server environment it is a costly option. If you wish to use ColdFusion locally, for development or learning purposes, there is a free development version available, but this version is feature-limited to prevent more than one user visiting the generated web pages.

PHP, in contrast, is completely free to use either privately or commercially, and for this reason there are no associated costs in running PHP on your own web server. PHP, like some of the other server technologies, can also be installed on a number of different web servers, and due to its easy installation, and lack of price tag, it has proven a very popular choice amongst host providers.

What Is PHP?

ASP

Active Server Pages is a proprietary technology, based around Microsoft's Internet Information Server. It allows you to combine HTML, Visual Basic Script (VBScript), and JavaScript with reusable ActiveX Components to create dynamic web pages.

For many developers this presents the ultimate in dynamic web page development because of the tight integration and interoperability between all of the components. Historically, ASP has proven to be costly to implement, due in part to its reliance on other Microsoft products. However, this is no longer a real issue, thanks to the large number of companies offering cheap ASP hosting packages.

In comparison to PHP, ASP can be unnecessarily unwieldy and slow. Much of the functionality that PHP offers as standard is not integrated into ASP's core code, which brings about a reliance on third-party code to extend and enhance it. ASP can present a very steep learning curve, especially to the first-time developer.

ASP.NET

Like ASP, ASP.NET is another proprietary technology, built around Microsoft's Internet Information Server and its own server variations called the .NET Web Server. Whilst ASP.NET is a relatively new kid on the block, it is a more developer-friendly language and is specifically geared towards the rapid development of web applications.

To achieve this, it provides the flexibility of allowing you to decide which programming language you wish to work with, with support for 25 different programming languages. It provides a wealth of new functionality, previously unavailable to ASP developers, and offers enhanced performance and reliability.

ASP.NET really is more of a programming language than a scripting language, and for this reason it is attracting more and more application developers every day.

Unfortunately, as ASP.NET is still relatively new, it is costly to implement in a production environment. There are only a very limited number of companies providing .NET support, though this number is slowly increasing, and while other companies are implementing versions of the .NET Framework for other servers, such as iNET, it will still be some time before this is a truly mature environment for development.

ASP.NET can prove to be especially difficult for the first-time developer to understand, and part of this is due to the number of languages that can be used for ASP.NET development.

Conversely, PHP is very easy to learn, especially if you are already familiar with technologies such as JavaScript. It is a stable and mature development language, which, like ASP.NET, is well suited to the rapid development of web applications. Whilst PHP does lack some of the complexity of ASP.NET, and what I am sure will prove to be flexibility in the future, PHP is constantly evolving and embraces new functionality wherever it is available. So much so that newer versions of PHP are even able to take advantage of elements of the .NET framework with relative ease.

CFML

ColdFusion Markup Language might sound like something that you write on the side of a nuclear reactor, but the truth is, that this is an extremely powerful and easy-to-learn language, as it is similar in many respects to HTML. Originally developed by Allaire in 1995, CFML started, like PHP, as a set of Perl scripts. It evolved rapidly into a full application server, and in 2001 the ever-evolving Macromedia purchased Allaire. At the time of writing the most recent version of the ColdFusion server is ColdFusion MX.

CFML grew in popularity for its clarity and ease of use. It is a tag-based language, like HTML, which makes it extremely easy to learn and fast to implement. CFML also has another great strength: it is extremely portable. When creating database connections, for example, often the code needs no modification when the pages are moved from a development server to a production server.

One other strength of CFML is the ability to create custom tags. This might sound a little daunting, but essentially, this feature allows any user at any time to take a portion of their own code, and create a tag that automatically executes their custom code. It is not unusual for a Cold Fusion Developer to have hundreds of "tag libraries" as they are known, as they increase the speed of development massively.

Unfortunately, some developers cite the very strengths of ColdFusion, highlighted above, as its ultimate weakness. Many developers don't like the idea of a tag-based language. It can make it difficult to determine which is server side code (code that runs exclusively on the server, whose output is sent to the web browser), and which is HTML mark up. This lack of structure can make it difficult for the developer with a programming background to really get to grips with ColdFusion. However, the removal of a formal syntax and structure system when using CFML makes it perfect for the neophyte developer.

JSP

Java Server Pages is available in various flavors. For many years Java was touted as being the ultimate in platform-independent coding. This was the promise, and to a degree, that promise was delivered.

The move from Java-based applications to its use as a method of dynamically creating web pages was a logical one. Certainly, the great thing about this architecture is that it can be run on any platform, on any machine, so it is a good candidate for portability and compatibility.

As there are a number of variations, at this point we should clarify how JSP is structured. First of all JSP is what is called a 'reference implementation' of Sun Microsystems Java Server Pages. In essence, Sun Microsystems determine how JSP should be implemented, and have developed a standard by which all versions of JSP should comply, called the Java 2 Enterprise Edition (J2EE).

There are various open-source and commercial implementations of JSP, including Macromedia JRun Server and Caucho Technology's Resin. Because there are various implementations, it can be difficult for the first time user to decide which version they should use. Different versions written by different software houses also bring a huge difference in quality, stability, and speed for each of these environments, as each has its own unique nuances.

In this respect, PHP really does have the edge. As there is a single development base, with a group of individual developers supporting, maintaining, and improving PHP at each stage it is stable, reliable, and much easier to implement than its JSP counterparts. It also means that there is no confusion about which "type" to use, as there is only one PHP.

JSP is a fairly flexible server technology too, as it allows you to extend and enhance its functionality in a similar way to CFML, providing support for third-party extensions, or "tag libraries". Its syntax and usage is also not dissimilar to PHP and JavaScript, as they all have a common inspiration root. However, whilst both PHP and JSP share a common background of sorts, JSP is much more difficult to learn and less user-friendly than PHP.

What Is PHP?

Dreamweaver UltraDev and PHP

Dreamweaver MX is the first version of Dreamweaver with native PHP support, but PHP developers have been using Dreamweaver UltraDev for quite some time now. How did they manage without the labor-saving tools that Dreamweaver is famous for providing? Well, it took some time, but they invented their own.

Since the very first version of Dreamweaver there has been only token support for PHP. When Macromedia purchased Elemental Software's Drumbeat, redeveloped it into the Dreamweaver Architecture, and released the first version of Dreamweaver UltraDev, there was wide criticism that there was no native support for PHP-generated pages. Developers couldn't understand the oversight, as PHP is currently the second most popular scripting language (source: *http://php.weblogs.com/popularity*). There was support for three server technologies, dubbed "server models", in UltraDev: ASP, JSP, and CFML. However, while UltraDev recognized PHP code when it was in use in a page, there was no built-in functionality to support this Server Model.

Unfortunately, the situation didn't improve at all for the PHP developer with the second version of UltraDev (confusingly called Dreamweaver UltraDev 4) until the middle of 2001, when a young talented developer called Dan Radigan began work on a project called PHP4UD.

One of the key features of all versions of Dreamweaver is that it is **extensible**. Using a combination of HTML forms and JavaScript routines it is possible to develop a type of macro called a behavior. Behaviors allow you to add additional functionality to your page in a visual way, without having to worry about the underlying code. Before UltraDev, these behaviors most commonly inserted JavaScript into your page and allowed you to easily add dynamic page interactions. When UltraDev was released, a new type of behavior became available: **server behaviors**.

Server behaviors work in much the same way as the original Dreamweaver JavaScript behaviors, however, instead of inserting JavaScript code, these behaviors inserted ASP, JSP, or CFML code into your page. Again, this was done in a visual way, and this formula proved to be very successful in developing web applications rapidly.

Along with JavaScript behaviors and server behaviors, there are a number of different types of extensions available as Macromedia wanted to provide as much flexibility as possible to the user. It was even possible to write an entirely new server model from scratch, to provide additional support for another server technology. PHP4UD was the first time that anyone had created this kind of extension.

After a number of beta releases, Dan handed development of this project over to a young Romanian company called Interakt. The next release of this server model saw some significant changes and enhancements to the functionality. To mark the significant leap in functionality the project was renamed to PHAkT.

PHAkT became the only way for PHP developers to fully utilize the power of UltraDev. This was something that was quickly recognized by many developers, who started to develop and share additional extensions for use specifically with PHAkT. These extensions ranged in complexity and design from simple scripts to format data in a specific way, to shopping cart management systems.

Chapter 1

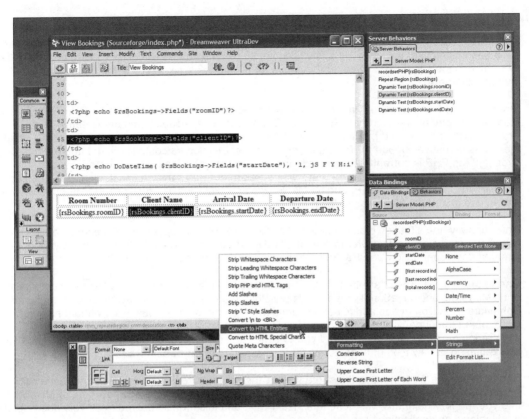

Recognizing the potential of the PHP Server Model at an early stage, Interakt also began work on an enhanced version of PHAkT, called ImpAKT. As PHAkT was released under the GNU Public License, or GPL, it was freely available to all for commercial or private use without charge. As ImpAKT was to be an enhanced version of PHAkT, it would be released under a commercial license, and provide a way to recuperate the costs associated with the thousands of hours of development time it took to bring PHAkT to its version 1 release.

The changes for PHP developers were massive. Especially for those who were used to not having any option but to hand code their pages. Now, there was not one PHP Server Model to use, there were two.

Thanks to the popularity of the new PHP Server Models, and the support given by the Extension Developer Community, Macromedia have finally provided support for PHP within Dreamweaver MX. This native support for PHP within Dreamweaver comes via Macromedia's own PHP server model, called PHP MySQL.

Introducing Dreamweaver MX

Dreamweaver MX sees a number of important changes. First of all, there is now only one product, as the functionality available in the previously separate Dreamweaver, UltraDev, and HomeSite packages have been integrated into one vastly superior tool.

What Is PHP?

Dreamweaver MX also sees enhanced support for more server models, including PHP, ASP.NET, and ColdFusion MX. This new version of Dreamweaver also boasts a new User Interface (UI) and enhanced support for extension developers, including a simplification of Server Model development. which will bring even more power and functionality in the future.

For the first time Dreamweaver MX allows you to choose the style and layout of the User Interface. If you are upgrading from a previous version of Dreamweaver, or UltraDev, this is good news as you can opt to work in an environment that you are already used to.

Choosing Your User Interface

When you start Dreamweaver MX for the first time, you are presented with a dialog that allows you to determine the UI style that you wish to use.

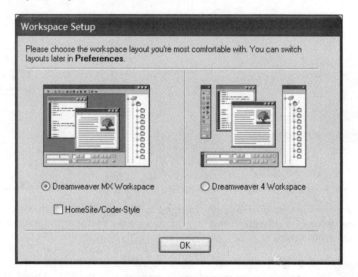

For the purposes of this book, we will presume that you select the Dreamweaver MX Workspace, as shown above. Of course all the tutorials and exercises in this book will work regardless of the layout that you opt for.

Once you have selected your preferred UI layout, Dreamweaver MX continues to load, and you are presented with your first view of its new look.

If you are familiar with earlier versions of Dreamweaver, you will see that there are a number of significant changes to the UI. One of the reasons for this radical change is that HomeSite, a sourcecode editing tool, previously provided as a separate tool on the Dreamweaver CD, is now fully integrated into Dreamweaver itself. Homesite has also seen an upgrade in this version of Dreamweaver, and is now called Homesite+, and while still available as a standalone product, the additional functionality of Homesite+ will not be made available separately. Unique features such as Code Hints – where the syntax of individual commands appear as tool tips as you manually enter sourcecode, and Snippets – where you are able to store pre-written portions of script for use at a later stage, are available directly through the Dreamweaver MX interface. We'll be looking at these features in Chapter 9.

Chapter 1

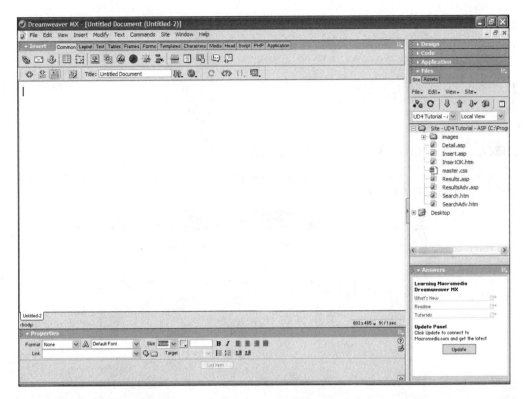

Given that there are a number of sweeping changes to the way that Dreamweaver MX looks, let's take a look at the different elements of the UI so that we may better understand their purpose within our development environment.

The biggest change, for those familiar with Dreamweaver's earlier incarnations, is the use of integrated panels. This provides a far more flexible approach to the UI, as predetermined panel-sets can be created that allow you to tailor the look of the UI, and the tools available, to a particular task at hand. As panels play such a vital role in the way that Dreamweaver MX works, the most frequently used panels are worthy of further exploration.

The Insert Panel

The Insert panel, as you can see from the image above, consists of a number of tabbed areas. Each tabbed area hides a different set of tools, which are there to help you realize your web site design.

Some of these "tabs" change dynamically, dependent on the type of document that you are working on. In the screenshot above, we have created a blank PHP page, and there is a tab in the Insert panel, called PHP. Clicking on this tab reveals a number of shortcut tools for when you are working in Code view. Similarly, if you are working on a ColdFusion page a number of other tabs appear, and the PHP tab disappears, because it is no longer required. Edit another PHP page, and the PHP tab

What Is PHP?

returns. This kind of change is called "context sensitivity", and it is specifically designed to help you find the tools that you need, when you need them.

The Design Panel

The design panel allows easy access to your Cascading Style Sheet (CSS) styles and HTML Styles.

Also, whilst not strictly a design element, the Behaviors tab allows you easy access to a series of built-in JavaScript behaviors. These are small pieces of code that allow you to add interesting and vital effects to your pages, allowing you to do everything from opening browser windows when a link is clicked, to controlling animations by manipulating Dreamweaver's timeline.

The Code Panel

The Code panel provides a number of useful tools and options. From here you can view the whole structure of your page using the Tag Inspector. This inspector displays your page in the form of a tree, and allows you to edit tags directly without having to enter Code view. This is a common tool found in many an Integrated Development Environment (IDE), and it is provided here to shorten the learning curve for those developers already familiar with such tools.

The Snippets tab provides you with the ability to easily store and retain pieces of prewritten code that you may want to reuse on other pages, or within other web sites. Of all of the new features available within Dreamweaver MX, this has probably been the most requested. The Snippets Library already comes preloaded with a number of useful pieces of code to get you started. Ranging from preset meta tags, to JavaScript functions that calculate the area of a circle, there is already something here for everyone, and space for much more! We'll take a more detailed look at the Snippets panel in Chapter 9.

The final tab in the Code panel is the Reference tab. Here you will find quick reference guides to all of the supported server languages. This tab is an extremely valuable tool, as it is also context sensitive. For example, if you are in Code view and you right-click (Windows) or control-click (Macintosh) a tag, attribute, or keyword, the Reference panel will open and display the full meaning of the element that you selected. Of course, this will not work for everything, as there might not be a reference book for the language that you are working with. (For example, at the time of writing, there isn't a reference for PHP. However, there is one available to download from the Macromedia Exchange at *http://www.macromedia.com/exchange*).

The Application Panel

The Application panel is where you will spend the majority of your time when creating the server-side interactions of your web site. This panel is split into 4 tabs: Databases, Bindings, Server Behaviors, and Components.

The Databases tab is what you might expect. It allows you to view the structure and layout of any databases that you have set up on your web sites. From here you can also add new database connections, making them available directly within the Dreamweaver interface.

What Is PHP?

When retrieving dynamic data for your web page, you must create something called a Data Binding. Data Bindings provide the essential link between the Dreamweaver development environment and your data. Using this tab, it is possible to create a number of different Data Bindings that retrieve information from databases, form fields, cookies, and much more.

In the Design panel section previously, we discussed behaviors. Through the Application panel we have access to even more behaviors. However, these behaviors do not insert JavaScript code into your page. They insert server-side code that provides you with the ultimate interaction between web site and visitor. This tab, too, is context-sensitive, as it changes depending on the server model that you are currently using. This provides unparalleled flexibility of development. If for example you apply the Dynamic Text server behavior while working on a PHP page, the server behavior will insert PHP code. However, apply the same Dynamic Text behavior while working on a CFML page, and the inserted code is, of course, CFML!

The Components tab isn't used when you are working on PHP pages. It is targeted specifically at other server models, such as ASP, that rely on proprietary or third party components to provide specific functionality. One such example for ASP is ASP Mail, which provides e-mail functionality to ASP web pages.

The Files Panel

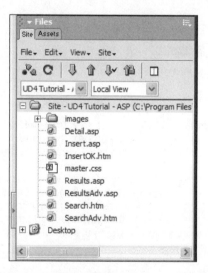

In prior versions of Dreamweaver if you needed to look at the files stored in either your work directory, or on your web server, you needed to open the Site window. The Site window was a user interface all of its own, with its own menus and functions. As most developers working on a web site constantly left this window open and running in the background, it makes logical sense, therefore, that its functionality was placed inside a panel within the main UI. This has been done with Dreamweaver MX, and the Site tab gives you full access to both your local and remote file systems. From here you can transfer files and folders to and from your work directory, without the need for a separate FTP (File Transfer Protocol) utility.

The Assets tab keeps track of all the external files, links, and colors used while creating your site, making them available for easy reference, modification, and reuse.

The Answers Panel

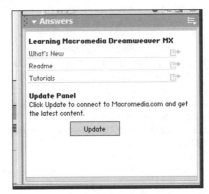

Another new functionality addition is the Answers panel. Here you can obtain rapid access to tutorials, Technical Notes and extensions directly within Dreamweaver. The information stored in this panel is retained for future reference, and is only modified when you click on the *Update* button.

The Properties Inspector

This panel allows you to control specific elements of your HTML tags and pages directly without entering Code view. Using its context sensitive nature, this panel constantly changes depending on the element that is selected on the page, providing a wealth of different options.

The example shown above shows all of the standard HTML text formatting options that are available when you select a region of text on your page. From here you can adjust the Format, Font, Size, Color, Alignment, and more. Once a change has been made within the Properties Inspector it is immediately shown on the working page. In this panel too, additional formatting options can be obtained by clicking on the *A* icon, which changes the panel and provides access to Cascading Style Sheet (CSS) formatting options instead.

Tabbed Document Windows

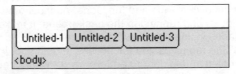

In earlier versions of Dreamweaver, working on multiple pages meant having to have multiple windows open. Whilst this was fine when working with 2 or 3 documents, it became unwieldy and laboriously slow when working with many more.

What Is PHP?

With this in mind, Macromedia has developed tabbed document windows. With this feature, all documents are opened within one window, and the user is shown tabs containing the filenames of these documents. These tabs are clickable, and allow for easy switching between multiple documents.

This approach is far superior, as it consumes fewer screen resources on the development computer and because the developer no longer has to break their workflow constantly when working on multiple documents.

With the development of more integrated tools within the Dreamweaver UI, there was a need for a more "task"-orientated approach to creating pages. Dreamweaver MX is able to create many types of different web-based documents, from HTML pages to Extensible Markup Language (XML) files. Because of this, a New Document wizard has been integrated into Dreamweaver to help you choose the type of document that you wish to create.

The New Document Wizard

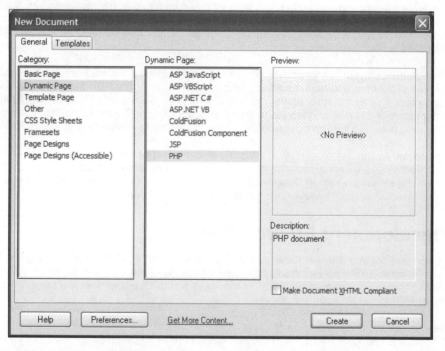

As you can see from the screenshot above, this approach is very similar to that used in many other software packages, most notably Microsoft Word. From this one window, you can create any kind of document that you need to. You can even create pages based on templates that you have created. This is a wonderful feature, as it allows you to create a page design and save it as a template, making the process of creating similar pages with differing content much quicker. This window will come in useful later when we look at the use of templates in greater detail.

Now that you are more familiar with the new user interface, we will look more closely at what this book is really about, the native implementation of PHP within Dreamweaver MX.

Dreamweaver MX and PHP

Developing something as complex as a server model is an extremely difficult task; it consumes a phenomenal amount of time, and resources. The prime reason for creating a server model for Dreamweaver is to easily create database interactions within your web site. For the other server models, this process was simplified as they all follow unitary methods for connecting to a database and retrieving information.

Unfortunately, PHP has a number of different standards for connecting to a database, and each of these utilizes a different set of commands. At present PHP supports at least nineteen different Database Management Systems (DBMS), all of which use a different set of commands to achieve the same task. Integrating support for nineteen different databases of course causes a number of logistical problems, as every tool that uses a database connection of some form would need to have nineteen variants.

Thankfully, there was a very simple solution. It is very common practice with web site host providers who provide PHP support, to include support for only one of these databases, MySQL. It therefore made sense for only that database system to be directly supported within Dreamweaver MX, and it is the DBMS we will be using for this book.

The PHP server model in Dreamweaver MX is very much a skeleton framework. If you compare the feature sets of the other integrated scripting languages, it is clear that PHP hasn't been given the same level of functionality as the other server models. This might appear a little disappointing at first, but due to the popularity of this scripting language, and the extensibility of Dreamweaver itself, it is only a matter of time before extension developers produce more tools to enhance your PHP experience.

Don't be fooled by the fewer number of tools. Everything that can be achieved with the other server model tools can also be achieved with the PHP server model, excepting Login Security, which at the time of writing wasn't present in Dreamweaver MX, and according to Macromedia sources, won't be in the final product either. However, we will be covering how to create a login system in Chapter 9.

The Development Environment

Before you can begin developing PHP pages, it is important to establish how you will test those pages. It is common for developers to have some form of test server, with which they can experiment before publishing their pages to the wired world. Over the next few pages, we will look at setting up PHP to run on your web server.

The most important thing to begin with, is to obtain a copy of PHP from the PHP web site (*http://www.php.net/downloads*). Here you will find a number of different versions of PHP, and this can become a little confusing, as it is well supported on a wide variety of platforms and web servers. For the purposes of working through this book, and for working with Dreamweaver MX, you should download the PHP 4.x version that is appropriate for your operating system.

The two most common flavors of PHP are for Windows and for Linux. The chances are that you are using a web server that is installed on one of these two platforms. For the purposes of this book we will assume that this is the case. However, if you find that your web server actually runs on a different platform from the above, you will find detailed and accurate information about how to install PHP in the downloadable archive for your platform.

What Is PHP?

It won't be long before you also notice that there are binary distributions and source distributions, and you'll probably wonder at the difference. Source distributions are versions of PHP's sourcecode, the actual C language code that makes PHP work. When working with a sourcecode distribution like this, you first have to use the right tools to compile the sourcecode to work on your chosen system. The compile process turns the sourcecode into an executable file and a series of libraries. Compiling code can be a complex task, but, if you have a web server that is hosted on a Linux machine, then it is actually rather simple, as all of the tools that you will need are installed by default. Unfortunately, these tools aren't included at all with a Windows installation, so it is recommended that you download the binary distribution in Zip format for Windows web servers. If you are using Linux on your development server, then it is recommended that you download the source distribution, or if you are using a flavor of Linux that uses the Red Hat Package Manager (RPM), you should find the appropriate files in your distribution's CD under the RPMS directory.

One important note should be made here, for the benefit of Macintosh developers who are using OSX. OSX is based on Darwin, which, like Linux, is a UNIX-like operating system. Because of these similarities many of the configuration options for Linux will also apply to OSX. Thankfully, those of you running OSX 10.1 or above will already have PHP installed by default, as it is now included in the default installation. There are a number of additional features of PHP that are disabled in the version of PHP distributed with OSX, however for the majority of tasks, and certainly for the ability to develop PHP pages using Dreamweaver MX, you can safely rely on the version you already have.

PHP-Compatible Web Servers

As previously mentioned, PHP will work on a number of different platforms and web servers. We have already talked about Windows and Linux versions of PHP, but what web server does PHP need in order to work?

PHP will actually work with the vast majority of web servers available, including Apache and Microsoft's Internet Information Server (IIS), both of which are the most common web servers in use today. If you find that you are using another web server, such as Xitami or a Netscape-based web server, you can find full instructions on how to configure these within the `install.txt` file included in your PHP download. Here we will concentrate on installing and configuring PHP on Apache and IIS.

Installing and Configuring PHP

Installing PHP might sound like a challenging task, especially if you have already looked inside the archive you downloaded from the PHP web site. Whilst the methods for installing PHP on both Windows and Linux machines are entirely different, they are both relatively easy.

Installation Shortcuts

Whilst knowing how to install PHP individually can be widely considered a good thing, it should not be forgotten that there are always alternative ways to achieve the same goal. Installing PHP is no different, and it is especially useful to know of the quicker alternatives, if you are pressed for time.

PHP itself is available as two different downloads from the PHP web site, `www.php.net`. There is a Zip file distribution, which requires a little bit of manual tweaking, and there is also a self-installing version of PHP available that uses the Windows Installer. Neither method is entirely foolproof, but in general the Windows Installer version is quicker with certain configurations.

Chapter 1

There are also a number of alternative, combination distributions available that not only install PHP, but also install MySQL and the Apache Web Server too. This is the perfect option, should you have no local web server to use for development purposes, or if you wish to use a web server other than Internet Information Server. There are two main distributions that fall into this category: PHPTriad and phpdev. Unfortunately PHPTriad has recently been discontinued, though its files are still available from *http://www.sourceforge.net/projects/phptriad*. phpdev is still under active development and can be obtained from *http://www.firepages.com.au*.

Installing PHP On Windows

The process for installing PHP on Windows is relatively simple, as you don't need to worry about compiling sourcecode. You can either use the Windows Installer, or follow these instructions. The process involves extracting the files from the archive you downloaded from the PHP web site, and moving the files and folders it contains to specific locations.

1. Locate the Zip file you downloaded and extract the contents to *c:\php*

2. Using Windows Explorer, move to the *c:\php* directory

3. Copy the file *php.ini-dist* to your Windows directory and rename it to *php.ini*.

    The Windows directory is slightly different dependent on your version of Windows. Typically, for Windows 95, 98, ME, & XP users this would be `c:\windows`, for NT & 2000 users this would be `c:\winnt`.

4. Copy the `php4ts.dll` file from your `c:\php` directory to your system directory (typically `c:\windows\system` for Windows 95, 98, & ME users, `c:\windows\system32` for Windows XP users, or `c:\winnt\system32` for Windows NT & 2000 users.

5. In some, but not all, distributions of PHP you might also find a file called `Msvcrt.dll`. If you find it there, you also need to copy it to your system directory, if it isn't already present.

6. Certain library files are required by different parts of PHP. For this reason, you should copy the contents of your `c:\php\dlls` folder also to your system directory.

7. Edit the `php.ini` file in your Windows directory using your favorite text editor (Notepad is perfect for this).

8. Find the line `extension_dir = ./` and change it to read `extension_dir = c:\php\extensions`.

9. Save the file, and close the text editor.

Now that the process of installing and configuring PHP to work on your Windows machine is complete, we need to tell the Web Server that you have PHP installed. This process is slightly different for Apache and IIS.

What Is PHP?

Configuring Apache 1.3.x

Historically there have been two ways to configure PHP to work with Apache. You could configure PHP to work as an Apache module, or you could configure PHP to work as a CGI process. Thanks to a security advisory report at `http://www.cert.org/advisories/CA-1996-11.html`, the CGI method is now not recommended under **ANY** circumstances. This is due to the fact that when PHP is installed as a CGI process, a hacker of proficient skill level can, under certain circumstances, access the PHP CGI Program and use it to run system-level commands on your web server. These commands can be anything from transferring the content of your database to a location of their choice, or even accessing your files with the intention of erasing or replacing them. This warning has been officially made as the risks of running any interpreter as a CGI program are too high, and cannot be ignored.

For this reason, we will configure PHP to run as an Apache module.

1. Open the Apache configuration file `httpd.conf` in your favorite text editor (again Notepad is fine for this purpose). This is a well-commented file, broken up into several independent sections. Each section relates to a specific part of the Apache Web Server configuration, and details everything from the address of the server and the administrator's e-mail address to the file types that Apache should recognize.

2. Within `httpd.conf` look for any lines that say "`LoadModule`". It is important that you do not change these lines, or their order, but the following line should be appended to this list:

    `LoadModule php4_module c:/php/sapi/php4apache.dll`

3. Now, within the same file, look further down and find the lines that begin "`AddModule`"; append the following two lines to the list.

    `AddModule mod_php4.c`
    `AddType application/x-httpd-php .php`

4. Save the file, and close your text editor.

All that now remains is to shut down and restart the Apache service (Windows NT, 2000, and XP users), to do this open a command prompt window and type "`net stop apache`" to stop the Apache Service, and "`net start apache`" to restart the service.

Configuring Internet Information Server (v4 or greater)

Like Apache, there are two ways to configure PHP to work with IIS. You can configure PHP to work as an ISAPI module, or you can configure PHP to work as a CGI process. As the ISAPI module is experimental, and for the moment considered unstable, it is not recommended that you use it in a production environment. For this reason, we will only look at installing PHP as a CGI process with IIS.

1. Start the Microsoft Management Console, also known as Internet Services Manager. Under Windows 2000 and Windows XP Professional this can be found in *Control Panel -> Administrative Tools*.

2. In Internet Services Manager, browse to *Internet Services Manager -> Computer Name -> Web Sites*. Right-click on *Default Web Site* and select *Properties*.

3. Select the *Home Directory* tab, and click on the *Configuration* button.

4. Under the *Mappings* tab, click on the *Add* button. In the new window, browse to the location of the PHP executable, in your `c:\php` folder.

5. In *Extension* type `.php` and ensure that the *Script engine* and *Check that file exists* checkboxes are checked.

6. Click *OK*, and you should return to the Management Console.

All that now remains is to shut down and restart the IIS service for the changes to take effect. To do this open a command prompt window and type `net stop iisadmin` to stop IIS completely. Typing `net start w3svc` restarts IIS with your new configuration options.

It is worth mentioning here that there is one final task for Windows NT, 2000, and XP users who use NTFS as their file system. In order for the above configuration to work you should additionally follow this procedure:

1. Using Windows Explorer, view the contents of your `C:` drive.

2. Right-click on your `c:\php` folder and select *Properties*.

3. Click on the *Security* tab, and then click the *Add* button.

4. A new window will open, entitled *Select Users Computers or Groups*. You should now scroll through the list of users and find an entry that begins `I_USER_`; the remaining part of this user's name should be the name of your computer. Click on this user once to highlight it.

5. Click the *Add* button and click *OK* to close this window.

6. Click OK once more to complete this modification.

Completing this procedure allows the web server to access this directory when it needs to use the PHP program to process your pages.

Installing PHP On Your Linux Web Server

If you're using Linux on your development server, then you need to follow these instructions. They are borrowed, in part, from the PHP & Linux Quick Install documentation, contained within the PHP sourcecode distribution. More detailed and up-to-date information on installing PHP on Linux can be found at the PHP Online Manual at *http://www.php.net/manual/en/install.apache.php*.

As with Windows, there are two ways in which PHP can be installed on your Apache web server under Linux. The first method is using a Dynamic Shared Object (DSO) much like the Windows Apache module, or a Static Module. DSO modules are far better in this respect, as they do not rely on you also having the sourcecode for Apache because they compile independently. This also means that should you wish to upgrade your version of PHP at any time, you don't have to also recompile Apache. For this reason, we will concentrate solely on compiling PHP as a DSO module.

What Is PHP?

1. Before you begin the compilation process, you must ensure that you are logged in as the root user.

2. Open a console window, or at the command line, browse to the location where you have stored your downloaded *tar.gz* archive.

3. To extract the archive, type: `gunzip -c php-4.x.x.tar.gz | tar xf -` (Note: replace `php-4.x.x` for the actual name of the file you downloaded. For example, PHP v4.2.0 is called `php-4.2.0.tar.gz`).

4. Type: `cd php-4.x.x` to enter the PHP directory.

5. To begin the precompilation process type: `./configure -with-mysql -with-apxs`.

6. Once step 5 has finished begin the compilation process by typing: `make`.

7. Step 6 can take a little while to complete, once it has completed type: `make install` to install PHP onto your Linux machine.

8. Find the file `php.ini-dist` and copy it to `/usr/local/lib/php.ini`.

The final stage in installing PHP on your Linux machine is to configure your web server appropriately. As most Linux distributions come with Apache pre-installed, all you need to do to is edit your `httpd.conf`, and add a line that looks like this:-

```
AddType application/x-httpd-php .php
```

Once this has been done, restart the Apache service, by typing: `apachectl restart` in a console, log in as the root user, and your server is ready to process PHP files.

We previously mentioned that OSX 10.1 comes with PHP installed by default. However, it should be noted that whilst PHP is installed, it isn't turned on by default.

Activating the PHP Module in OSX

Thankfully the OSX installer has handled the hard part of installing PHP to work with Apache under OSX. All that remains is to turn on the PHP module, and this is how we do it:

1. Open a terminal window

2. Navigate to the Apache directory by typing: `cd /etc/httpd`

3. Activate the PHP module itself by typing: `sudo apxs -e -a -n php4 libexec/httpd/libphp4.so`

4. That done, we need to inform Apache of the change, and configure it accordingly with the line:

   ```
   sudo perl -p -i.bak -e "s%#(AddType \S+-php[ -])%$1%i" httpd.conf
   ```

Now that this is done, if you are using a Linux or Mac OSX Server you should open a shell, or terminal window, and enter `sudo apachectl graceful` to restart Apache.

Chapter 1

Testing Your PHP Installation

We have now covered the installation and configuration of PHP on your machine, and all that remains is to check that the installation works. Thankfully there is a very easy way to do this. Create a new file in Notepad (or any other text editor), and enter:

```
<?php phpinfo(); ?>
```

Save the file as `test.php` and upload it to your web server. Once there browse the file on your web server and you should see something like this:

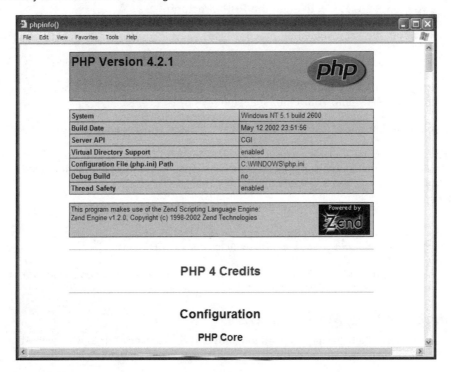

Troubleshooting PHP Configuration Issues

Nothing in life always goes quite to plan, as we all know. This is often the case with software installation. Here we will look at a list of possible issues that you might come across and their relevant solutions.

Because PHP is ever evolving, there are from time-to-time, version-specific issues that arise. It would be impossible to cover those here, due to the amount of time that PHP has been available. However, there are a number of issues that do occur, that are common over the various versions of PHP. These are detailed within the PHP install guide, that formed part of your download, and some of those are also included here for reference.

When Testing a PHP Page in Your Browser You Get a Blank Page

To determine whether or not any data has been sent to the browser view the source code of this blank page. If this reveals a sourcecode listing that begins with `<?php` or `<?`, then it means that your web server isn't properly processing the web page by sending it to PHP for interpretation. In this situation, you should check your PHP installation against the installation instructions given previously.

When Testing a PHP Page in Your Browser You Encounter a 500 Error

A 500 error occurs when something goes wrong with the server during processing. There is a simple diagnostic check, which might give further information.

Open a command prompt, and navigate to your `php` directory.

Under Windows type `php.exe -i` or under Linux type `php -i`. If the resulting output is a series of HTML tags then it is likely that this is a PHP configuration issue. As such, go over the configuration steps again for your web server to determine where the problem is.

If no HTML tags are returned, then you will receive some error messages. It might be clear from these messages what the problem is, enabling you to find a simple solution. If, however, this is not the case, you will find more information at the PHP Frequently Asked Questions (FAQ) page and discussion boards at *http://www.php.net/faq*.

Another common cause of this problem can be with Windows NT, 2000, and XP users who have not correctly assigned permissions to `IUSR_` to access the PHP executable. This process has previously been detailed in the *Configuring Internet Information Server* section.

The Specified CGI Application Misbehaved by Not Returning a Complete Set of HTTP Headers Visible in the Browser.

Follow the procedure given in the 500 error section, above.

Other Errors

Thankfully, while PHP is free to use, it is also very well supported. If you encounter other errors or problems, then there are two really useful resources to visit. First of all, there is the extensive PHP FAQ, as previously mentioned. Another great resource for installation issues is the dedicated installation mailing list. To subscribe to this mailing list, send an empty e-mail to *php-install-subscribe@lists.php.net*.

Chapter 1

Summary

We have briefly looked at the history of PHP and how developers were able to use previous versions of Dreamweaver to create PHP pages even though they weren't natively supported.

This chapter has taken you through the new-look Dreamweaver MX user interface, and has explained PHP's role within that interface. There is of course much more to the Dreamweaver interface than what we have covered here, as that subject alone could cover the content of a book in itself.

Dreamweaver is, and has always been, a revolutionary tool. Dreamweaver MX is no exception. With the natural integration of development tools, it is little wonder that this software is amongst the most popular web design packages available on the market today.

The addition of native PHP support to Dreamweaver can only be a benefit to the web design community as a whole, as it opens up extra possibilities to the developer. It should be noted here, that one of the greatest things about Dreamweaver as a development environment is that you can take all the skills that you gained from using one server model, for example PHP, and apply the same skills and processes to any of the other server models. Before you know it, you will be a multi-talented developer, which is as it should be.

We've also looked at installing and configuring PHP onto your development web server, a task that can appear quite difficult to the uninitiated, but one that is well worth the effort. This is the first step towards a dynamic development process, and one that we're sure will change the way you view web development in the future.

If you want to truly harness the power of PHP and Dreamweaver MX, though, there is one more tool that you will need to use, a database.

2

- Overview of MySQL
- Installing and configuring MySQL
- SQL and database primer

Author: Bruno Mairlot

What Is MySQL?

This book is about PHP development with Dreamweaver MX, and the only Database server support that Dreamweaver MX currently provides for the PHP language is MySQL.

This chapter will introduce you to the world of MySQL, independently of PHP and Dreamweaver. We will look at what MySQL is, how to install it, and how to administer it.

We will also give you an overview of getting started with SQL, the language used to communicate with MySQL. We will review the concept of databases and tables, how to create and delete them, as well as getting to know the structure of existing tables.

We will look at how to configure the MySQL server by creating accounts and setting up the permission system.

Finally, we will introduce you to two tools that will let you administer and issue SQL queries with a nice User Interface.

What Is MySQL?

MySQL is an SQL Database Server. Let's analyze each of these terms to help us define what exactly MySQL is.

Server

A server is a piece of software that runs in the background on a computer. It is built to keep running and executing specific tasks. All the way through this book, you will deal with two different servers: HTTP servers and MySQL servers.

Database

A database is a structured collection of data. It may be anything from the task list you use everyday, to information about the global population. A database is structured in a way that allows you to retrieve information easily and quickly depending on the kind of data it stores. You would not store a list of recipes the same way a big company will store its customer information. But the point these two databases have in common is that the information is easy to find and use.

MySQL is a relational database management system. An RDBMS defines relations between data structures. A relation between two data structures is a way to construct new virtual structures in a way that will enforce some constraints or conditions. This will help the user to construct a robust application. Most of the operations we will describe in this book are relational operations.

SQL

SQL stands for "Structured Query Language". The SQL language, which is commonly used on database software, will let you talk in a human-friendly way to the server to retrieve information from your database and manipulate the data in it. You may find many other flavors of SQL database server, for example Oracle, IBM DB2, Microsoft SQL Server, but they will all speak the same basic language: SQL.

Advantages of MySQL

MySQL has some advantages and disadvantages when compared to other databases. Let's take a look at some of them:

- MySQL is fast, very reliable, and easy to use. Other SQL servers are often fast and very reliable, but not very easy to use or configure. Some others are very easy to use, but neither fast nor reliable. MySQL has all these three qualities. It is also lightweight. The binary package of MySQL for Windows is only 12 MB. For comparison, Microsoft SQL Server weighs in at around 300 MB.

- MySQL is the server of choice when used with the PHP language. PHP provides a very strong support for MySQL, and due to its huge user base has been widely and thoroughly tested. Many web-hosting companies provide MySQL and PHP as a standard package.

- MySQL is open source. This means that you can have the sourcecode of MySQL and you are free to change it according to your needs. Hopefully, you won't need to, but the power of having MySQL open source is that if you did need to, it is very helpful to have the sourcecode to fit the server to your specific needs.

- There is a very large user base for MySQL and there are a lot of online communities focused on development and help. This means that if you have problems, there are plenty of people to ask for advice. This community has also created a number of third-party tools to help you get the job done. You will find some links to these tools at the end of this chapter.

- The biggest advantage of MySQL is that it is free. There are some cases where MySQL is not free, but for our goal, which is web application development, it is. For a free program, MySQL has a lot of advanced features like replication and a transactional system. It also runs on many platforms; you can run MySQL on Windows, Linux, FreeBSD, Solaris, and many others.

Disadvantages of MySQL

MySQL is not perfect. Its main disadvantage is that it lacks some of the more advanced features found on commercial database systems, which are also found on some of the other free database systems, like PostgreSQL. However, we won't need those features for the type of application that we're considering in this book.

Where To Get MySQL

MySQL can be obtained from many web sites and FTP servers. However, the official homepage for MySQL is *http://www.mysql.com*. Here you will be able to choose your operating system, choose the closest mirror to you, and choose between an HTTP or FTP transfer when you download.

On *MySQL.com* you will find a number of files available for download:

- MySQL is the most commonly used version of MySQL. It has no transaction system. All others features are included.
- MySQL Max is almost the same as the MySQL package, except that this one supports transactions.
- MySQL 4.0 is a development version of MySQL. It is not intended for a production environment, but is at your disposal for testing the new features.
- MySQL GUI and MyCC are graphical clients for administering a MySQL server.

There are many good products available to download for use with MySQL, we will review some of them at the end of the chapter.

Installing and Configuring MySQL

We will review a typical installation of MySQL. You will learn how to install and get started with the Windows version of MySQL.

Installation On Windows

Installing MySQL on a windows platform is very straightforward. The last stable version at the time of this writing is 3.23.49, so we'll focus on this version. But the installation procedure should be quite similar with other versions.

First, you need to download the binaries, which can be found at *http://www.mysql.com/*. Download the zip from the Windows section of this page. You will be directed to a list of mirror sites. Choose the mirror site that is closest to your location.

Once the download is complete, use WinZip to open it. If your WinZip version is recent enough, you should have an "*Install*" button on the toolbar. This will launch the installation process. If not, then decompress the files in the archive into a temporary directory, like `C:\WINDOWS\TEMP`, and then run the installation program in `C:\WINDOWS\TEMP\setup.exe`. Like most installation software on Windows, the process is very simple: all that you have to do is to click on *Next*. Once the installation software has finished, it will have created all the files necessary to run the MySQL server, but you still need to activate the services.

The win32 version of MySQL comes with a little application that will help you finish the installation. It is called `winMySQLadmin.exe` that you can find in the "bin" directory located in the main installation folder. If you installed MySQL with the default location, you should find it in `C:\MySQL\bin`. You need to run this program at least once just after the install process has finished. When WinMySQLadmin is run for the very first time, it will create the configuration file of MySQL, called `my.ini`. You will be asked for a username and password. This username will be the MySQL user that you will be able to connect with. Just enter the username and password as shown on screenshot below:

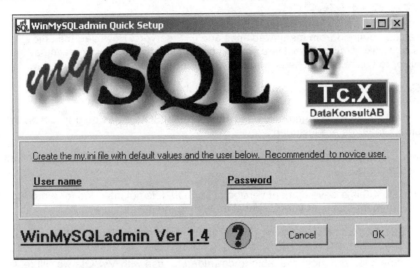

What exactly does the program WinMySQLadmin do?

First, it will create the configuration file for MySQL and WinMySQLadmin, `my.ini`, which we mentioned above. Next, it will create and register the "MySQL" service and start it. And finally, it will reduce to your taskbar as a small icon that will let you know the status of your MySQL server:

When the green light is on, it tells you that your MySQL server is running. If the red light is on, then your MySQL server has not been started. This icon is only shown when the WinMySQLadmin program is running and not necessarily when MySQL is running or not. You can have your MySQL server running without WinMySQLadmin.

You can stop the MySQL services, either by using the "*Services*" console that you can find in *Control Panel / Administration Tools / Services*. Select the MySQL service in the services list and then click on the stop button, situated in the toolbar.

You can also stop the MySQL services by entering this command in a command prompt: *net stop mysql*. The service can also be started manually by using the command: *net start mysql*.

MySQL Basics

Now that you have MySQL running, we can configure it.

The MySQL Console

The most basic tool to connect to your MySQL server is called MySQL. On Windows, it is called `mysql.exe`. The MySQL documentation also refers to this tool as the MySQL monitor.

This tool lets you type all your command and queries, and will return their results. As MySQL can be completely configured with SQL commands, you should be able to issue all the commands you'll need with this tool.

First you will need to find the location of this tool. It is situated in the `bin` subdirectory of your main install. If you are on Windows and installed MySQL in `C:\MySQL`, you will find it in `C:\MySQL\bin`. Next, open a command prompt, go into the `bin` directory, and type: *mysql.exe*.

The MySQL console welcome message should look like:

```
Welcome to the MySQL monitor.  Commands end with ; or \g.
Your MySQL connection id is 1 to server version: 3.23.49a

Type 'help;' or '\h' for help. Type '\c' to clear the buffer.

mysql>
```

You should be in the prompt of the MySQL monitor, which is where you will type all of your SQL commands, or queries. If haven't configured any users yet, you are running this connection as root. Therefore you have access to every database and all tables.

> Note: The MySQL Monitor can execute multiple queries in one command. All queries you enter in the MySQL monitor must end with a semicolon. But when you'll be writing SQL query in Dreamweaver MX or any other tool, you generally do not have to end them with a semicolon unless you want to execute more than one.

Introduction To Databases and SQL

First of all, we need to understand the database concept: in MySQL a Database is a collection of data and structures that are grouped under a regular name. The collections of data and structure that are stored in a MySQL database are called tables. The tables are the container of all the data in your database. These tables are structured in a list of column and rows, where the columns define the meaning of the data and the rows contains the data themselves.

The following diagram shows you a representation of a Server, with its database, and for each database, the table. In this schema, the server holds three databases: hotel, planning, and projects, with for each database a different number of tables and a different organisation.

Chapter 2

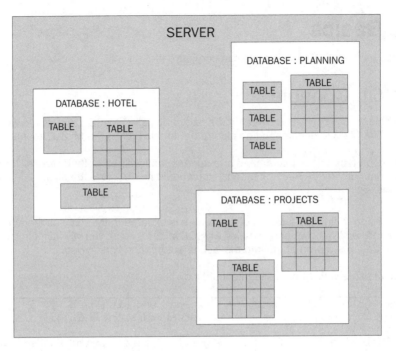

When you will be working with a database-oriented application, like the hotel reservation system that we will be looking at later on the book, you will focus on one database only. You will fundamentally work with the following database concepts:

- Tables
- Indexes
- Data (also called a RecordSet in Dreamweaver)

A table is a collection of data structured into columns and rows. You can think to it as a matrix of data. You will generally design the columns of a table and then fill it with rows containing the data.

Example of a Database

As an introductory example, we will present you how you could design a database to handle a company's employee and their working department. This company is called GlassMedia.

Suppose we have two departments in GlassMedia: the sales division and the marketing division. This company employs five people: John, Sally, Gene, Allan, and Robert.

Robert and Allan both work in the sales department and John, Sally, and Gene work in the marketing department.

To represent this information in a SQL server, we will construct one database called `glassmedia`, with two tables: `employees` and `department`.

What Is MySQL?

The following table shows you the conceptual representation of the database and its data.

DATABASE: GlassMedia			
TABLE: employees		**Table: department**	
name	**department**	**name**	**description**
John	Marketing	Sales	This department sells the company's products
Sally	Marketing		
Gene	Marketing	Marketing	This department composes brochures and advertisements
Allan	Sales		
Robert	Sales		

As you can see, the database holds two tables: 'employees' and 'department'. The table 'employees' has two columns: The name of the employee, and the department name into which this employee works. The table 'department' contains the list of the department and a short description of the department.

Suppose now that the company is going well and the sales department wants to hire a new employee. How would we update the database to store the new person's information?

We would just have to create a new record in the table 'employees' containing the new person's name, and the department 'sales'. We don't have to modify the table 'department', as there is no change in the department configuration of the company.

This little example shows you that you will represent an information concept (like an employee or a department) with a table. The column will represent all information you want to store about the concept, while a row will contain an instance of that concept. In the table 'employees', we have five rows, each containing the information related to one and only one employee.

This way, if some information changes for an object, others don't have to be changed as well.

The data stored in your database is stored in the table. You will access them through regular SQL queries. Most of your job when using the SQL server to design a database-oriented application will be to create the queries to interact with the data. Data access is done with the following four types of queries:

- SELECT – Returns a set of data from a table
- INSERT – Inserts new data into the database
- UPDATE – Sets a new value for existing data in a table
- DELETE – Deletes a record from a table

Selecting the Working Database

Every time you work with MySQL you must first specify which database you want to work on. First you need to know which databases are on your server. Issue the following SQL query in your MySQL Monitor:

```
SHOW DATABASES;
```

You will get a result like this:

```
MySQL> SHOW DATABASES;
+------------+
| Database   |
+------------+
| MySQL      |
| test       |
+------------+
2 rows in set (0.01 sec)
```

In this result you can read that the server has two databases: `MySQL` and `test`.

To create a database issue the SQL command:

```
CREATE DATABASE databasename;
```

where `databasename` is the actual name of your database. In our company example, we will use the database `glassmedia`. To create the `glassmedia` database, issue the following command:

```
CREATE DATABASE glassmedia;
```

This query will create a new database called `glassmedia`. You can now use that database. To use a database you will use the SQL command:

```
USE databasename;
```

In our example, the SQL command will be:

```
USE glassmedia;
```

Now, you are ready to use the database.

Note that the `USE databasename` SQL command will automatically switch the current working database to a new one. When you start the MySQL monitor, unless you specified the database in the command line, it won't know which database you want to use. Therefore the very first SQL statement you must issue is the `USE` command. After that, you don't need it anymore, unless you want to switch to another database.

Tables in MySQL

In this section we will give a brief overview of how to create a table, how to delete it and how to retrieve information for an existing table. In-depth coverage of the creation of a table will be given in Chapter 7.

Creating a Table

Tables are created using the CREATE TABLE SQL command. To create the table 'employees' from our above example, we will issue the following SQL command:

```
CREATE TABLE employees (
      name varchar(32),
      department varchar(32)
);
```

This command will create a table named 'employees' with two columns: name and department. These two columns are of the type varchar and of size 32. The varchar field type can be used to store a string of characters. When specifying the size 32, it means that the number of characters in an employee's name cannot be greater than 32.

To create the table 'department' we would issue the following SQL statement:

```
CREATE TABLE department (
      name varchar(32),
      description text
);
```

In this case, the column 'description' allows for a larger size.

To complete the example, suppose we wanted to create a table with more information about the employee, with the salary, we would do it this way:

```
CREATE TABLE employees (
      name varchar(32),
      salary integer,
      department varchar(32)
);
```

In this query, we see that the type of the column 'salary' is integer. This type indicates to MySQL that the value of this column can be only an integer number.

As far as we've illustrated, the CREATE TABLE syntax is:

```
CREATE TABLE tablename (
      field1 type1,
      field2 type2,
      ... ...,
);
```

As you can see, the CREATE TABLE statement requires the new table name, and a list of column definitions.

Deleting a Table

The SQL command to delete a table is:

```
DROP TABLE tablename
```

Chapter 2

where *tablename* is the name of the table you want to delete. In our `glassmedia` database, to delete the table '`employees`', we would use:

```
DROP TABLE employees;
```

Retrieving the Table Description

To retrieve the structure of an existing table, also called its definition, use the SQL command `DESC` as follows:

```
DESC tablename;
```

where tablename is the name of an existing table.

In the glassmedia database, if we want to know about the table '`employees`', we would use the following:

```
DESC employees;
```

If you issue this SQL command on the table '`employees`', you will get the following result in the MySQL Monitor:

```
C:\Program Files\mysql\bin\mysql.exe                                    _ □ ×
Welcome to the MySQL monitor.  Commands end with ; or \g.
Your MySQL connection id is 11 to server version: 3.23.49-nt

Type 'help;' or '\h' for help. Type '\c' to clear the buffer.

mysql> use glassmedia;
Database changed
mysql> desc employees;
+------------+-------------+------+-----+---------+-------+
| Field      | Type        | Null | Key | Default | Extra |
+------------+-------------+------+-----+---------+-------+
| name       | varchar(32) | YES  |     | NULL    |       |
| salary     | int(11)     | YES  |     | NULL    |       |
| department | varchar(32) | YES  |     | NULL    |       |
+------------+-------------+------+-----+---------+-------+
3 rows in set (0.00 sec)

mysql>
```

Configuring MySQL

As said previously, MySQL configuration is generally done via SQL queries. We will review some basic configuration options that will let you be ready for using it as a production environment. We will review the following configuration tasks:

- Configuring the MySQL database

What Is MySQL?

- Configuring the privileges system
- Creating a user.

> Note: The following commands are SQL queries and should be executed in the MySQL Monitor. The ending semicolon is included to help you in this software, but you should know that this character is used only to indicate to the MySQL Monitor the end of your SQL query.

The MySQL Database

In your MySQL monitor, issue the following sequence of SQL commands:

```
USE mysql;
SHOW TABLES;
```

The `SHOW TABLES` command will return the list of the table in the working database. The `'mysql'` database has the following tables:

- `columns_priv`
- `db`
- `func`
- `host`
- `tables_priv`
- `user`

These tables contain the MySQL user and privileges functionality. They are organized in an hierarchical manner.

- The table `user` is the host global privileges table. It contains the list of all users allowed to connect to your MySQL server, and their global privileges. Global privileges have precedence over all other privileges that you may specify in the other tables.

- The table `host` and `db` contain the information about the database access from a specific host. For example a user that connects from the local host can have access to every database, while if he connects from the network, have access to only some specific database, but it is still the same user, with the same password.

- The table `tables_priv` gives users access to specific table. In our glassmedia example, we defined the table `'employees'` with the salary of the people. This information is sensitive, and you may decide that all users cannot have access to that table except the boss. This table will contain the definition for these users.

41

- The table `columns_priv` gives users access to specific columns. Again, we can increase the granularity of the restrictions on the table `'employees'`. Finally you may decide to let all users use that table, but they can't look at the `'salary'` column, except for the boss.

To create a user in MySQL, you will handle the table user, and eventually give him the privileges you want. The MySQL privileges system is extremely flexible.

The Privileges System

In MySQL, the privileges system is based on the four tables: `user`, `host` and `db`, `tables_priv`, and `columns`. They are shown in order of priority.

The following picture shows a representation of the privileges level:

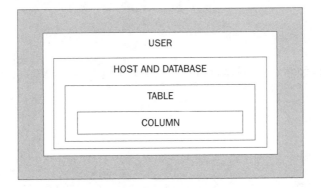

If a privilege is given in a higher level it will supersede the lower-level restriction you may have set. For example, if a user has the SELECT privileges on the User table, it will be able to do the SELECT on each database, each table, and each column of your database.

The Privileges Table Explained

The user table will contain the list of users allowed to connect to the server. It will also set the location from which they are allowed to connect. The host table gives access to a specific database only. The first level of security is about the connection itself. When a client tries to connect, MySQL will first look in the `user` table to see if it can connect, without even knowing about the database you're trying to access.

The following table present a brief description of the structure of the USER table, but the other tables work almost the same way.

`Host`	This column will contain the hostname from which the user is allowed to connect.
	If you want the user to be able to connect from everywhere, use the "%" value.
`User`	The username.
`Password`	The encrypted password.
	If you want to set up your own user directly by using this table, you need to use the SQL function `PASSWORD`() to make sure the password will be MySQL-encrypted.
`Select_priv`	These four privileges are the regular SQL query commands.
	Remember that if you set the value "Y" here, the user will be able to execute an SQL statement on **every** database.
`Insert_priv`	
`Update_priv`	
`Delete_priv`	
`Create_priv`	These privileges concern the `CREATE` and `DROP` statement.
`Drop_priv`	Note that the difference between a `DELETE` and a `DROP` statement is that the `DELETE` will affect only records in a table and leave the structure of the table unmodified, while the `DROP` statement will destroy completely the table or database.
`Reload_priv`	These privileges concern the MySQL server process. Giving these permissions to a user is rarely needed. Only the "root" superuser should have them set to "Y"
`Shutdown_priv`	
`Process_priv`	
`File_priv`	
`Grant_priv`	This privilege allows the user to grant privileges to other users.
`References_priv`	This privilege is not yet implemented.
`Index_priv`	Allows the user to create an index.
`Alter_priv`	Allows the user to alter the table structure.

Chapter 2

Allowing and Revoking Privileges

The `SQL GRANT` statement will help you manage all the privileges you may want to set up on a user.

To illustrate the concept of privileges, we will use the example of the boss and an employee account. We want the boss account to have access to any database from everywhere, while the employee's account to have access to the database `'glassmedia'` only, but he can access from everywhere.

To grant all privileges to the boss account, use the following SQL command:

```
GRANT ALL PRIVILEGES TO boss IDENTIFIED by 'mypasswordisnotgood'
```

This command will create an entry to the table `'host'`, with all privileges set to `'Yes'`. This user will be able to connect to the MySQL server from anywhere, with the username `'boss'` and the password `'mypasswordisnotgood'`.

Why isn't there any other entry? Remember the rule to check if a user has privileges. The first element we check is if the privilege is in the host table. If it is, no need to check further, this user has the privilege, therefore we won't need to specify the privileges for the boss account on lower levels.

Note that if the user does not exists when you issue the `GRANT` statement, MySQL will automatically insert it in the table `'user'`.

Now, we will create the employee's account, called `'emplaccount'` with password `'anewbadpassword'`. Creating this account is a little bit more complicated. We want the employee account to be able to connect to the server, but be able to use only the database `'glassmedia'`. In addition, the account has access to all tables in this database, but for the table `'employees'`, we don't want him to be able to `SELECT` the column `'salary'`. He will therefore have access to other columns of the table `'employees'`.

To create the employee's account, use the following query:

```
GRANT SELECT (name,department) ON glassmedia.employees TO emplaccount IDENTIFIED
BY 'anewbadpassword';
GRANT ALL PRIVILEGES ON glassmedia.department TO emplaccount IDENTIFIED BY
'anewbadpassword';
```

Note that there are two queries in the above statement. The first is to give the `SELECT` privileges on the columns `'name'` and `'department'` in the table `'employees'` from the database `'glasshaus'`. While the second gives all access to the table `'department'` in the same database. If you create another table later, you will need to grant the account `'emplaccount'` access to that table, by using another `GRANT` statement.

When using the `GRANT` statement, you should know that MySQL will act by supposing that for a specific level of privileges, everything you don't mention explicitly is granted.

For example, in the first `GRANT` statement, we didn't specify the host from where he can access the server. Then, if it is not specified, he can access from everywhere. On the second `GRANT` statement, we did not specify any column name, and therefore all privileges are granted on all columns of the table `department`.

What Is MySQL?

Now suppose we issue the following statement:

```
GRANT ALL PRIVILEGES ON glassmedia TO emplaccount IDENTIFIED by 'anewbadpassword';
```

There, we did not mention any table on the `'glassmedia'` database; therefore the user has all privileges on all tables.

The only element on which MySQL will not act this way is for the list of privileges. You always have to specify the exact list of privileges you want to give to a user, either by specifying `'ALL PRIVILEGES'` to set all privileges, or by specifying them by hand.

The names for the different privileges that GRANT understand are as follows:

```
ALL PRIVILEGES     FILE              RELOAD
ALTER              INDEX             SELECT
CREATE             INSERT            SHUTDOWN
DELETE             PROCESS           UPDATE
DROP               REFERENCES        USAGE
```

They are represented by the keyword *priv_type* in the GRANT syntax below.

The GRANT syntax explained:

```
GRANT priv_type [(column_list)] [, priv_type [(column_list)] ...]
ON {tbl_name | * | *.* | db_name.*}
TO user_name [IDENTIFIED BY "password"][, user_name [IDENTIFIED BY "password"]]
[WITH GRANT OPTION]
```

We will analyze each part of the GRANT SQL command:

```
GRANT priv_type [(column_list)] [, priv_type [(column_list)] ...]
```

This first part is the list of privileges you are granting to the user. The `column_list` element is a list of column specifiations. The list is separated by the "," character. Example: GRANT SELECT, UPDATE (dwmxhotel.*), DELETE (*.*)

```
ON {tbl_name | * | *.* | db_name.*}
```

The ON sequence identifies the database and table you are granting privileges on. You can use the table name, alternatively the * symbol means all tables, the *.* means all tables on each database and `db_name.*` means all tables on the specific database. If no database is specified, it will use the current working database. Example: ON dwmxhotel.*.

```
TO user_name [IDENTIFIED BY "password"][, user_name [IDENTIFIED BY "password"]]
```

This part represents the list of user you're working with. The list is separated by the "," character. The `user_name` element can be described with wildcards. The syntax for the user is `user@host`. If you want to let the user `dwmxphp` access from any host, you will use: `dwmxphp@'%'` (Note the ' characters).

The IDENTIFIED BY "password" is the plaintext password. MySQL will automatically encrypt the password when manipulating the `'privileges'` tables.

45

Chapter 2

When Do Changes Take Effect?

When the MySQL server starts, all privileges are read into memory. Database, table, and column privileges take effect at once, and user-level privileges take effect the next time the user connects. The server notices modifications to the 'grant' tables that you perform using GRANT or REVOKE immediately. If you modify the 'grant' tables manually (using INSERT, UPDATE, etc.), you should execute a FLUSH PRIVILEGES statement to tell the server to reload the 'grant' tables.

Additional Tools for MySQL

In this section, we will review some of the most common tools to administer a MySQL database on the Windows platform. Both of these tools provide a convenient way to execute SQL statements so you don't need to install both of them.

The purpose of an administrative tool is to provide a convenient interface to let you perform administrative tasks quickly and easily. Both of the tools we present here have their strengths and weaknesses, but they complement each other well. That's why we suggest installing both, and depending on the tasks you have, use either one or the other.

MyCC

MyCC is an open-source MySQL administration tool co-developed by MySQL AB and Jorge del Conde. It is a control panel that makes administering MySQL very easy, and is available for Windows and Linux platforms.

It is available for download from the MySQL web-site: *http://www.MySQL.com/* . It is currently beta software. That doesn't mean that it doesn't work correctly, but it is not yet a finished product, and will be updated very often.

At the current stage of the development, MyCC is more oriented for administrative tasks, like management of the server, creation of user, but has a very good SELECT statement interface.

Installing MyCC

MyCC binary distribution comes with an installer. It will install MyCC on your Windows platform exactly like many other installers do.

Connecting To a Database

When first you launch MyCC, it will look like this:

What Is MySQL?

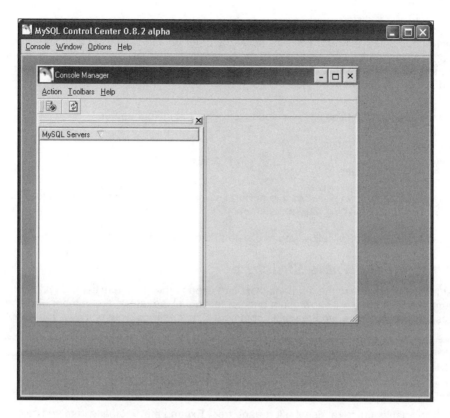

Clicking on the *Register Server* button will launch the *Database Connection Dialog*:

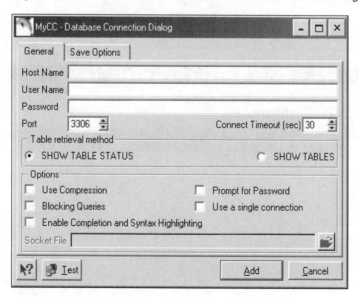

On this dialog, enter the hostname where your MySQL server is running, the user you want to connect with and its password. You may leave the other default options as they are. When you click on *Add*, it will just register a new server in the server tree interface. You will need to right-click on the server, and select the menu item *Connect*. Once you are connected to your server, the tree will expand in the following items:

- Databases: Contains all the databases registered in your server
- Server Administration
- User Administration

The Server Administration allows you to perform some administration tasks, like reloading the server, shutting it down, and flushing different elements.

The User Administration will allow you to create and set up the user privileges.

List of Tables and Table Structure

To get the list of table, use the left-pane tree, and expand the *Database* item. Click on the *Tables* subitem. The right pane will show you a grid containing all the tables, the number of records the size in bytes, the creation date, and the table comment. The following picture shows you an example:

Table	Records	Size (bytes)	Created	Type	Comments
department	0	0	2002-05-27 15:44:06	MyISAM	
employees	0	0	2002-05-27 15:43:47	MyISAM	

To analyze a table structure, use the left-pane tree. Expand the *Database* item and select your table. On the right panel you will see the structure of your table. The following picture shows you an example:

Field	Type	Null	Key	Default	Extra
name	varchar(32)	YES			
description	text	YES			

Executing a SQL Statement

To execute a SQL statement, you can use the *SQL* button. It will launch the *Query in Database* dialog box. The following picture shows you an example:

What Is MySQL?

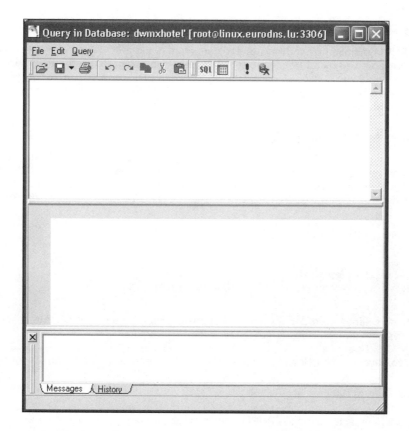

Enter your query in the upper panel, and click on the '*!*' button to run your query. Results will appear on the middle pane. If the result panel is not activated, click on the menu item *Query -> Result Pane*.

PHPMyAdmin

PHPMyAdmin is a very popular tool for administering a MySQL database. It is entirely written in PHP, so you need to have a working PHP server in order to run PHPMyAdmin. See Chapter 1 if you haven't set up a PHP server already.

PHPMyAdmin provides a very good interface to let you handle very specific records in a table, but will also let you configure the server and create users, though MyCC provides a better interface for that kind of task.

Obtaining PHPMyAdmin

The official PHPMyAdmin web site is *http://www.phpmyadmin.net*. On this page, you will find all the information to download PHPMyAdmin from Sourceforge, and you can find out about the latest version and about the changes made from previous versions.

Installing PHPMyAdmin

To install PHPMyAdmin, first you will need to decompress the archive you downloaded into a directory that is served by a PHP-aware HTTP server. If you want to test the PHP ability of a special directory, just write into a little `.php` file with the following PHP code: `<?php echo phpinfo()?>`. If you get the sourcecode, then your server does not handle PHP. If you get the whole PHP information, then your directory should be able to run PHPMyAdmin.

Connecting to a MySQL Server

Once you have installed PHPMyAdmin, open the file name `config.inc.php` with your favorite text editor (Notepad should be fine). This file contains the configuration options of PHPMyAdmin. In this file you will find the declaration of the server array that will contain the information needed like the hostname, the user, and the password. This part of the `config.inc.php` file will look something like this:

```
$cfgServers[$i]["host"]          = "localhost";
.
.
$cfgServers[$i]["user"]          = "dwmxphp";
$cfgServers[$i]["password"]      = "glasshaus";
```

Change these settings according to your server specification. The values used to describe the MySQL server are strings. Don't forget to leave the " characters.

You will also have to set the location of the PHPMyAdmin directory by altering the following lines:

```
$cfgPmaAbsoluteUri = 'http://localhost/phpmyadmindir/';
```

Where `localhost` is the machine PHPMyAdmin is running on and `phpmyadmindir` is the directory in which you installed PHPMyAdmin.

Running PHPMyAdmin

To access your PHPMyAdmin enter the URL of the directory you decompressed PHPMyAdmin in. If you get an error message try to add */index.php* to the URL.

The homepage of PHPMyAdmin looks like this:

What Is MySQL?

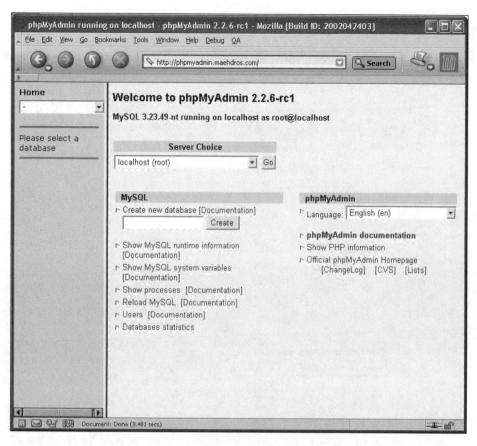

List of Tables and Table Structure

As alway, when using MySQL, you will first need to select your working database. To do that with PHPMyAdmin, use the dropdown menu in the left frame.

To get the list of tables and the information related to each table, click on the database name on top of the tables list, in our example click on the item `glassmedia`.

The table list shows like this:

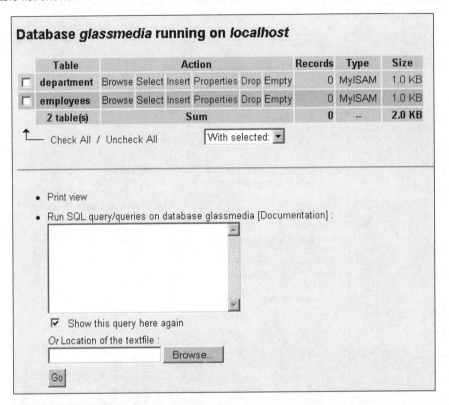

To get the information on a specific table, you can either click on the table name, on the left frame. Or if you are in the page showing database information, you can click on the *Properties* link with regards to your table name.

Executing an SQL Statement

To execute SQL statement with PHPMyAdmin, you must be on one of the two following pages:

- The Database structure
- The Table structure.

If you are on the *Database* structure page, you will have a text area where you can enter the query you want to run. Remember that you are not limited to the SELECT statement. You can execute every kind of SQL statement you wish.

If you are on the *Table* structure page, then you have almost the same text area, except that the content has been prepared for you. You will generally find an SQL query like: SELECT * FROM tablename WHERE 1.

Summary

In this chapter we have had a first look at the MySQL server. MySQL is a relational database management system, where data are structured into tables and relations. MySQL is the SQL server of choice when using the PHP scripting language.

The installation of MySQL under the Windows platform is almost straightforward, but don't forget that you will need to launch 'winmysqladmin' at least one time after the installation to setup the `'mysql'` service and have your first user ready to connect to the server.

In MySQL, the data is structured in a hierarchical organization: databases, tables, and columns. A MySQL server can hold multiple databases. The collections of data and structure that are stored in a MySQL database are called tables. The tables are the container of all the data in your database.

To create a table, use the `CREATE TABLE` statement. To delete a table from a database use the `DROP TABLE` statement. To get information about the structure of a table, use the `DESC TABLE` statement.

The configuration of the MySQL server is done mainly with the `'mysql'` database and the tables attached. The table `'user'` holds the account information. A user will be able to connect to your server, if and only if the account is present in this table. The table `'user'` holds the global privileges that supersede all other levels of privileges. The table `'host'` and `'db'` holds the accessibility for a user to a specific database and from a specific origin. The tables `'tables_priv'` and `'columns_priv'` hold the privileges access to a specific table and a specific column. Giving a privilege to a user is performed with the `GRANT` statement.

We also reviewed two tools to let you perform actions in an easy way, thanks to their user interface. The tool MyCC will be mainly used for database and server management, and to quickly issue a `SELECT` statement. The tool PHPMyAdmin is good for retrieving and editing records, but will also let you perform many other actions.

3

- Creating a site definition
- Creating a connection to the database
- Troubleshooting database connection problems

Author: Tim Green

Getting Started with Dreamweaver MX

In the first two chapters of this book, we have guided you through installing and configuring the development tools that you need to begin working successfully with Dreamweaver MX.

Now that you have a web server running PHP, and a MySQL database server configured and ready to use, it's time to get your teeth into what this book is really about: Designing PHP web pages in Dreamweaver MX.

We'll begin by giving Dreamweaver all the information it needs to work with your development environment, by creating a Site Definition. Once your site is defined, we'll take our first look at the juicier subject of Databases, and show you how to create a database connection within Dreamweaver, which will allow you to access the MySQL database we created in Chapter 2.

Summarizing this chapter, we will discuss some of the more common problems and errors that you might encounter, and provide you with simple, no-nonsense solutions, guaranteed to keep the development blues at bay.

The Essentials

Before you begin working through this chapter, you must ensure that you have the following:

- A web server configured to work with PHP (see **Chapter 1**).

- The Web Server Address, FTP Server Information (if applicable) and Authentication Information (Username & Password).

- A working MySQL Server (see **Chapter 2**).
- The MySQL Server IP Address and Authentication Information. (Username & Password)

All of this information will be required at some point over the coming pages, and is essential to providing you with the richest development experience possible.

Dreamweaver is a unique tool in the way that it allows you to view your web page within the User Interface. Certainly, there are many **WYSIWYG (What You See Is What You Get)** web page editors on the market today, but few, if any, offer the rich design experience that Dreamweaver presents. Indeed, Macromedia describes Dreamweaver as a "visual editor" in order to highlight this fact, and many Dreamweaver developers prefer this description.

One of Dreamweaver's best features is its ability to interact with your web server and application server, so that dynamic elements of your web page come to life within the UI, even before the page has been uploaded to your server.

With the above information to hand, we shall now take a look at the essential first steps you should take when creating any web site with Dreamweaver MX.

Creating a Site Definition

A site definition is the essential starting point to the development of any web site. With the information that is provided here, Dreamweaver will be able to accurately track the directory structure of your site, keep a watchful eye over all your internal (and external) hyperlinks and maintain a list of all images, movies, colors, and external files. Using the Site Definition, Dreamweaver is also able to provide you with a preview of what your page will probably look like without even uploading it to the server.

In essence, the Site Definition is the root of all the built-in site management functions. Without this information Dreamweaver will have no idea where to begin looking. So, to get the very best use out of the software, you need to provide it with all the information you can.

Dreamweaver employs two methods for defining sites. There is the Basic method, which employs a step-by-step Wizard that guides you through the Site Definition process, and there is an Advanced Definition process, which gives you complete control over every aspect of your site's definition.

It is often best to work through the Wizard, and then customize your definition by amending the properties in the Advanced Definition section. For this reason, we will cover the Site Definition Wizard only, as this will introduce you to the settings and properties that are also used within the advanced section.

Site Definition Wizard – A Step-By-Step Guide

The whole process of defining a site within Dreamweaver is made simple with the Basic Configuration Wizard, which walks you through the whole process. There are essentially four different ways to configure your site using the Basic Configuration Wizard:

- Edit and Test Locally

Getting Started with Dreamweaver MX

- Edit Locally and Upload to Remote Testing Server
- Edit Directly over a Network
- Edit Directly via FTP

These different configuration options have slightly different steps within the Wizard. For this reason we will cover each option individually.

The first two stages in "Defining a Site" with the "Basic Configuration Wizard" remain the same, regardless of the configuration that you have, so we will look at those now.

Naming the Site

To begin defining a site in Dreamweaver MX using the Site Definition Wizard go to the *Site* menu and click on *New Site*. The Site Definition Wizard will launch:

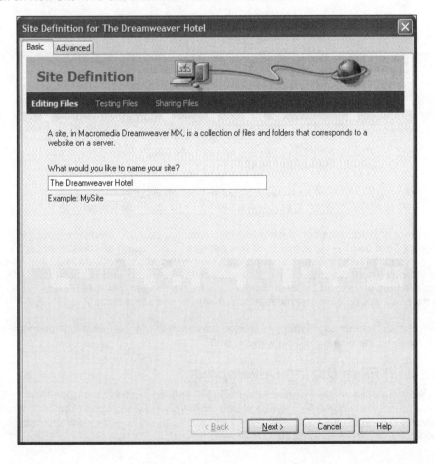

As you can see from the screenshot overleaf, the first stage in defining a site is to give the definition a name. In this case, we are defining a site for our example "*The Dreamweaver Hotel*". Here you should enter any name that is appropriate for the site that you want to develop. This name isn't used within your web site itself and won't be placed on any of your pages. It is an internal setting, which helps Dreamweaver to identify the site you are working on.

Once we have determined a name for the site we need to set up the Server Technology that the site will use.

Server Technology

First, you need to decide whether your site will be using Dynamic Scripting technologies (such as ASP, JSP, CFML, or PHP) or just rendering static HTML pages. Of course, for the purpose of this book, we will be using PHP and MySQL, so select the '*Yes, I want to use a server technology*' option. A dropdown containing the available options will then appear, and from it select *PHP MySQL*.

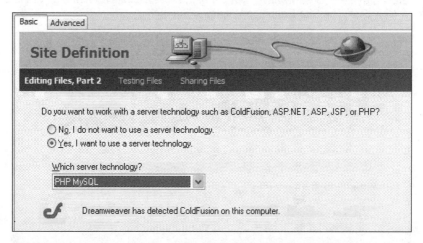

One important note from the screenshot opposite (which was taken on my own machine) is the reference to ColdFusion – "*Dreamweaver has detected ColdFusion on this computer*". You probably won't see this statement unless you have Coldfusion installed on your own machine. The latest version of ColdFusion, ColdFusion MX, has a special relationship with Dreamweaver MX, as these products are both developed by Macromedia. Due to this relationship, ColdFusion is automatically detected when installed on the same machine. There is no such detection for PHP.

With your Server Technology correctly selected we can now proceed to give Dreamweaver more information about the files we will be working with.

Working with Files During Development

This stage of the Wizard really sees the beginning of your site definition proper. From here, you determine where your source files will be stored while you are working on them, and whether your web server is a local machine, a remote machine on a local network, or a remote machine that requires an active Internet connection.

Getting Started with Dreamweaver MX

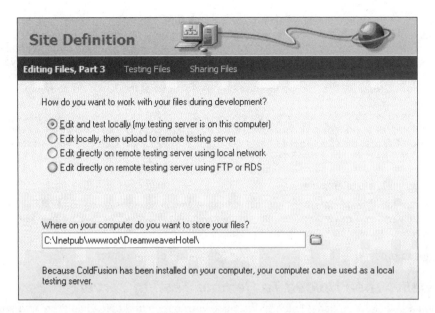

The subsequent steps in the Wizard are determined by your choice here. As each of the choices in this dialog produce different steps, we will look at the options and subsequent stages of the Wizard in more detail.

Edit and Test Locally (My Testing Server Is On This Computer)

You should select this option if everything is working from the same machine. This is the default selection, since many developers opt to run a web server from their development machine. If in Chapters 1 and 2 of this book, you opted to install PHP and MySQL onto your local machine, then this is the perfect option to choose. However, if you installed PHP and MySQL onto another machine that you have access to, either via the Internet or via a Network connection, then you should follow the instructions for **Edit Locally, Then Upload To Remote Testing Server.**

When selected, the only information that the Wizard requires is where you will be storing all of the files associated with your web site. To do this, you can click on the folder icon, and browse to the correct directory. Once you have done this, you can safely proceed to the next stage in the Wizard.

a) Communication with Your Testing Server

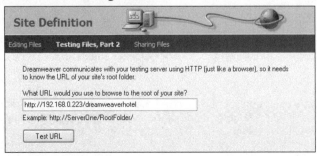

Chapter 3

In this stage of the Site Definition Wizard, you need to enter the web address used to view your web pages in your browser. Since you are editing and testing your files locally, this address can begin with either *http://localhost* or *http://127.0.0.1* – both of these addresses are synonymous, and point to the same location. If you were editing directly on a remote testing server, the address you entered would be prefixed with a different value (which would vary depending on your server and network configuration). Normally it would be the numeric IP Address of the server in question.

Once you have entered a value here, you should test the URL using the button provided, to ensure that everything is working fine. If you receive an error message flip forward to the section entitled **Connection Errors**, but if you get a message stating, "*The URL Prefix test was successful*", you can proceed to the next stage of the Site Definition Wizard.

b) Specifying a Remote Server

This stage of the Wizard determines whether your files will be transferred to another machine, or stored locally. As you have opted to edit and test your files locally, there is no need to specify a remote server at this stage, so you should select *'No'*.

Click *Next* to proceed to the summary of your Site Definition (see later).

Edit Locally, Then Upload To Remote Testing Server

You should select this option if you are designing your pages and uploading them to a server based on a different machine. This option normally applies if you have a secondary machine acting as a server that lives either on your Local Area Network or the Internet.

When selected, the only information that is required is the directory path to where your files will be stored on the local machine.

a) Testing Server Information

The next stage in defining a site consists of giving Dreamweaver the location of your testing server. To do this Dreamweaver needs to know how it should be connecting to the server.

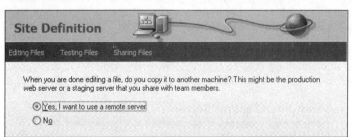

Taking a look at the dropdown under the heading *'How do you connect to your test server?'* you will see the options listed in a dropdown box. We will discuss these now.

I'll set this up later

You should select this option only if none of the other options in this dialog appropriately describe your configuration, or if you wish to enter all of the settings manually. For the purposes of this step-by-step guide to the Site Definition Wizard, this option will not be used.

Getting Started with Dreamweaver MX

Local/Network

You should select this option if your development files are stored either on your local machine, or a machine that is accessible through the network file system. When selected, you should enter the full path to the folder where your work is stored, or click on the folder icon and browse to the relevant folder.

The final piece of information required by this dialog asks whether or not you wish to refresh the remote file list automatically. The remote file list is shown in the Site panel within the Dreamweaver User Interface, checking this box ensures that all changes made to the contents of the local work folder are also reflected in the remote folder.

FTP

You should select this option if you edit your files locally, and then upload them to your testing server, or if you edit your files directly on your remote testing server. When selected, the dialog changes and you have a number of other settings to complete.

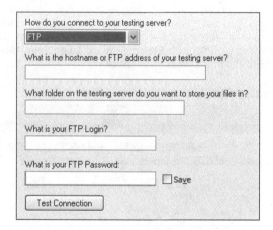

As you can see from the screenshot above, there are a number of additional settings that Dreamweaver requires to make an FTP connection to your server.

The hostname or FTP address of your server is likely to be the same as that of your web site itself. If your host provider, or system administrator has given you alternative FTP information, you should employ that here. To complete the configuration of this step, you should complete the name of the folder that your web site will be stored in. The FTP login and Password are essential for connecting to your server and should have been provided to you by either your host provider or network administrator.

When you have completed this form, perform the connection test, to ensure that the details you have entered are correct. If upon testing you receive an error message, then some part of the information you have entered is incorrect and you should double-check your settings. If the settings are correct, Dreamweaver will notify you of a successful connection.

RDS – Remote Development Service

As previously mentioned, the Remote Development Service is for use with a ColdFusion server. This option should not be used when working with the PHP Server Model.

Chapter 3

b) Communication with Your Testing Server

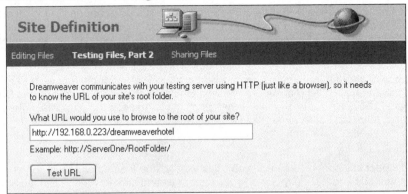

In this stage of the Site Definition Wizard, you need to enter the web address used to view your web pages with a browser. Once you have entered a value here, you should test the setting using the button provided, to ensure that everything is working fine. If you receive an error message flip forward to the section entitled **Connection Errors** later in the chapter. However you should receive a message stating, "*The URL Prefix test was successful*".

c) Checking in and Checking Out

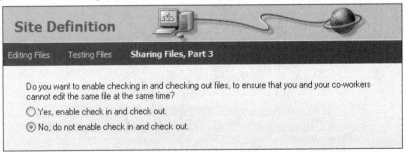

Dreamweaver utilizes a **check in – check out** system for users who work in a collaborative environment, or for users who work from multiple machines. Checking a file out to work on automatically makes that file unavailable to anyone else. This prevents other members of your workgroup from editing a file that you are currently working on. Checking the file back in automatically makes it available to anyone else who needs it for further amendment.

Selecting *'Yes'* at this stage presents a few more settings for completion, allowing you complete control over whether Dreamweaver should check out a file, or open a read-only copy of the file. So that other workgroup members can immediately see who is working on which file, you also need to enter your name and e-mail address for the purposes of identification.

You can now proceed to the summary (see later).

Getting Started with Dreamweaver MX

Edit Directly On Remote Testing Server Using Local Network

This option should be selected if none of the files you are working on will be stored on the local machine. This option normally applies if you have a secondary machine acting as a web server on your Local Area Network (LAN) and you want all of the development files to be stored on that machine.

This is a very common scenario if you are part of a Workgroup or if you are collaborating with other developers, but there are many developers who are able to run a dedicated web server themselves. This server might be for development purposes only, but it could also provide some remote access so that clients can view a project's development and evolution. If you access your web server via a LAN and do not wish to store your work files on your local computer then this is the ideal option.

When selected you can use the folder icon to browse your network file system to find the folder where all of the web site's files will be stored.

Communication with Your Testing Server

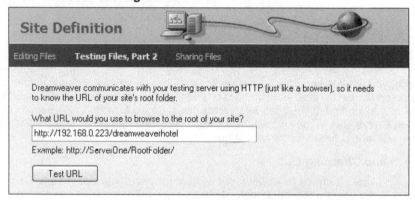

You need to enter the web address used to view your web pages in your browser. Once you have entered a value here, you should test the setting using the button provided, to ensure that everything is working. If you receive an error message flip forward to the section later in this chapter entitled **Connection Errors**, but you should receive a message stating, "*The URL Prefix test was successful*". You can now proceed to the summary (see later).

Edit Directly On a Remote Testing Server Using FTP or RDS

As stated earlier, **File Transfer Protocol** (**FTP**) and the **Remote Development Service** (**RDS**) are two technologies that allow you to connect to your web server in a relatively secure environment. RDS is a ColdFusion MX technology, and as such doesn't apply here, but FTP is a common method for transferring files to a remote file system, such as that on a web server on the Internet. When transferring web sites from your development server to your production server, you will undoubtedly make use of FTP.

Because FTP is a secure method of connection, it is susceptible to something called a 'Time Out'. Quite literally, the FTP Server will only allow you to remain connected for a certain period of time. Once that time has elapsed, you are immediately disconnected.

As I'm sure you will realize, with a development environment such as Dreamweaver MX this can cause difficulties, as frequent time-outs can slow the whole process of development, and in this instance it is necessary to dedicate a folder on your local machine for storing your development work.

Once you have completed your development, you can immediately transfer the files from your local directory to your web server, without leaving the Dreamweaver interface at all.

a) Testing Server Information

The next stage in defining a site consists of giving Dreamweaver the location of your testing server. To do this Dreamweaver needs to know how it should be connecting to the server.

b) Communication with Your Testing Server

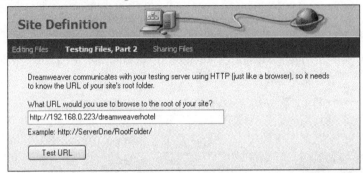

In this stage, you need to enter the web address used to view your web pages in your browser. Once you have entered a value here, you should test it using the button provided, to ensure that everything is working fine. If you receive an error message flip forward to the section entitled **Connection Errors** later in the chapter. You should receive a message stating, "*The URL Prefix test was successful*" and proceed to the next stage.

c) Checking in and Checking Out

Dreamweaver utilizes a **check in – check out** system for users who work in a collaborative environment, or for users who work from multiple machines. The setup is exactly the same as described in the "**Edit locally, then upload to remote server**" section.

Summary

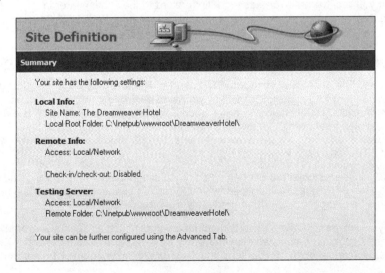

Getting Started with Dreamweaver MX

This stage of the Wizard allows you to review all of the values that you have entered. Should you need to amend any of the values, you can use the *Back* button to return to the appropriate step.

Once you have completed the Site Definition Wizard, and clicked *Finish*, Dreamweaver will automatically create a cache of all the files in your work directory and will automatically refresh the *Files* panel, to show the contents of your working directory.

Connection Errors

If, when initially testing your connection, you receive an error message similar to the one below, then it is likely that the root URL you entered for your site is incorrect.

If you do encounter an error similar to this, then you are given a clue as to the cause of the problem by the message *(HTTP Error: 404)*. This is a standard HTTP error, similar to the kind that you might encounter when browsing the web. In this case 404 means file not found, so it is likely that the address entered is incorrect.

Advanced Site Definition – An Overview

Whilst the Site Definition Wizard is an extremely user-friendly way of defining your site, it hides many of the configuration options available. This is necessary so that the Wizard can provide a simplified and unified approach to defining a site, but this isn't always enough. If you need to change specific configuration options, or access other configuration options not detailed in the Site Definition Wizard, then you need to access the **Advanced Site Definition**.

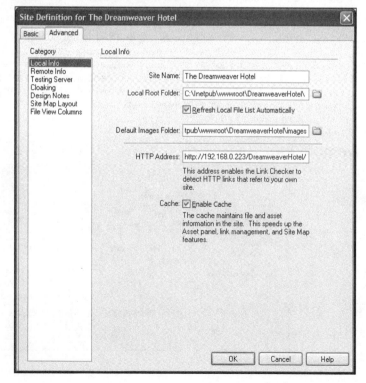

Chapter 3

The Advanced Site Definition can be accessed by clicking on the *Advanced* tab, when opening the Site Definition Wizard. The screenshot opposite displays the first category, *Local Info*.

As you can see, from the column on the left of the screenshot, there are a number of different categories. Some of these you will immediately recognize as steps within the Site Definition Wizard, and others will be completely new. Due to the nature of an Advanced Site Definition, it is impossible to cater for every applicable configuration scenario, so for this reason we shall work through each of these categories, and describe the options available to you, allowing you to make a more informed choice.

Local Info

The *Local Info* category is for defining the settings and options that are applicable to the development environment on the machine that you are using Dreamweaver on.

You will already be familiar with a number of the settings here, as they are similar to their corresponding settings in the Site Definition Wizard. However, other settings are new, and have not previously been covered.

Default Images Folder is one such setting. This allows you to specify a folder within your web site that is dedicated to storing all the images that are used within it. This is normally a good practice, as some web sites may use literally hundreds of images in different places. Placing these images in a central directory makes them easy to find and easy to manage. Dreamweaver has its own reasons too for wanting to know where your images will be stored, as it can better keep track of all your site's images and make them available within the *Assets* tab in the *File* panel. Dreamweaver also uses this information to track links to your images, and uses this information whenever you insert an image stored outside your web site's root folder, to determine where an image must be copied to.

The other option, which you will probably be unfamiliar with, is *Enable Cache*. Cache technology is crucial in the day-to-day working of the Internet. It speeds up connections around the world, and gives users a better experience in general. A cache essentially stores a local copy of the file in question, allowing it to be more quickly accessed, and Dreamweaver's cache works in exactly the same way. By default this option is checked, and when you are developing it works transparently, allowing you to view pages more quickly. Whenever you add, amend, or delete a file in the web site the cache is recreated so as to remain accurate and consistent. It is usually a good idea to leave this option at its default setting.

Remote Info

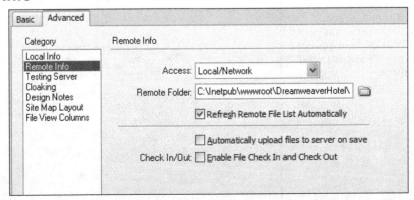

The *Remote Info* category is largely the same as in the Site Definition Wizard, however there is one additional option here, not covered in the Wizard.

Automatically upload files to server on save does exactly that; uploads your files to the web server, whenever you save them. This is perfect if you're working one a number of different web pages at the same time, so you can be sure that you don't forget to upload on of the files. However, this option does require that you have an active Internet connection if you connect to a remote server via FTP.

Testing Server

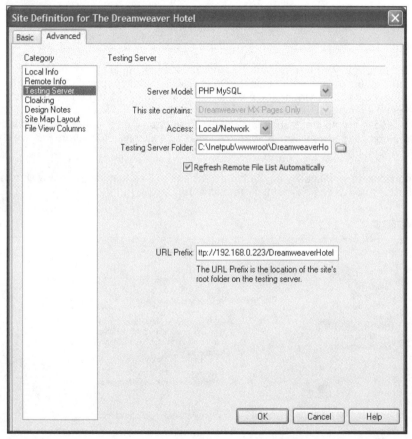

One piece of useful information that is completely hidden from you in the Site Definition Wizard is the fact that you can independently configure a testing server to work with Dreamweaver MX. This allows for some developers who have a Development Folder, a Test Site, and a Production Site. We have previously discussed all of the options and settings available here in the Site Definition step-by-step guide.

Cloaking

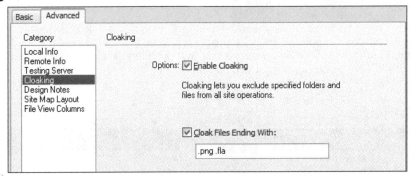

Cloaking is a completely new addition to Dreamweaver's functionality, and allows you to specify types of files that you do **not** want uploading to your web server. Typically these are files that are created during the development of some portion of your web site, but are not used as part of the end product. A good example of this is a Macromedia Flash source file (called an FLA). These files are the canvas used to create the flash animation itself, but aren't used in the final animation. Of course, if these were uploaded to your web server, they would be accessible to everyone, which isn't necessarily appropriate.

By enabling cloaking, and specifying the file extensions of files that you do not wish to be uploaded to the web site, you can ensure that they remain safe.

Design Notes

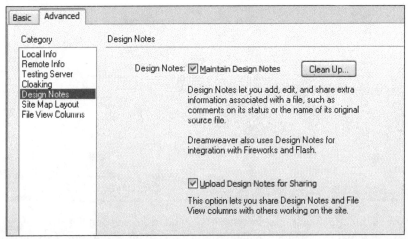

Design Notes are useful during the production of a web site, as they allow you to make essential notes about design ideas and tips about a particular file directly within Dreamweaver. If you like, Design Notes are Dreamweaver's version of a PostIt note, and are accessible (optionally) to whomever you share web development tasks with.

By default Design Notes are maintained, but you can turn this feature off, though this isn't really recommended, as Design Notes are used to store more than just your information about a file. They also store internal system values, such as recordset information, and can be shared amongst development teams by enabling the Design Notes-sharing option.

You can purge all design notes from a site at any time by clicking the "*Clean Up...*" button.

Site Map Layout

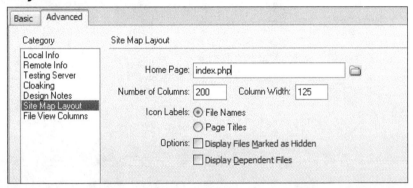

One of Dreamweaver's most useful features is its ability to diagrammatically show you the structure of your web site. This allows you to view the relationship between various pages easily, as well as see at a glance any broken or orphaned links within your site.

All site maps are generated in relation to a specified homepage, so if you wish to take advantage of Site Mapping features, then you should specify the very first page of your site here.

Number of Columns and *Column Width* allow you to control the size of the generated site map, while the *Icon Labels* options allow you to determine which icons in the site map have descriptive text next to them.

Display Files Marked as Hidden ensures that all files (hidden or otherwise) are shown within your site map, so that you can properly see their relationship to other files in your site, whilst *Display Dependent Files*, displays a list of every file referred to in each page.

File View Columns

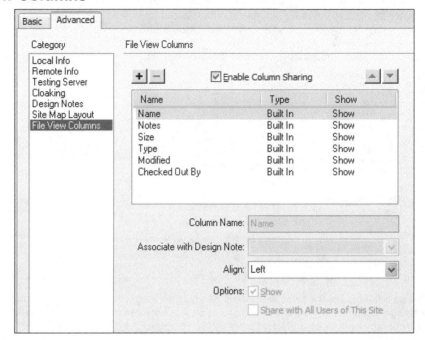

File view columns are only available when you click on the ⊞ icon in the *Site* tab of the *Files* panel.

This opens up a larger window showing each file within your site, along with a number of associated properties. This category of the Advanced Site Definition allows you to change the order of the columns, add a new column, or delete a column. The actual columns themselves represent properties of each file, and these may be either typical file-related properties, or internal pointers to Dreamweaver references.

For example, it is possible to include a column that will specifically map to a value stored as a design note. However, this truly is advanced usage, and is beyond the scope of this book. If you wish to find out more about the customization of the File View Columns, you should consult the Dreamweaver MX User Guide.

Now that we have defined our site, and Dreamweaver has all the settings it needs to manage your workflow, all we need to do is to configure a connection to your MySQL database, and you are ready to begin using the full power of the Dreamweaver MX development environment.

Creating a Database Connection

Database connections are very simple to create. Thankfully Dreamweaver MX handles the majority of this process for you. Armed with your MySQL server information, we shall now look at creating a connection to your database.

Getting Started with Dreamweaver MX

To begin creating a database connection we have to turn to the *Application* panel, and the *Databases* tab. Before we proceed, if next to the minus button it says "*Document Type: HTML*", then you must close the currently open document, and create a new PHP File. Why do you have to do this? Well, this comes back to Dreamweaver's Context Sensitivity that we discussed in Chapter 1. Dreamweaver changes the way it works depending on the task at hand and makes available only the tools that you can use. Unfortunately if the default open document is a plain HTML file, Dreamweaver will not allow access to any of its dynamic behaviors, including connections, as they do not apply to a standard HTML page.

Now you have a new blank PHP file open, we can proceed with creating the connection. Returning to the *Application* panel, click on the plus sign and then click on MySQL Connection.

Before we complete this dialog, it is worthwhile noting that there is a standard naming convention for connections. Whilst not entirely necessary, they can help you identify a reference to the connection if you ever delve in *Code View*. With connections the naming convention is to prefix your chosen name for the connection with the string `'conn'`. In this case, as we are using the Dreamweaver Hotel example that we have already introduced, we will call this connection `'connHotel'`.

The MySQL Server value for this dialog should be the hostname or IP Address of your MySQL Server. If your web server is at *www.mysite.org,* then you would enter *www.mysite.org* in the MySQL Server textbox.

> The username and password information represent the authentication information for your MySQL Server, not your web server. This is often the most common mistake to make when creating a connection.

When you have entered all of the above information that is relevant to your site, click on the *Select...* button. This will open a new dialog that will allow you to choose your database.

Upon selecting the database from this dialog, click *OK*, for the name of that database to be entered into the connection dialog. All that now remains is to test the connection by clicking the *Test* button.

If you have entered the correct details, you will be presented with a message informing you that the connection has tested successfully. When this happens, click *OK* to complete the Connection Definition process.

With this is done, Dreamweaver MX automatically updates the *Databases* tab of the *Application* Panel. From here you can readily see all of the tables and columns within your Database.

Connection Troubleshooting

You could be forgiven for thinking that a dialog as simple as the connection dialogue doesn't pose any problems. As always, this could never be further from the truth.

Here are some common error messages that occur when creating a MySQL Connection:

There are a number of reasons why something similar to this error might occur. The most common of these are that the authentication information is incorrect (that is wrong username or password) or that the MySQL Database has been set to deny remote connections. The denial of remote connections is not a standard MySQL configuration option, and it is therefore unlikely to occur when you are running your own server.

If you receive an error similar to the one above, then Dreamweaver has been unable to locate your MySQL Server. It is likely that either the server is not running, or that the wrong MySQL Server address has been entered.

Summary

In this chapter we have looked at how to configure Dreamweaver to work with your Development Environment. We have walked through the new Site Definition Wizard, and explained each step of the configuration so that it will apply in each of the four types of development environment available.

We have also looked at the creation of a MySQL Connection that allows Dreamweaver to fully interact with your database, so that you can take fullest advantage of all the functionality that Dreamweaver MX has to offer.

Now that the site is defined and ready to use, let's look at creating our example site, The Dreamweaver Hotel.

4

- Site planning
- Flowcharts
- Planning the database

Author: Tim Green

Planning the Web Site

When designing any web application or web site, there are a number of steps that can be taken to make the whole process much easier. Planning a web application need not be a meticulous process, but it should be thorough, as there are always elements that could be expanded on, removed, amended, and replaced at any time. Knowing that these changes occur, whether by natural evolution or by client decision, is an essential part of working with any form of scripting technology or database, and planning will make your life much easier.

Over the next couple of chapters we will be looking at a number of different steps that can be taken in both the planning of the web site itself and in the development of the database. Not all of the steps mentioned here would be relevant to all of your projects, and it is very possible that additional steps may need to be taken with more complex projects. However, what we provide here is an essential grounding, a starting point on which you can build.

In this chapter, we will look at the structure of a dynamic web site. We will take an initial design brief, and from there plan the features, functionality, and form of the site itself. We will also look at the type of data that the site will need in order to fulfill the brief, and determine an initial plan for structuring our database. We will also examine the processes of the site itself, and begin to map them with the aid of flowcharts.

When we talk about designing a web site, one of the most common analogies used is the "Virtual Store"; due in some part to the large increase of eCommerce and eBusiness web sites that are available today. It is often used in Business to Business (B2B) seminars, as an easy introduction to the less technically minded about the subject in hand.

In many respects, building a web application does not really fulfill this typecasting. By definition, "virtual" relates to something in the imagination, or something that is created or simulated by using some form of computer technology, in this respect it accurately defines the end product. For the serious web professional though, these "Virtual Stores" take form well before finger has touched keyboard. When you are building a real store, in the real world, before you do anything you must get the right information down on paper in the form of a blueprint, otherwise the whole structure collapses, and the same rules apply for the creation of a virtual store.

As a web professional, you are responsible for the overall structure of this store, how it functions, how it feels, and how it is perceived. In the real world you would be called an architect.

Architecture of a Dynamic Web Site

Web sites are curious things; they all derive from the same, basic hierarchical structure. An entry point (the Homepage) that branches off into a number of subpages, each of which branch off or loop back to other pages, and so on.

Given this structure, the vast majority of web sites follow the same kind of navigational pattern. It is one that is long established, and has its roots in the earliest of web pages. Before the prevalence of images, movies, Shockwave, and other mediums, web sites were a strictly 'text only' affair, not at all exciting by today's standards, but revolutionary at the time.

With the upsurgence of different mediums, and of course faster connection speeds, it was soon possible for web designers to experiment with different forms, structures, and navigational components. Of course, experimentation is a necessary process, and one that is for the benefit of all (though judging by some sites you wouldn't always believe that).

One thing that seems to be a constant is the hierarchical structure of a web site, probably because the societies of the world are built on hierarchies, as our families, our places of work. In fact the more you look into it, the more you will see hierarchical structures, and it therefore seems logical that the web is presented in this way.

When considering a hierarchy in the context of a web site, there are a number of factors that we need to take into consideration. It must be simple; you must at all times know where you are, where you want to go, and where you have been. Many developers believe that if you have more than four levels to a web site's hierarchy that visitors soon lose interest in the site, get lost, or feel overwhelmed, and there is a good reason for this. Psychologically, hierarchies with more than 4 levels will tend to make you feel like a small cog in a big wheel, and given the "Virtual Store" example this is exactly what we don't want the visitor to feel, the visitor is a customer, and (forgive the cliché) the customer is King.

To better illustrate the steps towards achieving our goal, we shall be concentrating exclusively on the design and planning process behind our example web site, **The Dreamweaver Hotel**. Feel free to expand on these processes as you see fit for the development of your own web site.

The Brief

Every web site begins its life as a set of particular instructions and requirements, otherwise known as a brief. Some clients prefer to give only a basic indication of what they want, without elaborating too much on the detailed aspects of the site itself. Others will provide a brief so comprehensive that little more information is required before work can commence. Of course there are advantages and disadvantages with both kinds of brief, but it is your job as a web designer to ensure that your customer is delighted with the final result.

The Dreamweaver Hotel, our example site, is no different in this respect. The following brief summarizes particular requirements that the web site's design and functionality should completely satisfy.

Planning the Web Site

1. Each page in the site should open quickly in the browser.
2. The site should be compatible with all major browsers.
3. The web site's relative design and complexity should reflect the fact that the hotel is small and family-run.
4. The client likes the prudent use of white space, but insists that the hotel's color scheme, orange black and white, be employed throughout, to be sympathetic to the 'Corporate Image'.
5. Visitors should be able to check current availability of rooms, according to specified criteria (Grade, Room Type, and Arrival and Departure dates).
6. Visitors should at all times be allowed to amend or cancel their bookings.
7. Hotel Staff must be able to retrieve a list of bookings at any time through an Administration Area.
8. The Duty Manager must be able to manage Administration Area Access for Hotel Staff.
9. The booking system must be able to integrate with the current billing system, possibly so that in the future a business customer with an account can check their balance.
10. Each page of the site should be of uniform and distinctive design.
11. The site should contain the following types of content:

    - Hotel Information and Brief History.
    - Travel Information, including appropriate local area maps.
    - Room information, detailing the differing facilities of each room based on grade, or type of room.
    - Contact Information for the hotel, including Telephone and Fax numbers, e-mail address, and hotel's address.

As you can see, this brief isn't overly complicated, though it does make specific demands on the design and functionality of the web site itself. This is more than enough to start planning the site and developing an initial design concept. Some areas of the brief may require additional information, particularly regarding rooms and booking information.

Determining Site Features

The Dreamweaver Hotel requires a number of different elements. First of all, there is the client-facing site that allows a customer to check the availability of rooms based on date criteria that they specify. If a room is available, then the visitor is given the opportunity to place a reservation and give their credit card details to act as a security against the booking. The customer can return at any time and view their bookings, and make amendments or cancel them as appropriate. As well as this, there are the usual informative sections including Hotel Information, Travel Information and Map, details of rooms and suites and of course contact information.

Chapter 4

The second part to the site is the Administration section. This allows a designated hotel representative to check bookings and manage staff user names and passwords.

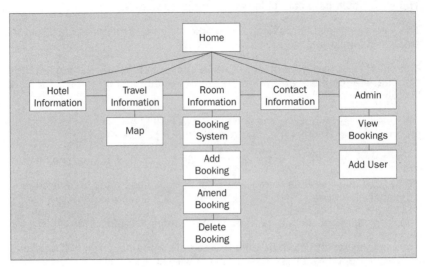

The overall site structure is something like the diagram above. Whilst there aren't many pages, we can limit the number of physical pages by looking at the types of page we have to create.

Hotel Information, Travel Information, Map, Room Information, and Contact Information will all contain static information provided by the client. As these pages do not use any other functionality of the web application itself, these pages can be created as standard HTML pages using our design template.

Many web designers who use a scripting technology often opt to store static information of this kind within the database itself. Then, with the addition of some extra administration pages, a system is integrated to allow the customer to maintain the 'static' content of their web site themselves. This might be above and beyond the initial design requirements, but creating functionality like this is usually a good idea. Experience has shown that of all the last minute amendments required by the client, the integration of some way to easily edit page content is usually around the top of the list. This is called **latency**, or the adding of features without activating them. It is generally a good idea to do this whenever possible, as it speeds development and later redevelopment, and creates a more professional and scalable end product to the customer.

Having now determined the site feature set, we need to establish how the content provided by the client for the site is integrated into the overall design and layout. As all of the information is to be stored in our database, we now need to determine the database structure.

Planning the Database Structure

Like the web site itself, a database has its own internal structure, hierarchy, and set of rules. As such, you should approach the design of a database in much the same way as you would approach the design of a web site.

Planning the Web Site

For the Dreamweaver Hotel, there are specific types of information that we need to store and retrieve. What we really need to determine, is the precise nature of that information, how we will store it, and whether that information is related to any other information that might be stored elsewhere.

The starting point for all public enquiries on the site is the visitor seeking a room. We can safely establish what information we need to store for the room, and build upwards from there.

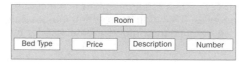

The diagram above outlines the information that we need to store in this database. As The Dreamweaver Hotel is not a large hotel, it isn't necessary to store prices in a different table and create a relationship. Though of course, this might be a more practical approach if you are working on a database for a hotel with a few hundred rooms.

As there are various elements of this table that will be used within the search functionality of the site, we are going to create a couple of indexes to help speed up this process. As the Bed Type will be a criterion that the customer can specify, we will make this column into an index, and we will do the same for the only other obvious column, the Room Number.

As we begin to build on this first table, we immediately know that there will be some relationships, but it is important to establish which relationships these are. I find that the best method for me is to get a large sheet of paper and list out, longhand, all of the information that I need in each table. Once this is done, I start to look for common denominators, or information of the same type, and put them together. Before too long, you'll find that there is enough common information to justify another table. Continue this process until there is no other shared information.

What you have been doing here is to establish relations. In the image below you will see a screenshot of the table layout and relationships for all of the room-related information.

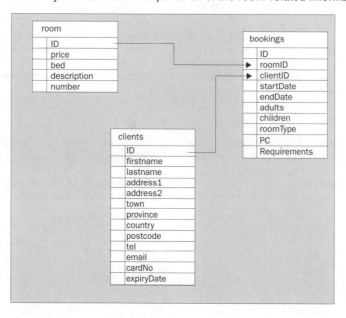

79

These relationships between tables will help immensely when coding the pages that make up the site. Now that we know how the database will work we need to plan the functionality of the site, so that we can fully understand the processes involved. Of course, we need to also remember that the design of a database is an iterative process. In the future, during development of the site, or with any later site amendments or additions, certain aspects of the database structure may require change. It is not uncommon for additional functionality to be added to a site at a later date. This additional functionality will have its own set of data requirements which may force the amendment of some, or all of your existing database tables. It is worth considering the possible additions that could occur within the site, and build a degree of latency into your database for these future additions.

Determining Site Functionality and Features

When developing a web application of any type it is worth planning out the logical steps to achieve the functionality that you require. Certainly, this will vary greatly depending on the type of site that is being developed, but as we have seen previously, it is always worth spending that little bit of extra time in determining a road map of activity.

For our example, the functionality of the site may appear quite clear, but it is worth mapping out the requirements and steps envisioned. This enables you to provide a clear description to the client of your plans for the web site. In this way, you both know whether or not you are on the right track.

Flowcharts

Flowcharts have long been used to describe systems of all kinds, and have been a common tool in IT development and systems for many years. Their great strength is that using them you can define the individual elements of a system or process without having to deal with the specifics of implementation. They act as a roadmap and guide that allow you to see where you are in the current stage of development, where you have been, and where you are going.

A flowchart is a diagram comprised of a number of simple icons, each with a special meaning, which help define entire areas of work into a simple visual medium. They are perfect for charting processes and navigation and are very easy to learn. Diagrams are a good way to clarify and conceptualize your ideas, systems, and processes, and provide a clear and unambiguous medium for communicating them.

The Basics

Flowcharts consist of a number of unique symbols, each of which can be used in a simple and informative way to illustrate the ideas you wish to communicate.

In the following sections we will be using a number of these symbols to communicate elements in our web application's process, so it is essential that we explain their concept here.

The Document Symbol

In the early days of computing, the document symbol was representative of a paper medium, something that was actually printed out and read. Of course, this still applies today; however, the document symbol is an obvious and logical symbol to use for a web page. In the context of the systems and processes detailed later in this chapter, the document symbol will represent exactly that: a web page.

The Decision Symbol

As you might expect from the name of this symbol, it represents a conditional segment within the flowchart. Typically, the Decision Symbol will provide only Yes/No answers, and these are reflected in the flow of the diagram.

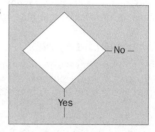

The Process Symbol

There are actually two types of process symbol, there is the symbol illustrated on the right, which denotes a named process, system, or module, and there is a standard process symbol, represented by a simple rectangle which represents any processing function.

As we are working with web pages and scripting technologies, each segment of PHP code that we use can be referred to as a named process, or function, hence its use here. The process symbol is far more complex than you might initially realize, as each Process symbol can also contain its own flowchart. We won't be dealing with flowcharts on that kind of level in this book; however, it is something to take into consideration, especially if you are dealing with exceptionally large processes or systems.

A standard process symbol allows us to indicate the use of a technique or formula to transform our data. A typical use for this is when we perform a mathematical calculation without referring to an external subroutine.

```
<?php
$width = 100;
$length = 25;
$area = $width * length;
?>
```

A named process symbol, however, allows us to indicate the use of an external function or subroutine, which performs our task. Given our mathematical example above, the corresponding named process could be something like this:

```
<?php
$width = 100;
$length = 25;
$area = calculateArea($width,$length);

function calculateArea($theWidth, $theLength) {
    return $theWidth * $theLength;
}
?>
```

Of course this is only a very simple example. However, named processes do play a very important part in the optimization and reuse of your code. If, for example, you have a number of sections within your page where you perform the same kinds of calculation, or data transformation, it is usually a good idea to take the common components of these calculations, and turn them into a function, allowing for later reuse, less coding, and easier debugging.

The Manual Input Symbol

This symbol represents manual entry, or input, via a screen or keyboard. For our purposes it represents the information that is typed into a form and submitted for processing.

Of course there are many more icons that can be used in flowcharts, and each has their own, unique meaning. A good example of flowcharting software is Microsoft's Visio, which also allows you to create flowcharts of all types; not only for application logic, but also for a myriad of other different uses. More information about Visio can be found at *http://www.microsoft.com/office/visio/default.asp*.

The Booking System

The booking system process that we wish to use for The Dreamweaver Hotel consists of the customer arriving at our site, entering their required dates of arrival and departure, and the kind of room that they wish to stay in. Using this information, the site searches the relevant database tables (bookings and rooms) to establish that it is possible to make the reservation. If the reservation is not possible then the visitor is given the opportunity to specify an alternative set of dates, or alternative room type. If there is a suitable room for the period stated, the system allows the customer to complete the booking by entering their personal information and credit card details to secure the room.

> The use of a credit card on any web site, should only be done using a Secure Socket Layer (SSL). As the installation and configuration of SSL is beyond the scope of this book, we will not be employing SSL for the purpose of our example site. For this reason, you should remember not to employ any of the pages created within a production environment. When creating eCommerce or eBusiness systems, SSL is a necessary process, and is covered by many online mercantile services, such as Authorize.net (*http://www.authorize.net*), Verisign (*http://www.verisign.com*), or CCNow (*http://www.ccnow.com*) to name a few.
>
> If you would prefer to use your own server, then you can obtain further information about SSL from *http://www.openssl.org*. To successfully use SSL within your PHP scripts, you will need to install a PHP extension called cURL. More information about cURL, including download options, can be found at *http://curl.haxx.nu*.

Planning the Web Site

As the credit card will be processed either when the client checks out, or if the client doesn't show up for their booking, there is no requirement for an online credit card transaction, so this simplifies the whole process, as there are no merchant facilities required.

By creating a flow chart for this process, we can better understand the steps required, and also have a complete understanding of the application logic required to make this system work.

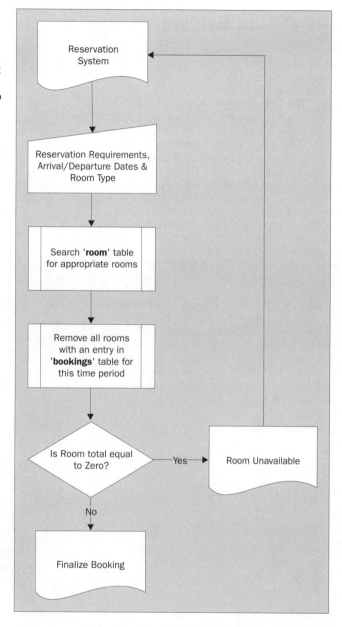

As you can see from the chart, there are two essential processes. The first process is the search for appropriate rooms, and the second process involves searching the *bookings* table and removing all rooms that are previously booked. Thankfully, while this may sound like a difficult thing to do, it is really only a matter of devising the correct SQL statement to query the database.

Chapter 4

The Billing System

Another essential process is the Billing System while we won't be covering the entire billing system within our example web site, we do need to understand the billing process that the hotel uses. This is a good example of a future addition to the site functionality, which we have already taken into account by creating a billing table. Of course this would be an Administrators system, and wouldn't be available to the web site visitor.

Again, this is a relatively simple system. Upon the entry of a room number all information relating to that room, details of the booking, any room service charges, etc. can be established and calculated. Most hotels operate a policy of charging a fee if the client does not arrive at the hotel and it is for this reason that the credit card information is taken.

Of course, this system is really is an extension of the manual system, but it is worth understanding the process. It may not be entirely relevant to the project at hand, but by better understanding what information is used by the client, you can gain a better insight into what information you need to gather in the development of the site.

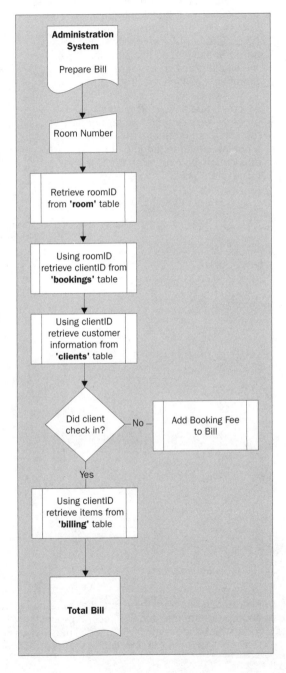

Planning the Web Site

The Administration System

For the purposes of our example site, only a simple administration system will be created, allowing for the addition of new administration users, and for checking the online bookings. Of course, this system could be more complex, and could incorporate the billing system and other processes relevant to the needs of the hotel staff and managers.

The Administration System comprises three separate processes: Login System, User Management, and Booking Analysis. Here we will take a brief look at the login system, and define the process flow.

The Login System

This process describes the actions to be taken when a login is attempted in the administration section. First of all, the user visits the login page, and enters their username and password details. The password information is then encrypted and, along with the username, is compared to the information stored in the users table. On a successful login, the visitor is sent to the correct entry point page. If incorrect information is entered, the login will fail.

These are all fairly basic and easy systems. As an exercise you could try to map out similar processes, perhaps for the View Bookings feature for the Administration section. Flowcharts are very useful for illustrating processes, and though their use has seen some decline in many circles, the truth is that they are a very powerful tool, and an easy-to-use resource.

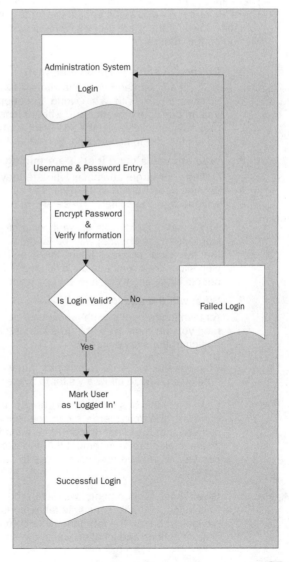

Chapter 4

Planning the Design

Design is a tricky concept, as it is all a matter of taste. What one person considers a good design, another person will consider as bad. Yet, good design does matter, and it is how you apply the fundamentals of design that really matter. Usability is another major factor that you should take into account, as the way that your site 'feels' to the visitor plays an important part in the perception of your client. Popular sites are often the most simple to use, the most intuitive, and this should be a strong consideration in whatever design you wish to implement. The credo "Know your audience, design for your audience, test for usability, and solicit feedback from your audience." is something that you should take to heart. Further information about web usability can be found in "*Usability: the Site Speaks for Itself*", from glasshaus (ISBN 1904151035).

There are a number of principles of good design, search the Internet and you'll find a few thousand. There are concepts and ideas and, in the large part, it really is a matter of working things out for yourself. However there are a few simple steps that are common amongst all of the principles you will find on the Internet.

- **Define the site's purpose and goal.**
  Without purpose and goal, the site will have no function. With no function, it can be the greatest looking site in the world, but people just won't want to use it. There is also a great design principle at work here, without function there is no form. In other words, until you properly establish what the site is for – what it is to achieve – and establish what the client needs the site to accomplish, you cannot properly develop any kind of meaningful form.

- **Who are you aiming it at? Determining who it is for.**
  Define your target audience: who are they? Are they colleagues, customers or friends? What do they need from the site? Will they all speak the same language? Will the site be visited by anyone with disabilities? These are all essential questions.

  At the end of the day we all want something, in some form. If a site has no value to me, then I won't visit it, and neither will you for those very same reasons. You must provide something that the visitor will want. I think this is perhaps the hardest thing to achieve when constructing web sites. We often have our own ideas of what people want, but very often, what we *think* people want, and want they *actually* want are two very separate, very different things.

- **What will the site look like?**
  As mentioned earlier, with function comes form. When you know what the site has to do, then you are more fully able to account for everything during the actual construction and design of the site itself.

  With our site, we have determined that we need to show a few informative pages about the hotel itself, and to allow a visitor to make, amend, or delete a reservation.

  Essentially this has determined our site navigation, which for our example site is not at all complex, and from there we can determine the 'Look' of the site. Referring to our brief, we can see that the client has pre-determined a color scheme of white, orange, and black. There is also the requirement that the site should be quick to load, cross-browser compatible, and be relatively simple to use due to the fact that this is a small, family-run hotel.

  Given these requirements, we have produced a layout for the site, which meets all of them. This layout comprises a single table, containing two images that form the layout, with a navigation bar on the left-hand side, comprised of images that change according to the visitors actions and location within the site, making it easily navigable.

Planning the Web Site

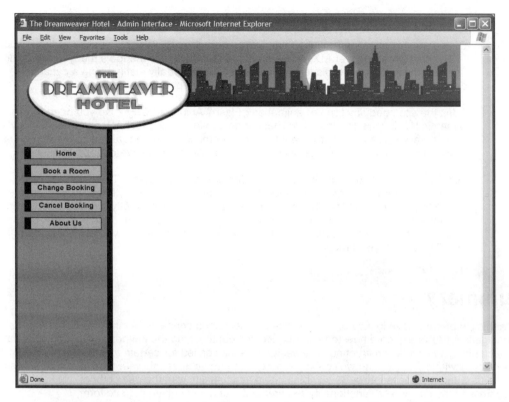

Of course, this design can be built on as required, but it more than suits the purposes of our example.

- **How do you get around? Navigation**

    Thankfully, for our purposes, the navigation of the site is relatively easy. In fact you will have noticed that it is already in place in the screenshot above. Unfortunately the same cannot be said for many sites. People spend hours, days, or even weeks in trying to determine a simple navigational method, or methods. In truth, it is a massively difficult process. It has been shown that 80% of people will use 20% of the navigational methods presented to them. This seems to imply that you need to employ more than one navigation system for your site, and ideally you should, whether that is a combination of images serving as buttons, along with text links or dropdown menus, the decision really is yours. You might want to check out "*Constructing Usable Web Menus*" from glasshaus (ISBN 1904151027), for more practical examples of how to do this.

    However, you should always remember that the best navigational methods are the simplest ones, which again is a usability requirement. Don't try to be too clever with navigation, as there are many people who won't find it as intuitive as you do. Anyone who works in an IT Department, or teaches web skills to newbie surfers will tell you that the most common question is "What do I click now?" – something that web designers hate to hear! The best advice that I can offer, when it comes to web site navigation, is to find someone who would likely be a visitor to the site. Sit them at a computer and have them use your web site. Listen to any comments that they might make, and learn from them. Sometimes, going back to the 'grass roots' is the only way we can learn.

87

- **What do you need to get the job done?**

    Of course, this question has been semi-answered already. After all, you're reading a book on PHP within Dreamweaver MX, so we presume that these are the tools that you are going to use. Are these the right tools for the job? Does the site really justify being a dynamic, database-enabled web site, rather than a static HTML page?

    Does the site need any form of animation? Flash? Animated GIFs? Do you need to use Dynamic HTML (DHTML) scripts? There is no sense in using technology for technology's sake, unless you are going to use it to its true potential. If there really is no need to be using scripting technologies and databases, then don't use them, they're not appropriate.

    For our purposes PHP and MySQL are perfect for the job in hand. They are fast, cost-effective and offer the right level of functionality for the task. Sometimes, we can be in such a rush to use the latest tool that we don't necessarily use it correctly, or to its best potential. So these factors are well worth considering. If you haven't already done this, look back over your project; look at the features, and look at the site's needs. Are you still using the right tools? Good, now let's move on.

Summary

In this chapter we have looked at some of the principles and concepts behind site design and navigation. We've explored how to build our site without touching the keyboard, as building is as much planning as it is constructing. The design brief has called for certain functionality to be employed within the site, and we've explored how we can achieve this with the aid of flowcharts to help us work out process flow. By combining this functionality with the design brief, we have addressed the design and functionality requirements, and have given the site form.

In the following chapter, we will look at putting this all together, by finally putting finger to keyboard, and implementing our site design and constructing our database.

Planning the Web Site

5

- Setting up the database
- Creating the tables
- Using templates

Author: Tim Green

Beginning Site Development

Now that we have looked into the essential steps in planning a web site and its database, we can concentrate on creating the site.

In this chapter we will look at our example site – The Dreamweaver Hotel, in more detail. To begin with, we will establish the database tables and structure that we need to store the site's content and information by employing lessons learnt in Chapter 2.

Once we have created the database tables we will look at creating our first pages, based on a sample layout, and introduce the new Dreamweaver MX templating system. This will allow us to standardize our layout, so that we can concentrate on the development of the rest of the site.

Setting Up the Database

Now that we have established exactly what information we need to store in the site's database, and what information we require from people who visit our site, we can implement a simple site database that will hold all of the information that we require.

In the last chapter we looked at the structure of our database, but did not explain how we were going to achieve it. We've previously introduced a number of tools that allow us to manipulate the content and structure of our MySQL database, using **Structured Query Language** (**SQL**). Now all we need is the relevant sequence of SQL Statements to create that structure for us.

The bookings Table

When a web site visitor makes their reservation online, all of the reservation information is stored in the `bookings` table. This table is created with the SQL statement below, and forms the backbone of the online reservation system.

```
#
# Table structure for table 'bookings'
#

CREATE TABLE bookings (
  ID tinyint(11) NOT NULL auto_increment,
  roomID tinyint(11) NOT NULL default '0',
  clientID tinyint(11) NOT NULL default '0',
  startDate date NOT NULL default '0000-00-00',
  endDate date NOT NULL default '0000-00-00',
  adults int(11) NOT NULL default '1',
  children int(11) NOT NULL default '0',
  roomType varchar(30) NOT NULL default '',
  roomOptions int(8) NOT NULL default '0',
  networkConnection int(8) NOT NULL default '0',
  PC int(8) NOT NULL default '0',
  requirements varchar(250) NOT NULL default '',
  PRIMARY KEY (ID)
) TYPE=MyISAM COMMENT='Room Booking Table';
```

The `bookings` table is related to two other tables, the `room` table, and the `client` table which is indicated by the columns `roomID` and `clientID` respectively. During the registration process, the web site visitor's details are stored within a separate table, the clients table, which we will cover shortly.

Information about a particular booking, `client` and `room` is retrieved with the creation of a specific SQL Query statement, similar to this:

```
SELECT CONCAT (clients.firstName, ' ', clients.lastName) AS CustomerName,
bookings.startDate AS ArrivalDate, bookings.endDate AS DepartureDate
FROM clients, bookings
WHERE clients.ID = bookings.clientID AND clients.firstName = 'John' AND
clients.lastName = 'Smith';
```

Assuming the table contained some data, this SQL Query would return all arrival and departure dates, for all bookings made under the name "John Smith" in a format similar to the table below.

CustomerName	ArrivalDate	DepartureDate
John Smith	2002-02-12	2002-02-14
John Smith	2002-05-15	2002-05-15

The clients Table

This table stores all of the customer's information when the customer places an online reservation. It should be noted that more information about the customer can be requested, but it is always recommended that you ask only for the information that you absolutely need.

The SQL used to create the `clients` table looks something like this:

Beginning Site Development

```
#
# Table structure for table 'clients'
#

CREATE TABLE clients (
  ID tinyint(11) NOT NULL auto_increment,
  title varchar(10) default NULL,
  firstName varchar(30) NOT NULL default '',
  lastName varchar(30) NOT NULL default '',
  address1 varchar(100) NOT NULL default '',
  address2 varchar(100) default NULL,
  town varchar(100) NOT NULL default '',
  province varchar(100) NOT NULL default '',
  country varchar(40) NOT NULL default '',
  postCode varchar(20) NOT NULL default '',
  tel varchar(20) NOT NULL default '',
  email varchar(100) NOT NULL default '',
  cardNo varchar(16) NOT NULL default '',
  expiryDate date NOT NULL default '0000-00-00',
  PRIMARY KEY  (ID)
) TYPE=MyISAM COMMENT='Customer Table';
```

As you can see from this table, most of the information stored here is quite pertinent to that of a hotel booking. The data contained in this table is retrieved from the reservation booking form, during the online reservation process.

The room Table

This table contains all of the information about every room in the hotel, its price, type etc. Yet again, the structure of this table is rather simple, consisting of only five columns. The statement used to create this table is this:

```
#
# Table structure for table 'room'
#

CREATE TABLE room (
  ID int(11) NOT NULL auto_increment,
  price int(11) NOT NULL default '0',
  bed tinyint(4) NOT NULL default '0',
  description text,
  number tinyint(5) NOT NULL default '0',
  PRIMARY KEY  (ID),
  INDEX bed (bed),
  INDEX number (number),
  ) TYPE=MyISAM COMMENT='Room description';
```

The creation of this table leads us to the last table in this database.

The users Table

This table is used exclusively for administration and staff access to the 'secret' parts of the web site. In this table you will find information about each authorized user, their names, usernames and encoded passwords:

```
#
# Table structure for table 'users'
#

CREATE TABLE users (
  ID int(8) NOT NULL auto_increment,
  username varchar(20) NOT NULL default '',
  password varchar(20) default NULL,
  firstName varchar(30) NOT NULL default '',
  lastName varchar(30) NOT NULL default '',
  status varchar(10) NOT NULL default '',
  PRIMARY KEY  (ID)
) TYPE=MyISAM;
```

Creating the Tables

Now that we have established the SQL required to create our tables in the database, we need to use the tools, previously introduced in Chapter 2, to create these tables.

Using phpMyAdmin

As we have seen before, phpMyAdmin is a very powerful web-based tool, and is useful for managing a database structure when it is stored on a remote server.

To begin, visit your phpMyAdmin site, and click on the entry in the left frame that represents your Hotel database. In our example site this database is called `dwHotel`. If you haven't yet created the database, you can do so by entering the name in the field provided and clicking "*Create*". Once you've selected your database, you should be able to see a section of the page in the main frame similar to the image below:

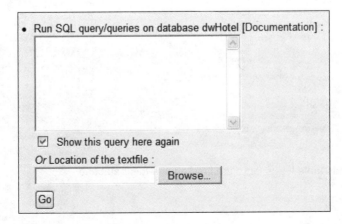

This section allows us to directly enter the SQL that we have already given, to create the table and all its columns. To use this section, simply enter the SQL as it is given earlier and when finished, click on the '*Go*' button. It is best to do this a table at a time, so as to lessen the chances of an error.

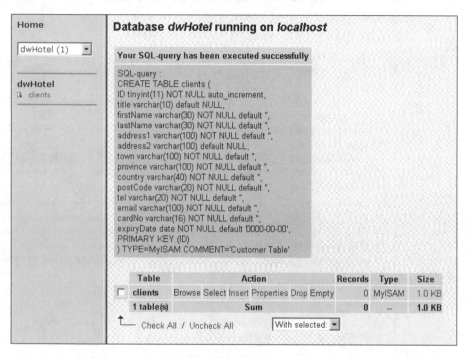

Once done, you should see a page confirming the SQL statement that you have just entered, similar to the above screenshot which details the results of creating the `clients` table. To confirm that the table has been created successfully, and to your specifications, click on the name of the new table in the left-hand frame to take you to the table structure page.

In our example above we have created the `clients` table using the following SQL:

```
CREATE TABLE clients (
  ID tinyint(11) NOT NULL auto_increment,
  firstName varchar(30) NOT NULL default '',
  lastName varchar(30) NOT NULL default '',
  address1 varchar(100) NOT NULL default '',
  address2 varchar(100) default NULL,
  town varchar(100) NOT NULL default '',
  province varchar(100) NOT NULL default '',
  country varchar(40) NOT NULL default '',
  postCode varchar(20) NOT NULL default '',
  tel varchar(20) NOT NULL default '',
  email varchar(100) NOT NULL default '',
  cardNo varchar(16) NOT NULL default '',
  expiryDate date NOT NULL default '0000-00-00',
  PRIMARY KEY (ID)
) TYPE=MyISAM COMMENT='Customer Table';
```

This SQL statement produces a table structure resembling the screenshot below. You will note that immediately you can compare the SQL statement overleaf, to the corresponding entries in this table.

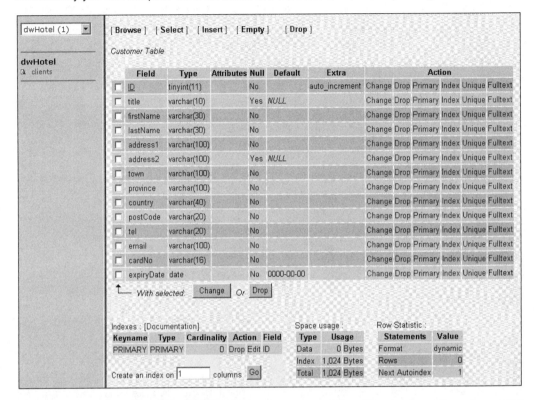

Of course this is a quick and painless method for creating tables when you have the relevant SQL statements already. If you don't have the relevant SQL already prepared, then you can visually create your table using phpMyAdmin's Table Wizard.

The Table Wizard

To begin using the table wizard, you must ensure that you are working with the correct database. To do this, visit your phpMyAdmin page, and click on the relevant database name in the left-hand frame. You will see a section in the main frame that resembles the image below.

To begin using the table wizard enter the name of the table you wish to create, and the number of fields, or columns, that the table will contain. In the screenshot above, you will see that this time we are creating the `bookings` table, which contains a total of twelve fields. Once this has been done, click on the '*Go*' button, to proceed to the next step.

Beginning Site Development

Field	Type [Documentation]	Length/Values*	Attributes	Null	Default	Extra	Primary	Index	Unique	---	Fulltext
ID	TINYINT	11		not null		auto_increment	●	○	○	○	☐
roomID	TINYINT	11		not null			○	○	○	○	☐
clientID	TINYINT	11		not null			○	○	○	○	☐
startDate	DATE			not null			○	○	○	○	☐
endDate	DATE			not null			○	○	○	○	☐
adults	VARCHAR	8		not null			○	○	○	○	☐
children	INT	8		not null			○	○	○	○	☐
roomType	VARCHAR	30		not null			○	○	○	○	☐
roomOptions	INT	8		not null			○	○	○	○	☐
networkConnec	INT	8		not null			○	○	○	○	☐
PC	INT	8		not null			○	○	○	○	☐
requirements	VARCHAR	250		not null			○	○	○	○	☐

Database *dwHotel* - table *bookings* running on *localhost*

Table comments:

Table type: Default

Save

* If field type is "enum" or "set", please enter the values using this format: 'a','b','c'...
If you ever need to put a backslash ("\") or a single quote ("'") amongst those values, backslashes it (for example '\\xyz' or 'a\'b').

[Documentation]

We now proceed to enter the information for each column, as seen in the above screenshot. When creating a database table like this, you are presented with a number of options to help you determine the precise nature of the columns within that table. We have previously discussed some of these options in Chapter 2; if you want to know more about the available data types, the documentation links will take you directly to the MySQL web site.

You will notice from the screenshot that there are a couple of discrepancies, between what is entered onto the page, and our SQL Statement for the creation of the `bookings` table. The missing elements are the default values, because in our example above no default values have been entered.

This has been purposely done to illustrate a feature of phpMyAdmin. When creating a column that requires a zero default value that is **NOT** NULL, if no value is entered then the software will assume that the value is zero. This is an essential point to remember, as if you require the default value to be anything else, you must explicitly state the value you wish to be used.

When you have completed this form, and are happy that you have chosen the data types, lengths, attributes, and values that you require for each field in your database, click on the '*Save*' button to create the table. You are then taken to another page that confirms the SQL statement that phpMyAdmin created to generate the table.

Chapter 5

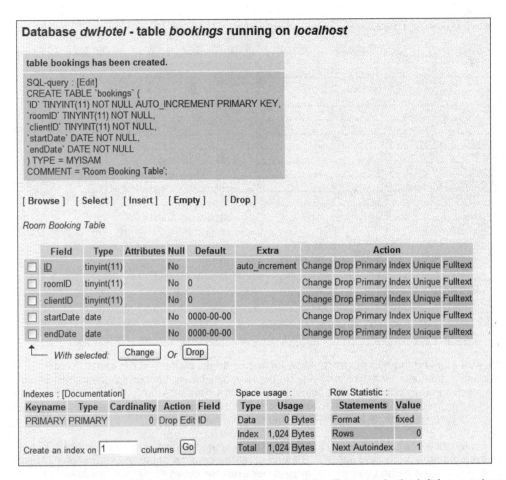

Once again, when the table has been successfully created, it will appear in the left frame, where you should click it, and verify that the table is indeed constructed the way you wished it to be.

The Table Wizard in phpMyAdmin is not a wizard in the strictest sense, but it does allow you to easily and visually create your table and columns, which can be more appealing than dealing with raw SQL Statements.

Continuing with the theme of table creation, we will now explore how to achieve similar results using a database management tool that is installed with MySQL itself, the MySQL Monitor.

Using the MySQL Monitor

As mentioned in Chapter 2, the MySQL Monitor is an integral part of MySQL, and is installed automatically when you install MySQL onto your local system. Even if you have no plans to run a MySQL Server locally, it is useful to install MySQL anyway, and prevent the service from starting (by removing it from the Start Up folder in the Start Menu, or by disabling the MySQL Service in the Administration Tools of Windows NT, 2000, and XP). I recommend doing this, as the tools that are installed are useful even if you are connecting to a MySQL Server on another machine.

Beginning Site Development

We can modify our use of the MySQL monitor using some extra settings, called switches, when we start the program. The syntax of this command can be seen below, all the highlighted sections of this command should be replaced with the actual settings for your MySQL server.

```
mysql -u username -p -h mysqladdress databasename
```

To access the MySQL Monitor using the above syntax, in either Windows, Linux, or OSX, we can enter a command similar to the one below.

```
mysql - u dwmxphp -p -h 192.168.0.223 dwHotel
```

There are various command-line switches that can be used, and it may be necessary for you to use additional switches that are peculiar to your MySQL configuration. The most commonly used switches and their syntax are included in the table below for your reference.

MySQL Monitor Syntax

Usage: mysql [OPTIONS] [database]

Name	Command	Description
Compress	`-C, --compress`	Uses a compression algorithm when communicating with the server. Occasionally used to speed up communication with the server. This option will only work if the server supports compression.
Database	`-D, --database=[databaseName]`	Specifies the name of the database to use.
Execute	`-e, --execute=[SQLCommand]`	Connects to the server, executes the given command, and then immediately exits the MySQL Monitor program.
Force	`-f, --force`	Continues, even if an error is encountered.
Host	`-h, --host=[Host Address]`	**Connects to specified MySQL Server. This is useful for connecting to a remote web hosting machine.**
HTML	`-H, --html`	Produces output in HTML.
MySQL Monitor Help	`--help`	Displays a full list of all the command-line switches that can be used with the MySQL Monitor.

Table continued on following page

Name	Command	Description
Password	`-p[password], --password[=[Password]]`	**Password to use when connecting to server. If password is not given it will be asked for.**
Port	`-P, --port=...`	Port number to be used for connection.
Start Logging	`--tee=[filename]`	Stores all commands and results that appear on screen into a separate file.
Stop Logging	`--no-tee`	Stops logging commands and results to the file.
Username	`-u, --user=[UserName]`	**User for login if not current user.**
Version	`-V, --version`	Output sversion information and exits.

The switches that we have used in the command line are highlighted in the above table for clarity. There are many more command-line switches available, for more information on these you should type `mysql -help` at the command prompt.

When you have typed the command line that you need to use to connect to your MySQL server, press *Enter*, and the MySQL Monitor will attempt to connect to your database. On a successful connection you will receive the MySQL command prompt from which we can enter SQL Query commands, and directly communicate with the server.

If you haven't already done so, you can create the `dwHotel` database using the command:

```
CREATE DATABASE dwHotel
```

Then select this database with the command:

```
USE dwHotel
```

As in the previous examples for phpMyAdmin we will proceed to create the `clients` table. To do this, we simply type out the SQL as it has previously been given, ensuring that we follow the SQL to the letter, as mistakes here will produce an error, and we will have to retype our work.

```
mysql> CREATE TABLE clients (
    -> ID tinyint(11) NOT NULL auto_increment,
    -> title varchar(10) default NULL,
    -> firstName varchar(30) NOT NULL default '',
    -> lastName varchar(30) NOT NULL default '',
    -> address1 varchar(100) NOT NULL default '',
    -> address2 varchar(100) default NULL,
    -> town varchar(100) NOT NULL default '',
    -> province varchar(100) NOT NULL default '',
    -> country varchar(40) NOT NULL default '',
```

```
    ->    postCode varchar(20) NOT NULL default '',
    ->    tel varchar(20) NOT NULL default '',
    ->    email varchar(100) NOT NULL default '',
    ->    cardNo varchar(16) NOT NULL default '',
    ->    expiryDate date NOT NULL default '0000-00-00',
    ->    PRIMARY KEY  (ID)
    ->  ) TYPE=MyISAM COMMENT='Customer Table';
```

Here we can see what the SQL looks like when we type it out in the MySQL Monitor. As you can see, each line of the SQL statement is prefixed with ->. The MySQL Monitor does this automatically whenever you enter a command without ending the line in either a semi-colon, or \g, and it signifies a multi-line SQL Statement. The moment that the MySQL Monitor encounters either a semi-colon, or a \g entry, it will assume that the command is complete and it will automatically execute it.

You should bear this in mind if you are wishing to delete tables, or columns in your database, as the MySQL Monitor will not check first if you are sure, it will just action the statement. So here I would urge a real sense of caution if you ever make any amendments or changes using this software.

Query OK, 0 rows affected (0.01 sec)

When you reach the semi-colon at the end of the SQL, press enter, and you should receive the above message. Now that we have created the table, we need to check that it is built according to our specifications. To check the structure of a table we use the following SQL Statement:

```
mysql> SHOW COLUMNS FROM clients;
```

This will work for any table. All you need to do is to supplement `clients` for the name of the table that you wish to view the structure of. Using this command will return an output similar to the one below.

```
+------------+---------------+------+-----+------------+----------------+
| Field      | Type          | Null | Key | Default    | Extra          |
+------------+---------------+------+-----+------------+----------------+
| ID         | tinyint(11)   |      | PRI | NULL       | auto_increment |
| title      | varchar(10)   |      |     |            |                |
| firstName  | varchar(30)   |      |     |            |                |
| lastName   | varchar(30)   |      |     |            |                |
| address1   | varchar(100)  |      |     |            |                |
| address2   | varchar(100)  | YES  |     | NULL       |                |
| town       | varchar(100)  |      |     |            |                |
| province   | varchar(100)  |      |     |            |                |
| country    | varchar(40)   |      |     |            |                |
| postCode   | varchar(20)   |      |     |            |                |
| tel        | varchar(20)   |      |     |            |                |
| email      | varchar(100)  |      |     |            |                |
| cardNo     | varchar(16)   |      |     |            |                |
| expiryDate | date          |      |     | 0000-00-00 |                |
+------------+---------------+------+-----+------------+----------------+
13 rows in set (0.00 sec)
```

As you can see, like **phpMyAdmin**, it is very easy to compare this layout with the SQL Statement itself, to ensure that the table has been created in exactly the way that we wanted. If during this process something has gone wrong, don't worry. We will look at how to change your database tables in Chapter 7, where we also discuss Advanced SQL usage.

Once you have finished creating your tables, you should close down this tool. To do this, simply type *EXIT*, and you are returned to your command prompt.

Now that we have looked at how to create our database tables, we need to put them to use. Dreamweaver MX includes an enhanced template system, which allows us to standardize our page layout, so that all we need to be concerned about is creating our template, and then entering all of our content.

Using Templates To Standardize Layout

When developing a web site, you often need to repeat the same design features on a number of different pages. To do this you could simply copy and paste all of the relevant sections of HTML code from a previously created page, and then add the rest of the page content.

While this method does indeed work, it isn't very efficient. Say, for example, you are creating a web site for a client, who at the last minute makes a sweeping design change, such as they change the size and color of their logo? If you have used the above method, then your only recourse is to manually edit each page to effect the change.

Dreamweaver allows you to have more control over the creation process, and in so doing it uses two technologies that help you in the generation of web pages, **templates** and **libraries**. If you create a number of web pages based on a template within Dreamweaver, if the client does decide to change the size and color of the logo, you only have to change **one** file, the template. Once it has been changed, Dreamweaver automatically adjusts **all** the pages that have been created using that template.

A library is like a template in many ways. The biggest difference though, is that while a template contains information about the layout of an entire page, a library is more focused, containing information about an element within that page, like a menu or a navigation bar.

To better understand how templates and libraries work, we shall make full use of them when creating our example site, The Dreamweaver Hotel.

Getting Started

For our example, we start by creating the overall 'Look' of the site, in a graphics package such as Macromedia's Fireworks MX, though you can of course use your preferred software package. I use Fireworks because it is designed to integrate with Dreamweaver, and it allows you to easily break an image up into its component parts, also known as **slicing**. This allows us to easily create a table-based layout, as Fireworks exports all the necessary HTML for use within Dreamweaver.

Beginning Site Development

Creating the Layout

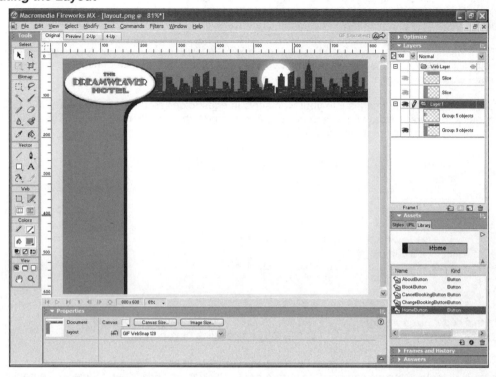

This layout has been constructed in such a way that when it is broken up, or sliced, there will be only two images creating the layout. These two images comprise the horizontal graphic at the top of the image, and the vertical bar on the right. The image below demonstrates how this looks when slicing the image in Fireworks.

Once this has been done, you can export the sliced images directly from Fireworks MX into Dreamweaver by using the **Quick Export** feature, which automatically creates the images and HTML code necessary, and puts that code within Dreamweaver.

The process is similar if you aren't using Fireworks. Simply use the selection tool in your chosen graphics package to choose the area that you want to slice. Once selected, copy the region and paste it as a new image. Repeat this process for each slice in your layout.

Once done, save the images into your web site's images folder. You then need to create a table layout within Dreamweaver MX, and insert the images into the appropriate places. The HTML code necessary for this is not at all complicated.

```
<table width="800" border="0" cellpadding="0" cellspacing="0">
  <tr>
    <td colspan="2"><img src="images/dwHotelLayout_r1_c1.gif" width="800" height="130"></td>
  </tr>
  <tr>
    <td width="190"><img src="images/dwHotelLayout_r2_c1.gif" width="190" height="470"></td>
    <td width="610" valign="top"> </td>
  </tr>
</table>
```

In this code `images/dwHotelLayout_r1_c1.gif` is the horizontal slice, and `images/dwHotelLayout_r2_c1.gif` is the vertical slice of your image.

Now that we have the general layout of the page, we should save it as a template. The template is not yet complete, but we can build on it from here. Clicking on "*File*", then "*Save As Template*" will open a dialog box like the one below.

Enter the name of the template in the "*Save As*" textbox, we have called this template `dwHotel_Layout`, and then click on "*Save*". You should immediately notice a change in the *Files* panel, a new folder called *Templates* is created, along with a new file called `dwHotel_Layout.dwt.php`; the `dwt` part of this filename stands for **Dreamweaver Template**.

Beginning Site Development

Adding Elements To the Template

Now that we have the basic layout of our template set, we need to add a new element to the layout, the Navigation Bar. The bar in our site consists of five buttons, pointing to the 5 sections of our site on which we wish to concentrate: *Home, Book a Room, Change Booking, Cancel Booking,* and *About Us*.

These buttons can be created using your preferred graphics package. For our example, we used Fireworks MX to create the buttons, and at the same time we produced a number of variations to illustrate each button's rollover state. We can now insert these images into our template using Dreamweaver's Navigation Bar Object.

Creating the Navigation Bar

First of all, we need somewhere in our template page to place the navigation bar. We can do this by using the layer tool to draw out the area we wish to use. Layers are extremely useful as we can use them to accurately place anything onto the page. The layer tool can be found in the "*Insert*" panel's "*Common*" tab as in the screenshot overleaf, or by clicking *Insert -> Layer*.

Chapter 5

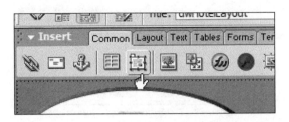

When you hover over this symbol, a tool-tip will say **Draw Layer** to confirm that this is the tool you wish to use. Click on it once and the cursor will change to a crosshair symbol (**+**).

To add a layer to the page, point to the section of the page where you wish the layer to be, left-click and hold the mouse button down, and drag the mouse pointer so that a rectangular area is drawn to the size you require. When done, let go of the left mouse button, and the layer is created leaving you with a rectangular element on your page similar to the image below.

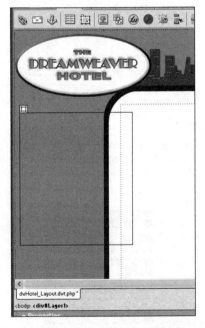

If the layer is not in exactly the right place, its position can be modified by clicking on the layer itself, and either dragging the layer into size and position, or by adjusting the layer's properties directly within the properties panel. Before we can proceed with the insertion of the navigation bar, we need to place the insert cursor within the layer, to ensure that our navigation bar goes inside the layer. This is easily done by clicking anywhere within the rectangle itself.

Now we can use Dreamweaver's Navigation Bar behavior. This is found, once again, in the *Insert* panel's *Common* tab, or by clicking *Insert -> Interactive Images -> Navigation Bar*

Beginning Site Development

Clicking this button once opens a new dialog window that provides us with total control over the look, feel, and function of the navigation bar. This dialog can appear to be a little complex, so we shall explain it in detail here.

The Insert Navigation Bar Dialog

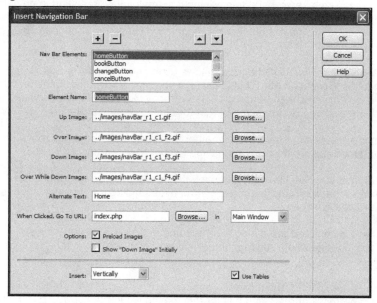

As you can see from the screenshot, there are a number of options available in this dialog, however despite this, it is easy to use.

When you first open the dialog, there will be no entries at all, so the first place you should start is with the "*Element Name*". This should be a unique name for each of the buttons within the navigation bar. The visitor does not get to see these names, as they are used internally by the generated code itself; however, it is always best to use names that have some form of meaning, so we have chosen *homeButton, bookButton, changeButton, cancelButton*, and *aboutButton* for each of the navigation bar elements. For now, we shall concentrate on the creation of the home button.

Next, you should select the images that you have created for each of the navigation button states for the home button, which we looked at earlier. To select each image for each button state, click on the *Browse* button and find the relevant image. If the image is stored somewhere outside of your web site's root folder, then Dreamweaver will ask you whether you want to copy the image to a directory within the folder, which you should do. This is extremely important, as it will affect the path to that image when the navigation bar is inserted.

Next you should enter appropriate Alt text for the button, which will appear in a tool-tip when the visitor moves the mouse cursor over it, and be shown in the image placeholder when the page is loading.

The "*When Clicked, Go To URL:*" section allows us to specify the page that this button points to, the menu to the right of this allows us to control which frame the page should open in, if we are using a frame-based site. As we aren't, we leave this option at its default setting.

The next section defines whether we want images to be preloaded or not. Preloading is a technique that is used to ensure that graphics are downloaded to the visitors web browser in advance of them being used. This is essential to achieve the correct effect when the visitor moves the mouse pointer over a button. Without preloading, when the user points at a button, the image will have to be downloaded from the web server, and this will incur a small delay, resulting in no rollover image being visible until it is downloaded. Preloading avoids this delay, and ensures that the rollover image is immediately visible the moment an event is triggered. This option is checked by default, so we will leave it this way.

The "*Show 'Down Image' Initially*" checkbox allows us to specify that the down image is used initially for this button in the navigation bar. This is useful if you are not using a template, but wish to ensure that the navigation bar reflects the page you are currently working on. We don't use this in a template, as this would specify the same button for each repeated page.

The "*Insert*" menu allows us to determine whether the navigation bar is horizontal or vertical in alignment. For our purposes, we want the navigation bar to be vertical.

Finally, the "*Use Tables*" checkbox allows us to specify whether the navigation bar makes use of tables to control the bar's layout. For better control over spacing and positioning, it is usually a good idea to leave this box checked.

Now that we have completed the dialog for the home button, we should repeat the above steps for each of the other buttons in our navigation bar. When complete, click "*OK*", to insert the bar into our layer.

When initially inserted, all of the buttons will appear to be on top of each other, with no spacing in between. This is perfectly normal, and it is for this reason we left the "*Use Tables*" checkbox checked in the "*Insert Navigation Bar*" dialog. To add spacing to the table, first select one of the images in the navigation bar, and then look just above the "*Properties*" panel within Dreamweaver.

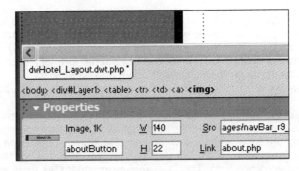

Beginning Site Development

Here we can see some of the basic structure leading up to the image that we have just selected. If we now click on `<table>` we instead select the navigation bar's table. This automatically changes the properties panel, so that it is relevant to a table. In this panel, we change the "*CellSpace*" attribute from zero to six, which automatically spreads out the buttons, and improves the layout of the navigation bar.

Now that we have successfully created the navigation bar, we can save this as a **Library Item** within Dreamweaver, so that it can be reused elsewhere within the site. We do this, because we might need to create an alternative template within the site at a future time. By creating a **Library Item** now, we can ensure that the same navigation bar be used throughout, and if we ever need to add or remove options to this bar, changing only the library item will automatically update all templates that contain it, and subsequently all pages based on those templates!

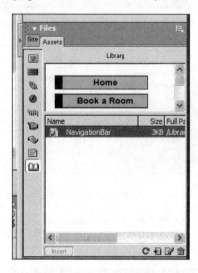

To turn the navigation bar into a Library Item, we keep the bar's table selected, and click on "*Modify->Library->Add Object to Library*". This immediately places the bar into the *Assets* tab of the *Files* panel; if you look there now, you will see that the name is `'untitled'`, which we should change to something more meaningful.

Now that we have created our layout, and inserted the navigation bar, we have nearly completed our template. All that remains is to define the area where we will be placing content.

109

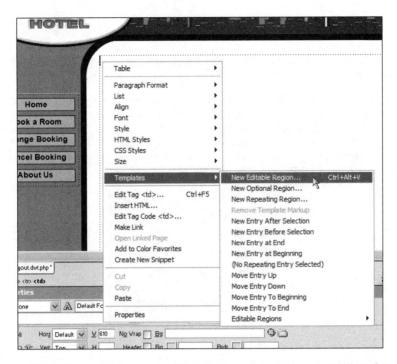

To do this, we click in the main blank area within the template design, just below the point where the horizontal and vertical images meet. Once selected right-click (Control Click for Macintosh) and go to *Templates->New Editable Region*, this opens a new dialog window that allows us to assign a name to this editable region. As this is where the main content of each page will be located, we call this page *MainContent*.

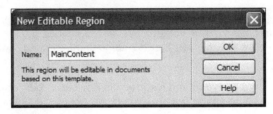

Our template is now complete, and we can save the file and close it.

Accessing Your Templates

You might be wondering now, how we actually use this new template that we've just created. Well, this has been made very simple within Dreamweaver MX. If you click on *File -> New* you'll see that the "*New Document*" dialog has a "*Templates*" tab. Click on this, and you will see a list of all your defined sites. Within each entry, you have easy access to all of the templates created within each site. All we do is click on the site we have defined; select the template from the list, and click "*Create*", to create a new page based on this template.

Beginning Site Development

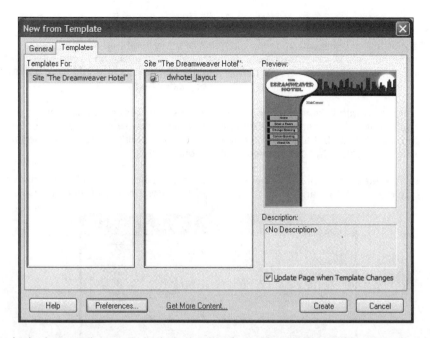

We have looked at templates now in their simplest form. However, there is a great deal more flexibility and power offered to us via the new advanced template features in Dreamweaver MX. Whilst, for the purpose of this book, it isn't necessary to study these features in depth, it is useful to know what these features are and how they can be used.

Advanced Template Features

Dreamweaver MX introduces a wealth of new template-related features, all of them designed to assist in the consistent production of a web site. Some of these more advanced features might, on the surface, appear to be esoteric, but all of them are useful.

Nested Templates

Nested templates are probably the most useful of all the new templating features. A nested template is a template that is based on another template.

They are useful for creating pages that each share a common theme, the general site layout, but has specific elements that are completely unique to them. You often find this kind of layout in sites like www.ebay.com where specific design elements are determined by a selected category, yet the overall look of the site remains the same.

To create a nested template, simply create a new document using your existing template, and then save that document as a template too. In this way, the nesting template is generated, and you can add whatever design elements to the page that you require.

The only restriction on this is that you can only work within the editable regions of the previous document. This can cause some confusion, especially when you want to create design elements in your nested template that fall outside of the original editable region.

Chapter 5

Editable Tag Attributes

Editable Tag Attributes allow you to define elements of a tag itself that can be modified in subsequent pages. This is a great addition, as historically, if you wished to change only the background color of a table that was contained within a template, you would have had to create a completely alternative template containing this minor modification.

The same holds true with links and other HTML elements that were previously locked inside a template, and remained unchangeable. Editable tag attributes allow you to lock all of the HTML elements you wish to lock, but allow some room for maneuverability by specifying parts of an HTML tag, like background color, that can subsequently be changed.

Editable tag attributes are created by opening the template, selecting the element that you wish to use, say a table or an image, and going to *Modify->Templates->Make Attribute Editable*.

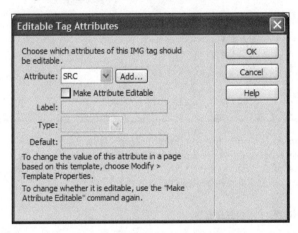

In the dialog box that opens, you are given complete access to all of the attributes available for the selected object. If you cannot see the appropriate attribute in the menu, click *Add* and enter the name of the attribute you wish to add, and then click *OK*.

Once you have selected the attribute you wish to make editable from the list, enter a unique name for this template element in "*Label*". The Dreamweaver MX manual recommends that you use a name that is both a combination of the type of object (image, table, etc.) and the attribute that is editable, and I would recommend that you maintain this convention for clarity.

In the *Type* menu, there are a number of options. These specify the type of data that can be entered for this attribute from a choice of *Text*, *URL*, *Color* or *Number*. The "*Default*" text box, will initially display the current value for that attribute within the template. However, if you wish this to be different, you can amend that value here. In the screenshot above you can see that we have selected an image within our template. By selecting the *SRC* attribute we can directly access the content of that attribute and change it as necessary. When the *OK* button is clicked, this attribute is made editable, enabling this image to be changed on pages created with this template.

Repeat the above procedure for each attribute that you wish to make editable without having to close this dialog box and starting over, simply select the next attribute you wish to make editable from the "*Attribute*" menu.

Beginning Site Development

Optional Regions

An optional region within a template allows you to show or hide an element based on a condition. The conditions are based on Template Parameters, which can be added to the template. Template Parameters are in essence variables, which can be set a particular value, and the conditions used for Optional Regions are based on these parameters.

This might all sounds a little confusing, after all, why would you want to do this? Well, simply put, these can be very useful when working with Nested Templates, as it allows you to control which of the new design elements are visible, and which aren't.

For example, say you have 3 categories within your site all with different design elements. Optional Regions and Template Parameters allow you to:

1. Create a Master Design Template

2. Create a Nested Template based on your Master Design Template with all of your new design elements.

3. Create a new template based on your Nested Template for each of your categories.

In this way, you can standardize layout and fully control the way your site looks without having to create a separate nested template for each different design possibility.

To insert an optional region in a template, open your template for editing, and select the element you wish to tie an optional region to, click on *Insert->Template Objects->New Optional Region*. This will open the New Optional Region dialog.

Inserting an Optional Region

The screenshot below shows how the New Optional Region window appears when it is first opened. As you can see there are two tabs within this window, "*Basic*" and "*Advanced*", that allow you determine how your optional region will display.

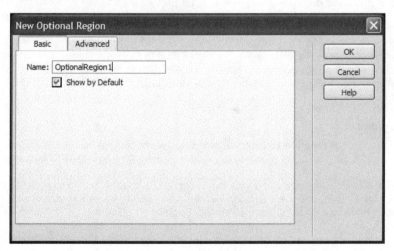

In the "*Basic*" section of this window, you can simply determine whether or not this region is shown or hidden by default when your template is used. To apply the optional region to your template using the Basic options, you should enter a unique name for this region in the "*Name*" field, and check or uncheck the "*Show by Default*" option.

The unique name that you enter here, also serves another purpose. When using **Advanced Optional Regions**, the name that you enter here creates a parameter of the same name that you can refer to in other Optional Regions. In this way, you can create complex templates where certain regions will display only if specific regions are also visible.

If you require even more control over how the optional region is handled by Dreamweaver, then clicking on the "*Advanced*" tab will present you with some more options, as shown below.

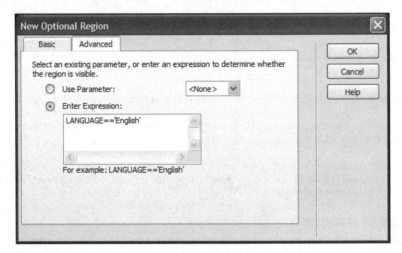

Here you can create conditions that allow you to specify when a region should be displayed. These conditions can be based on a parameter, or another previously created optional region, or a conditional expression. In the screenshot above we have used a conditional expression that will display the inserted region if the current language is English.

Just as there are Optional Regions, there are also Editable Optional Regions, which allow you to modify the condition in pages based on that template. Editable Optional Regions provide the same functionality as Optional Regions, with the added advantage that the contents of these regions can be modified at any time.

Repeating Regions

Just as you can have Repeating Regions within your dynamically generated web site, when using recordsets or other data sources, you can also have Repeating Regions within your templates.

Repeating Regions in templates allow you to have multiple instances of a specific element in your template, usually a table, and are especially useful when you are creating pages that have a recurring element in their design, like the product page of an eCommerce web site for example.

Repeating Regions are created by selecting the element you wish to repeat in the template and then clicking *Insert->Template Objects->Repeating Region*. In the dialog box that opens give the Repeating Region a unique, but identifiable, name, and then click OK.

When using Repeating Regions, it is important to understand that no element of the region will be editable unless you add an Editable Region within it.

As you can see from these advanced template features, there is a lot more to the creation of templates than meets the eye. Of course you don't have to use any of these advanced features at all in your pages, but if you work with other developers, or you concentrate purely on the design elements of a website while someone else works on the actual content, knowing more about templates and the way they work can help you to work safely in the knowledge that your designs won't be accidentally modified.

Summary

In this chapter we have explored the fundamentals of setting up your MySQL database for our example site. The lessons learned here can easily be implemented across your own sites, as the principles and techniques detailed remain relevant regardless of the site being developed.

We've learned new MySQL techniques, by exploring the power of the command-line, an often feared but extremely powerful tool, and seen how an installation of MySQL on our development machine can be beneficial even if our MySQL database is on another machine, as the associated tools and utilities, such as the MySQL Monitor, can be a great bonus.

From setting up the database we have begun to design our example site – The Dreamweaver Hotel, and have designed and implemented a template and a library object that allow us to have central control over the site's look, without having to worry about the difficulties of updating a great number of pages for a minor design change.

Finally we've explored the possibilities and benefits of using templates when creating a web site, and have briefly looked at the new advanced templating techniques that are available only within Dreamweaver MX.

Now that we've done all this, we're ready to begin developing web pages that interact with our database, using the power of PHP, MySQL, and Dreamweaver.

6

- Adding records
- Updating records
- Deleting records
- Designing the pages

Author: Gareth Downes-Powell

Manipulating the Database

In this chapter we will start building our Dreamweaver Hotel Booking System, to allow guests to book a room, and to change and cancel their bookings.

We will look at the main Dreamweaver MX Server Behaviors, to add, update, and delete data in our database tables.

We will be creating Simple and Advanced Recordsets, to retrieve data stored in our database tables, and will learn how to create SQL queries with dynamic parameters, to select specific records.

Finally, we will be looking at using URL parameters, to pass data from page to page, so that we can keep the user records and the booking records tied together.

Database Operations within Dreamweaver MX

Almost every web site on the Internet now uses a database of some form. Whether it's to run a simple guestbook, or a complex E-Commerce system, databases are an essential part of modern web site design.

In this chapter, we're going to design a hotel booking system for The Dreamweaver Hotel. Guests will be able to make a booking, log in and change an existing booking, and also cancel a booking.

As we build the booking system, we are going to encounter a number of different database operations: to add records to a database, to update existing records, and to delete records.

The Hotel Booking System

Our first job is to plan the system, and decide which pages we need, and which operations they need to perform. In Chapter 4 we discussed the basic design of the booking system, in this chapter we're going to create the actual pages that make up its three sections. We're also going to look at each of the three sections for adding, modifying, and deleting records individually, and define the actual pages that will carry out the operations for each section.

Chapter 6

Making a Booking

Our first set of pages allows the user to make a booking. First we need to get the user's name and address details. If the user has booked before, then we will already have their details in the `clients` table in the database. We need a way of pulling that user's record from the database though, and ignoring the others. We do this by asking the user to enter their e-mail address, as this will be unique to each user.

If the user hasn't booked at the hotel before, then we need to collect the user's details before they actually make the booking, and insert them into the `clients` table. Next we need a page to allow the user to enter their booking details, and again insert them into the database. Lastly, we'll display the user's booking details, so that they can print them out and keep them as a permanent reminder of their booking details.

We can cover all these functions with the following four pages:

- `add_user_record.php`
- `book_a_room.php`
- `booking_details.php`
- `confirm_booking.php`

We will look at the roles of each of these pages in turn, and how they link to each other.

add_user_record.php

As the name suggests, this page allows the user to add their name and address details to the database. We will insert the user's data into the `clients` table in the database we created earlier in the book.

This page will add the user details to the `clients` table in the database by using the **Insert Record Server Behavior**. After the record has been inserted, we will redirect the user to the page `booking_details.php`, where the user can enter their required booking details. We pass the user's e-mail address to the booking details page, so that we can correctly tie the user to their booking.

book_a_room.php

This is actually the first page the user sees when they select "*Book a Room*" from the Main menu. If the user is a new user, we have a link to the `add_user_record.php` page above, which allows them to enter their details. If the user has booked with The Dreamweaver Hotel before, we can pull their details from the database. To do this we ask them to enter their e-mail address and we use this to find their details, by searching the `clients` table for the e-mail address the user supplied.

booking_details.php

This page allows the user to enter their booking details, which we will insert into the database table, `bookings`, again using an Insert Record server behavior. As a reminder the database structure for the `bookings` table is shown opposite.

Manipulating the Database

```
# Table structure for table 'bookings'
#

CREATE TABLE bookings (
  ID tinyint(11) NOT NULL auto_increment,
  roomID tinyint(11) NOT NULL default '0',
  clientID tinyint(11) NOT NULL default '0',
  startDate date NOT NULL default '0000-00-00',
  endDate date NOT NULL default '0000-00-00',
  adults int(11) NOT NULL default '1',
  children int(11) NOT NULL default '0',
  roomType varchar(30) NOT NULL default '',
  roomOptions int(8) NOT NULL default '0',
  networkConnection int(8) NOT NULL default '0',
  PC int(8) NOT NULL default '0',
  requirements varchar(250) NOT NULL default '',
  PRIMARY KEY  (ID)
) TYPE=MyISAM COMMENT='Room Booking Table';
```

When the booking form is submitted, we will add the booking record to the database, and we will then redirect to the `booking_confirm.php` page, and again we will pass the user's e-mail address, so that we can locate the correct record on the next page.

confirm_booking.php

This page will pull the users details, and also the booking just created from the database, and displays it on the page, so the user has a copy of their booking details. It also shows the user their booking number, which they will need if they want to change or cancel a booking in the future.

Changing a Booking

The next section we will look at is to allow the user to change their booking. To do this we need to get some information from the user so that we can identify them, and select the correct booking record from the database.

We can't use the user's e-mail address this time, as one user can have a number of different booking records. Instead we ask the user to enter their booking number, which is unique, so that the correct booking record can be selected from the `bookings` table in the database. Once we have the correct booking record, we can read the user's ID number, and we can then retrieve their name and address details from the `clients` table.

We also display the existing details from the bookings record, and allow the user to modify them. We can then update the record in the database, and then again we display the details so the user can print them out.

The following pages will perform these operations.

- `change_booking.php`
- `change_booking_details.php`
- `booking_updated.php`

We will now look at each of these pages individually.

change_booking.php

This page will allow the user to enter a previous booking, so that they make alterations to it. The form will submit to the next page, `change_booking_details.php`, and the booking ID is passed to this page.

change_booking_details.php

This page will display the user's booking details, by using the booking ID passed from the previous page, `change_booking.php`.

The user can now change their booking details. When the form is inserted we use the Update Record server behavior. We pass the client's ID and booking ID to the next page, `booking_updated.php`.

booking_updated.php

This page takes a booking ID number, and a client ID number, and pulls the correct records from the database, to confirm to the user that their booking has been changed, and show the details of the new booking.

Canceling a Booking

The last section will allow the user to cancel their existing booking. To do this we need the user to enter the booking ID that they want to cancel. We can then delete the record with the same booking id from the `bookings` table. Finally we show the user a message to confirm that the record has been canceled. We will do this with the following pages:

- `cancel_booking.php`
- `booking_cancelled.php`

Again, we will look at each page:

cancel_booking.php

This page is to allow the user to cancel their booking. We allow the user to enter their booking number, and then we use Delete Record server behavior to delete the record. Finally, we redirect to the next page, `booking_canceled.php` passing the booking ID.

booking_cancelled.php

This page displays a message to the user, confirming their booking has been canceled. It uses the booking ID number passed to it from the previous page to show the user the ID of the booking that was deleted.

Building the Pages

We now have all three sections planned, so we can start building the pages. First, create a folder called `bookings`, into which we can place the pages. Next create pages from your template, and save them with the following filenames in the `bookings` folder:

Manipulating the Database

- `add_user_record.php`
- `book_a_room.php`
- `booking_details.php`
- `confirm_booking.php`
- `change_booking.php`
- `change_booking_details.php`
- `booking_updated.php`
- `cancel_booking.php`
- `booking_cancelled.php`

At this stage do not add anything to the pages, just save them with the filenames shown above and close the pages. We do this now, so that when we are using the database server behaviors, we can select the page to link to, as the page exists in the `bookings` folder, even though we may not have worked on it yet.

Creating the Bookings Pages

The logical place to start is with the bookings pages, so that we can create some bookings that we can use to test the other sections.

Adding user records – add_user_record.php

The first page we are going to create, is `add_user_record.php`, so open this page in Dreamweaver MX.

Creating the Page

Design the page, so it looks similar to the screenshot overleaf:

Chapter 6

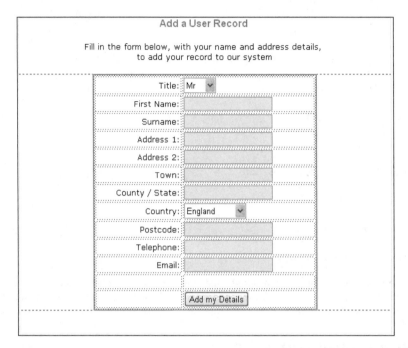

First, place a form on the page by selecting *Insert -> Form* from the main menu bar. Name the form `userform`. There is no need to set an action for the form. On the page above we have used a table to hold the form fields, so all the fields line up neatly with each other. The fields for first name, surname etc. are text fields, and are inserted by placing the mouse cursor at the desired location, and then *selecting Insert -> Form Objects -> Text Field* from the main menu bar.

Once you have inserted a text field, you can click on it, and its settings will be shown in the properties inspector panel, as shown in the image below:

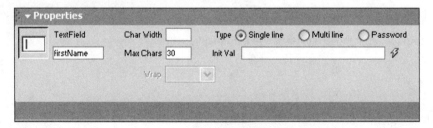

Manipulating the Database

Set the text fields up with the settings shown in the table below:

Form Field	Text Field Name	Max Characters	Type
First Name	firstName	30	Single line
Surname	lastName	30	Single line
Address1	address1	100	Single line
Address2	address2	100	Single line
Town	town	100	Single line
County/State	province	100	Single line
Postcode	postcode	20	Single line
Telephone	telephone	20	Single line
Email	email	100	Single line

You may have noticed that we have set all of the text field names to be the same as the database field they insert into. This allows Dreamweaver MX to automatically match the field data to the correct fields in the database. You don't have to do this, but it makes the process easier, if you do.

The "*Maximum Characters*" field allows you to set the maximum number of characters that the text field will accept. We have matched this to the field length in the database, so that a user can't enter more characters than we can store in the database field. Lastly, we set all the text fields to be single line, as they will only be holding small pieces of data.

We have created a drop-down menu for the title field, which was created by selecting *Insert -> Form Objects -> List/Menu* from the main menu bar. This inserts an empty drop-down menu. Select the drop-down menu, and from the properties inspector, shown below, name the menu title, and then click the "*List Values*" button.

When you click the "*List Values*" button, the following dialog box appears, which allows you to enter the labels and values for the drop-down menu.

123

Chapter 6

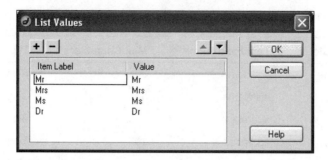

To add a new menu item, click the + button, and you can then insert the item label and value. The "*Item Label*" field is shown to the user as the menu item in the drop-down, and "*Value*" is the corresponding value that will be inserted into the database, when that option is selected.

Enter the following data into the List Values dialog box:

Item Label	Value
Mr	Mr
Mrs	Mrs
Ms	Ms
Dr	Dr

If you need to delete a row, simply select the row, and click the – button. When you have entered the values above, click OK.

The Country drop-down menu is created in the same way as the title drop-down above, and is named country, but you need to enter the menu options below, again by clicking the "*List Values*" button on the properties inspector.

Item Label	Value
England	England
United States	United States
France	France
Spain	Spain
Italy	Italy

Our last job is to create the button the user clicks to submit the form. You can add this button by selecting *Insert -> Form Objects -> Button*. Change the button label to "*Add my Details*". This completes the design of the page.

Manipulating the Database

Creating User Help

We are now going to add some prompts for the user, to explain the data they need to enter. First click on the `firstName` text field, to select it. Select the *Behaviors* tab, on the *Design* panel, so that it looks like the image to the right:

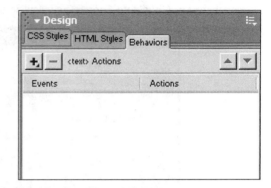

Click the + button, and select *Set Text -> Select Text of Status Bar* from the menu options that appear. A dialog box will open similar to the one shown below:

Enter the following in the dialog box:

Please enter your First Name

Click *OK*, and the dialog box will close. You will now see the action "*Set Text of Status Bar*" in the *Behaviors* action. You will see however, that the Event is set to "*onMouseOver*". This means that when the user moves their mouse over the `firstName` text field, the status bar will display "*Please enter your First Name*". For the event we require, change it from "*onMouseOver*" to "*onFocus*". The *Behaviors* panel should now look like the image to the right:

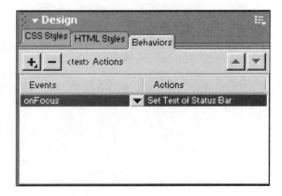

Now when the user's cursor is in the `firstName` text field, either by using the tab key or by clicking in it, the Help message will be displayed in the browser's status bar. This is especially useful on complex forms, to allow you to add instructions for the user.

Repeat the above procedure for each form field, adding appropriate Help text for each field.

Validating the Form

We now want to add another behavior to validate the form data the user submits.

125

Chapter 6

Click on the "*Add my Details*" button, and from the *Behaviors* tab on the *Design* panel, click the + button and then select "*Validate Form*". The following dialog box appears:

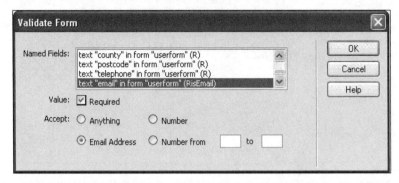

In the "*Named Fields*" box we have a list of all our fields that exist in our form. We can select whether fields are required, that is, they cannot be left blank, and we can also check for various types of data.

Select every field in "*Named Fields*" as "*Required*", except for Address2, which can be left empty if it doesn't apply to the user. Set the data type for each form field that is required as "*Anything*", except for the e-mail field, which should accept an "*Email Address*" only. Finally click "*OK*", and the action is added to the button.

Note that this isn't actually PHP, but client-side JavaScript, so the form will not be submitted to the server unless it has been validated.

Adding the Insert Record Behavior

Our last job on this page is to actually insert the record into the database when the form is submitted.

You should already have a database connection defined in Dreamweaver MX for connection to the mySQL database. You can check this by looking on the *Databases* tab on the *Application* panel, and you should see your database connection as in the screenshot below:

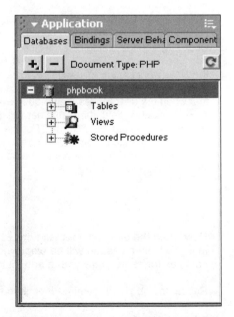

126

Manipulating the Database

If you haven't got a database set up, click the + button, and select MySQL Connection, and enter your database connection details for your database, as in the figure below.

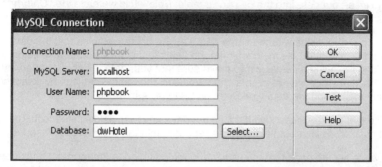

Once you have your database connection established, select the *Server Behaviors* tab, so the panel looks like the image to the right.

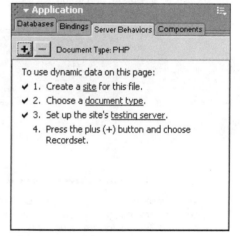

Click the + button, and select "*Insert Record*" from the menu options. The *Insert Record* dialog box appears as shown below:

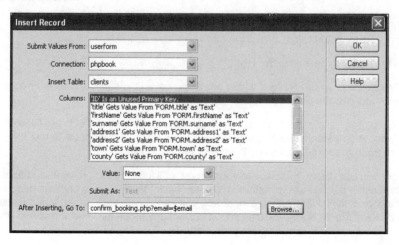

127

From the "*Submit Values From:*" menu select *userform*, which is the name we gave to our form earlier. Select your database connection from the "*Connection:*" menu, and *clients* from the "*Insert Table*" menu, as we want to insert our data into the `clients` table. Below this we have the "*Columns"* menu that shows all our database fields, and the name of the form fields as well as their data types.

As we created our form fields with the same name as the database fields that the data inserts into, Dreamweaver MX automatically matches the form fields to the correct database fields. It's always worth double-checking the column items, just to make sure that your data is being inserted into the correct database fields. If any options are mismatched, you can change the settings by selecting the form field from the Value menu, and the data type from the "*Submit As:*" menu.

You will notice that the database field ID does not have any form fields linked to it. This is because the ID was created as an Auto Number field, and the record number is automatically inserted by the database.

Lastly we need to set the page that the user is redirected to, once the form data has been inserted. Click the "*Browse"* Button, and then click the "*Parameters"* button on the dialog box that appears. The *Parameters* dialog box is shown:

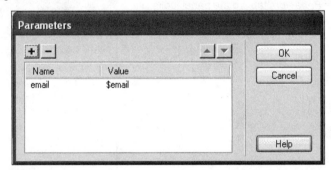

These parameters are added to the URL of the page that we redirect the user to, and can carry addition information from page to page. Click the + button to add a new row, and enter e-mail for the parameter name, and $e-mail for the value. This means that when the page is inserted the value from the e-mail field, which is referred to by placing a $ in front of the field name, is added to the URL Click "*OK"*, and then click on the `booking_details.php` page, and click OK.

Now, if a user with the e-mail address `test@test.com` submitted the form, the user would be redirected to:

`booking_details.php?e-mail=test@test.com`

The e-mail field value is passed in the URL.

Click "*OK"* to close the *Insert Record* dialog box if you haven't already, and all the necessary code is automatically added to the page by Dreamweaver MX.

So to recap, our page allows the user to enter their data, it validates all fields are filled in (apart from address 2), and then it inserts the data into the `clients` table, and redirects to the `booking_details.php` page passing the user's e-mail address.

At this stage, you can upload this page to your server, call it up in your browser, and enter a test record. You can then use a database administration tool, to check the data you typed has been entered correctly, and into the correct fields. If any data is incorrect, you can double-click on the Insert Record behavior, and the dialog box will appear again, allowing you to correct any problems. The completed page when viewed in a browser looks similar to the screenshot overleaf:

Manipulating the Database

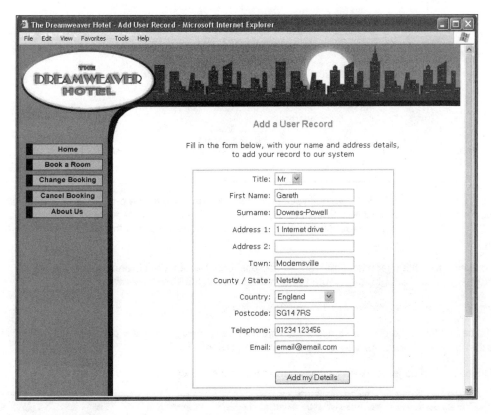

The Book a Room Page – book_a_room.php

This page is a fairly simple page, and is the page the user goes to when they click "*Book a Room*" from the main menu on the web page.

Open the `book_a_room.php` page that you created earlier, and insert a form, giving it the name `bookingform`, as shown in the image below:

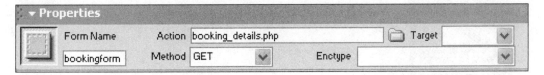

Set the form action to the `booking_details.php` page, and set the form method as GET. This means when the form is submitted, it will send the form data to the `booking_details.php` page, and adds the form values to the URL.

The rest of the page is shown in the image below:

> **Book a Room**
>
> If you have already booked a room with us before, enter your email address in the box provided below, otherwise Add yourself as a New User.
>
> Email Address : [   ]
>
> [Book a Room]

The text field is named `email`, with Max Chars set to 100, the same as the e-mail field in the database. Next, add a button, and change its label to "*Book a Room*". Create a text link to the `add_user_record.php` page, so that the user can create a new record if they haven't made a previous booking.

To summarize, the user enters their e-mail address, and the form data is sent to the `booking_details.php` page, with the e-mail address in the URL as shown below:

`booking_details.php?e-mail=test@test.com`

Notice that this is exactly the same format as the `create_new_user.php` page, so that whichever page submits to `confirm_booking.php` the same data is sent.

The completed page viewed in a browser is shown in the screenshot below.

Manipulating the Database

Making a Booking – booking_details.php

This page allows the user to actually enter their booking details. First open the page `booking_details.php` that you created earlier. The page should be laid out in a similar way to the screen-shot below:

```
                    Email Address Not Found!

            Click here to enter your email address again,
                  or to register as a New User.

       Thank you, name surname, please enter your Booking Details below
    --------------------------------------------------------------------
              Arrival Date: [            ] (yyyy-mm-dd)
            Departure Date: [            ] (yyyy-mm-dd)
                Room Type: [Single  v]
       In Room Extras Required: [ ] Network Connection
                                [ ] PC
           Number of Adults: [1 v]
          Number of Children: [0 v]
              Room Options:  [ ] Smoking    [●] Non Smoking

         Special Requirements: [                    ]
                               [                    ]
                               [                    ]

                              [ Book a Room ]
```

First of all we have some ordinary text telling the user their email address is not found, and to ask them to click the link to go back to the `book_a_room.php` page. Later in this section we will set this text to only be shown if the user's email address is not found.

Next create a line with the following text:

Thank you, name surname, please enter your Booking Details below.

Again, later in this section we will change name and surname, to be the user's first name and surname read from the database.

131

Chapter 6

Creating the Form

Add a form to the page, and name it `bookroom`. There is no need to set a form action as the Insert Record server behavior does this for us. Leave the form method set to `POST`, which is the default. Again we created a table to hold the form fields so they are neatly lined up.

First create the two text fields, to hold the user's arrival and departure dates, and give them the following settings:

Form Item	Name	Max Chars	Type
Arrival Date	`arrivalDate`	10	Single Line
Departure Date	`departureDate`	10	Single Line

Next, insert a drop-down menu, and call it `roomType`, and add the following, after clicking the "*List Values*" button in the properties inspector.

Item Label	Value
Single	Single
Double	Double
Suite	Suite

We now come to the in-room extras required, with two options, Network Connection and PC. We use check-boxes for this data. Create a checkbox by selecting *Insert -> Form Object -> Check Box*. Click on the new check box, and the properties inspector will appear with checkbox settings, as shown below:

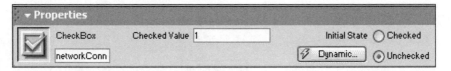

For the checkbox name, enter `networkConnection`, enter 1 for the "*Checked Value*", and select "*Unchecked*" for the "*Initial State*". This means that when the checkbox appears unchecked initially, and if its checked by the user, it will have a value of one, which we can write to the database. Create another check box, called PC, again with a checked value of 1, and unchecked for the "*Initial State*".

We next have two drop-down menus, so the user can select the number of children and adults staying in the room. Create these two drop-down menus, and name them `adults` and `children`. The `adults` drop-down has the following menu items:

Item Label	Value
1	1
2	2

Manipulating the Database

Then set the `children` drop-down to have the following menu items:

Item Label	Value
0	0
1	1
2	2

We now come to the room options, which gives the user a choice of a smoking or non-smoking room.

To do this we use a radio group, which is a set of options, of which only one option from the group can be selected at any one time. When you select an option from the group, all the other options are deselected. This is useful for situations like this to make the user select one from a series of options, and stopping them from selecting more than one.

To insert the radio group, select *Insert -> Form Objects -> Radio Group* from the main menu bar, and the following dialog box will appear:

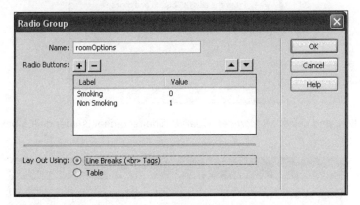

Give the radio group the name `roomOptions`, as this is the field in the `bookings` table that the data will be inserted into. Change the labels to read "*Smoking*" with a value of 0, and "*Non Smoking*" with a value of 1. Select "*Lay Out Using Line Breaks*", as we don't want another table inserted. Click *OK*, and the option group will automatically be inserted. Drag the circular buttons to a more suitable location.

Our last field is for the user to enter any special requirements they may have. It's a text field, but it allows multiple lines of text to be entered. Create the field by selecting *Insert -> Form Objects -> Text Area* from the main menu bar. Select the text area and the properties inspector will look like the following:

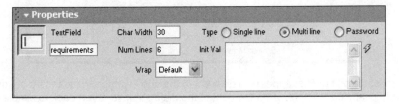

133

Chapter 6

Note this is the same as for a text field, but the "*Multi Line*", instead of "*Single Line*", option is selected. Enter requirements for the text area name, 30 for the char width, and 6 for the number of lines, to give the user a decent sized area in which to type. Lastly, insert a button and give it the label "*Book a Room*".

Creating the Database Recordsets

Now we've created our form, we can start creating the database interactions. We first want to open a recordset that contains the user's name and address details, which we can find by using the e-mail parameter, sent in the URL to this page from the preceding pages. On the "*Application*" Tab, click the "*Bindings*" Tab, as shown below:

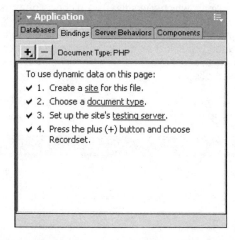

Click the + button, and select "*Recordset (Query)*". The recordset builder dialog box will appear as shown below:

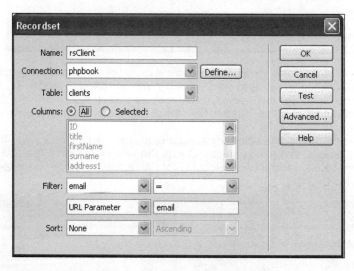

If the recordset dialog box that appears is different to the above image, it means it's in advanced mode, so click the button labeled "*Simple...*" on the right of the dialog box, to revert back to simple mode. We'll be looking at the advanced mode later on in the chapter.

Manipulating the Database

For the recordset name enter `rsClient`. It's advisable to name your recordsets like this, so that you can easily identify the recordset later. Select your database connection from the "*Connection"* menu. Select the `clients` table from the "*Table"* menu, as this is where the user's record is stored. We can now build our query quickly and easily.

From the "*Filter"* drop-down menus, select:

`e-mail   =   URL Parameter   e-mail`

This does exactly as it reads, and opens a recordset containing a record where the e-mail field in the database matches the e-mail parameter in the URL. We don't need a sort, as we're only expecting one record to be returned. Lastly click *OK* to create the recordset. The recordset `rsClient` will now appear in the "*Bindings"* window, and clicking on it to open its tree shows the following:

As you can see all the fields in the recordset are shown.

We are now going to go back to the top of our page, to the text above the form, which is set out similar to the image below:

> **Email Address Not Found!**
>
> Click here to enter your email address again,
> or to register as a New User.
>
> Thank you, name surname, please enter your Booking Details below

In the last sentence, we have name and surname. We want to replace these with the values from the `rsClient` recordset. First highlight name, by clicking at the start of name and holding the mouse button down dragging across it.

Click on `firstName` in the recordset field list, and click the insert button. Dreamweaver MX adds a placeholder showing that the data for name is dynamic, and will be replaced with `firstName` from `rsClient` when the page is viewed in a browser. Highlight *surname*, select *surname* in the Bindings window, and again click *insert*.

135

The sentence should now look the same as the image below.

The user's first name and surname will now be substituted into the text when the page is viewed in a browser.

Hiding and Displaying Text

If we look at the top of our page again, we have the two sections of text, one saying the e-mail address has not been found, another thanking the user and asking them to enter their booking details. Obviously we don't want the user to see both sections of text; only one or the other, depending on whether the user's e-mail address was found in the `clients` table.

Now we know that if the recordset we created, `rsClient`, contains a record, then the user's e-mail address and details have been found. If the user's e-mail address is not found, then the `rsClient` recordset will be empty. We can now add server behaviors that display or hide the text, according to the state of the `rsClient` recordset.

First select the whole text block that tells the user their address has not been found, including the text with the link underneath. Click the "*Server Behaviors*" tab, which is next to the "*Bindings*" tab we have been looking at, on the *Application* panel. Click + to add a server behavior, and select *Show Region -> Show if Recordset is Empty* from the menu. The following dialog box will appear:

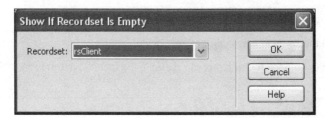

From the recordset menu, select *rsClient* and click *OK*. The PHP code will automatically be added to the page, and you will see the server behavior appear on the *Server Behaviors* panel. Next select everything from the start of the sentence thanking the user to the end of the form, right at the bottom of the page. Click + to add a server behavior, but this time select *Show Region -> Show if Recordset is Not Empty*. This time the dialog below appears:

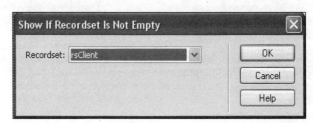

Manipulating the Database

Again select the rsClient recordset, and click *OK* to apply the behavior. Your page should now look similar to the screenshot below:

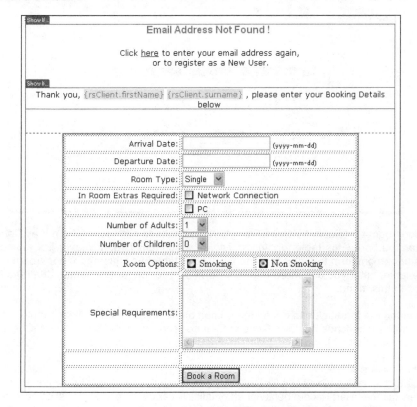

Note that the two regions we created are marked automatically by Dreamweaver MX, so we can see which data is in which region.

Inserting the Record

Now we've created our page, we can add the server behavior to insert the record into the database.

Before we do this however we will create a hidden field on our form, which we will use to hold the ID number of the user, obtained from the `rsClient` recordset. Select *Insert -> Form Objects -> Hidden Field* from the main menu bar to insert a hidden field. Click on it, and enter its name as `clientID` in the properties inspector; don't type anything in the value field.

Again, click the hidden field to make sure it's selected, and click on the ID field in our `rsClient` recordset on the "*Bindings*" tab. Next click the "*Bind*" button, which binds the ID field in the `rsClient` recordset to our hidden field. This means that when the page is viewed in a browser, the value of the hidden field will automatically be set to the value in the ID field of the `rsClient` recordset.

Now we've done all the preparation, we can finally apply the Insert Record behavior. Click back to the "*Server Behaviors*" tab, and click the + button to add a server behavior. Select "*Insert Record*" from the menu. The *Insert Record* dialog box appears as shown overleaf:

Select bookroom for "*Submit Values From:*", your database connection from the "*Connection*" menu, and the `bookings` table for "*Insert Table*", which tells Dreamweaver MX to use the values from the bookroom form to insert into the `bookings` table. For this page, bookroom is the only form available, but if you use more than one form on your page, the names of all the forms will be displayed in this menu.

As we created the form fields to match the names of the fields in the bookings table, Dreamweaver MX automatically matches the form fields to their corresponding database fields. Check through the list to make sure that all the data is being inserted into the correct place.

We want the user to be redirected to the `confirm_booking.php` page once the data has been inserted, so browse to this page and select it for the "*After Inserting, Go To:*" field. We do not need to set any parameters, as the Insert Record behavior automatically carries across any existing parameters, that is, the e-mail parameter, and adds it to the URL.

You can now upload this page to your server, open the `add_user_record.php` page and enter your details. When you add your details, you will be taken to our `booking_details.php` page, and your name should be showing in the greeting at the top of the page. When viewed in the browser, the page will look similar to the one opposite:

Manipulating the Database

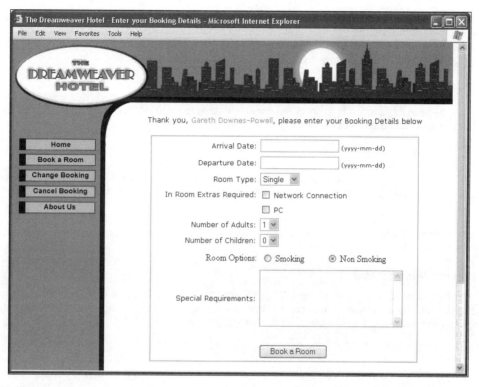

If the user entered an e-mail address on the `book_a_room.php` page, and the e-mail address is not found, then the page will show the following:

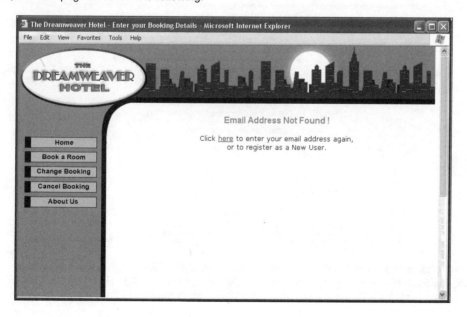

Chapter 6

These two pictures show the Show Region server behavior in action. Both show the same page, but one showing with a record in `rsClient`, the other when `rsClient` is empty. The Show Region server behavior is extremely useful, as you can use the same page to cover different scenarios, cutting down the number of pages you have to design, saving you time.

Confirming a Booking – confirm_booking.php

The last page in this section is to show the booking details to the user for confirmation. To do this we use two recordsets, and data from the `bookings` and the `clients` table.

First, we use the e-mail address that is passed to this page in the URL parameter e-mail, to open and find the last of the user's bookings in the `bookings` table (which will be the booking) they just made. This gives us the user's booking details to display on the page. From the booking record, we get the client's ID number, and we use this to pull the users name and address details from the `clients` table.

We then display all this data on the page, so the user can print off a copy or save the page, as confirmation of their booking details.

Creating the Page Layout

First open the `confirm_booking.php` page you created earlier. Create a form, but don't set an action. We're not actually using this form to submit data, just so we can use form elements to display existing data. Lay the page out in a similar way to the screenshot below:

```
                    Booking Complete

Thank you, your booking is complete, and we will email you with more details shortly.

              Below are your details for confirmation:

          Booking ID: Booking-ID
                Name: client-title client-firstname client-surname
             Address: client-address1, client-address2
                      client-town, client-county
                      client-country, client-postcode.
        Arrival Date: booking-arrivaldate (yyyy-mm-dd)
      Departure Date: booking-departuredate (yyyy-mm-dd)
           Room Type: booking-roomtype
In Room Extras Required: ☐ Network Connection
                         ☐ PC
    Number of Adults: booking-adults
  Number of Children: booking-children
        Room Options: ○ Smoking      ○ Non Smoking
Special Requirements: booking-requirements
```

Again we've used a table to set out the data neatly. Create placeholders for the dynamic data we are going to be inserting into the page. The placeholders are labeled so that they show the table their data comes from, and the fieldname, to make it easier when we come to add the dynamic data later on.

Manipulating the Database

As the fields for Network Connection, PC, and Smoking and Non Smoking are entered in the database tables as 1 or 0, we add form elements to show this data in a way the user can understand. Again the "*In Room Extras Required*" options are checkboxes, and the "*Room Options*" field is a radio group with the same settings as on the bookings page, Smoking, 0 and Non Smoking, 1.

It doesn't matter this time what the fields are called as we are not using them to insert data into the database, only to display it. For the same reason we do not need to add a submit button to the form, as we do not want it to actually be submitted, but you need a form if you want to use form elements.

Creating the Recordsets

We are now going to create the recordsets that pull the correct data from the `clients` and `bookings` tables. First we want to retrieve the correct client data, which we can do using the URL parameter e-mail which is passed by the `booking_details.php` page. Click on the "*Bindings*" tab, and click the + button, and select "*Recordset*".

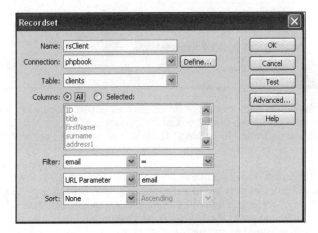

Enter `rsClient` as the recordset name, and select your database connection. Select *clients* as the table to pull the data from. For the filter, select from the filter options:

e-mail = URL Parameter e-mail

Again this finds the record in the `clients` table, where the address in the e-mail field matches the e-mail parameter in the URL. We know that there definitely will be a record, as `booking_details.php` will not allow you to add a booking unless you have entered an e-mail address that exists in the `clients` table. Leave "*Sort*" as "*None*", as we should only find one matching record. Click "*OK*" to create the recordset.

Advanced Recordsets

We now need to add another recordset, to pull a booking record from the booking table. Click the + button on the *Bindings* tab, and select "*Recordset*".

This time we're going to use an advanced recordset, so click the "*Advanced...*" button, which is on the right-hand side of the Recordset dialog box. The dialog box expands to look like the image opposite:

141

Chapter 6

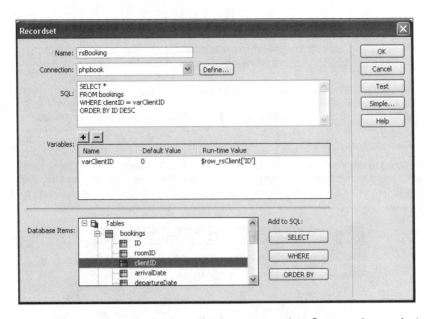

Enter *rsBooking* for the name, and select your database connection. Once you have selected your database connection, the "*Database Items*" box at the bottom is populated with all of the tables and fields in your database, which you can see by clicking "*Tables*" to expand the tree, and then clicking the `bookings` table, to show all its fields.

Place the mouse cursor on the `bookings` table, in the *Database Items* window, and then click "*SELECT*". The SQL will automatically be added to the SQL box. Next click on the `clientID` field in the `bookings` table, and click "*WHERE*", and more SQL is automatically generated. Lastly click on the ID field in the `bookings` table and press the "*ORDER BY*" button, and the order by statement is automatically added. You will need to manually add DESC to the end of the ORDER BY statement, as we want the records in descending order of ID. If we wanted the records in ascending order we could have added ASC.

Now we come to the reason we are using the recordset builder in advanced mode. We want to select a booking from the booking table, where the `clientID` is equal to the value of the ID field in the `rsClient` recordset we created. This way the results from one recordset are used to search for data from another recordset, which is extremely useful.

In the middle of the `Recordset` dialog box, you will see a box labeled "*Variables*". Click + to enter a new variable, and the variables parameter box will appear, as shown overleaf.

For the name enter `varClientID`, enter 0 for the default value (which is substituted in if there isn't a value when the page is run, to stop errors occurring). Lastly for the "*Runtime value*" enter:

```
$row_rsClient['ID']
```

This takes the value of ID from the `rsClient` table when the page is opened in a browser. The format is always:

```
$row_RECORDSETNAME['FIELDNAME']
```

Click "*OK*" to create the new variable. You can retrieve data from any field, in any recordset using the above format, just replace `RECORDSETNAME` with the name of your recordset, and `FIELDNAME` with the name of the field you want to pull the value from.

When you use this technique, of using data from one recordset to select records from another, you need to make sure that you create the recordsets in a logical order. For example you can't use a recordset field value to select records from a table, if the recordset from which you're taking the value hasn't already been created.

Our last job is to add our new variable to our `WHERE` clause. At present we have for the `WHERE` clause:

```
WHERE clientID =
```

Change this to

```
WHERE clientID = varClientID
```

This takes our run-time variable, and opens a recordset containing records where the `clientID` matches the value in `varClientID`, which in turn comes from the ID field of our `rsClients` recordset. We sort the bookings into descending order, using the `ORDER BY` clause, so we get the last ID number of that user, which will be the record we just added.

Click "*OK*" on the Recordset dialog box, to create the recordset.

Now in the *bindings* tab we have two recordsets, `rsClient` and `rsBooking`, with all the fields the tables contain. We can now populate our page with this data, by highlighting each placeholder and inserting the appropriate field. When you have done this to each placeholder, your page should look similar to the screenshot overleaf.

Chapter 6

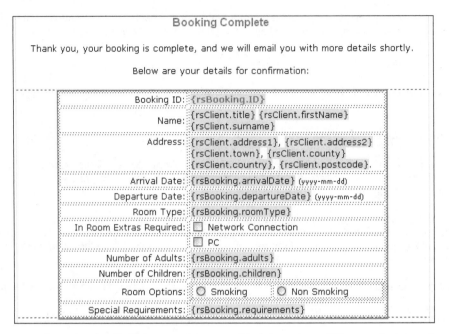

Another way of merging results from more than one table is by using a SQL `JOIN` between the `bookings` and the `clients` table, this involves a more advanced SQL statement. This, and other advanced uses of SQL, is covered in Chapter 7.

Dynamic Form Fields

Our last job on this page is to make the correct values show in the "*In Room Extras*" checkboxes, and the Room Options radio group. Select the first check box, for "*Network Connection*", and then click the "*dynamic*" button on the properties inspector. The following dialog box will appear:

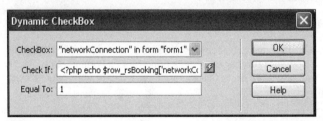

For the "*Checkbox*" field, select `networkConnection`, which is the name of the checkbox. For "*Check If*", press the lightning bolt icon, and select the `networkConnection` field. Finally enter 1, for "*Equal To:*". Click *OK* to continue.

This means that if the value in the field `networkConnection` in the `bookings` table is equal to 1, the box will be displayed with a check mark in, if not the box will be empty. Repeat the same process for the PC Check box, setting it to "*Check*" if the value of the PC field in the `bookings` table is equal to 1.

Lastly select one of the options in the radio group for *Room Options* and click the "*dynamic*" button in the properties inspector. The following dialog box will appear:

Manipulating the Database

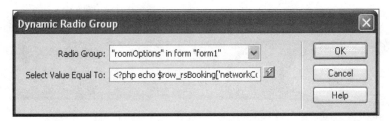

Select `roomType` for the Radio Group, and for "*Select Value Equal To:*" click the lightning bolt icon, and select the `roomType` field from the `bookings` table, then click "*OK*". Now when the page is viewed in a browser, the option with a value matching the `roomType` field in the `bookings` table will be selected.

Finally, at the bottom of the page below the form, add the following text:

If any of the booking details are incorrect, click here to change them.

We are now going to make the words "*click here*" a link, which takes the user directly to the `change_booking_details.php` page, automatically selecting the correct booking record.

Highlight the words "click here", and click the link button on the properties inspector. In the dialog box that appears, select the `change_booking_details.php` page, and click the "*Parameters...*" button. Select the following options from the dialog box that appears:

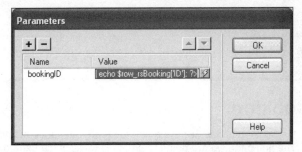

for the *Name* type `bookingID`, and for the *Value*, select the ID field from the `rsBooking` recordset, by clicking the lightning bolt icon. Click *OK*, and then *OK* again to create the link. When the user clicks on the link, the booking ID number will be sent to the `change_booking_details.php` page, in the URL, in the following form:

http://php.buzzinet.co.uk/~phpbook/booking/change_booking_details.php?bookingID=10

This ensures the correct record is selected on the `change_booking_details.php` page, as we are mimicking the action of the `change_booking.php` page, which we create, and look at in detail in the next section.

We now have our first section completed. Upload `confirm_booking.php` to your server, and you can then book a room and see the results in your browser. The screen should look similar to the one overleaf:

Chapter 6

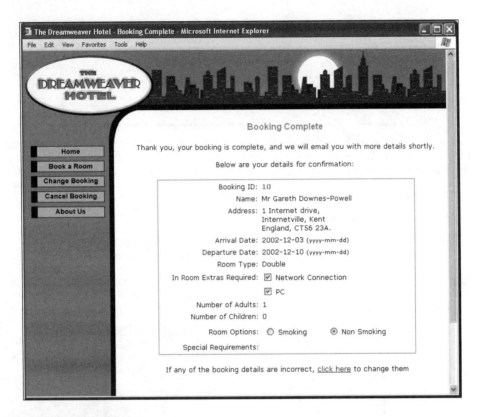

Changing a Booking

Now we have created the booking pages, we are going to create the pages that will allow the user to change their booking. The first page we are going to create is to allow the user to enter their booking number, and is a fairly simple page.

Changing a Booking – change_booking.php

Open the `change_booking.php` page that you created earlier in the chapter. Our first job is to create the form on the page.

Creating the Form

Insert a form onto your page, and change its name to `changeform`, and set the form action to `change_booking_details.php`. Create the page layout so it looks similar to the screenshot below:

Manipulating the Database

Name the text field `bookingID`, and set its "*Max Characters*" attribute to 5, by using the properties inspector.

When the user selects "*Change Booking*" from the *Main* menu, this is the page that is loaded. They can then type in their booking ID, and the form sends this data to the `change_booking_details.php` page. The image below shows this page when viewed in a browser:

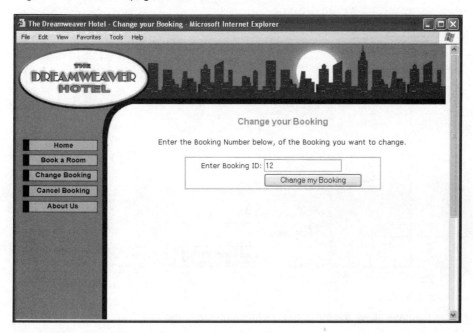

Save this page and upload it to your server so we can use it later.

Changing the Booking Details – change_booking_details.php

This page is similar to the `booking_details.php`, which we created in the last section. This page is opened when the form on the previous page, `change_booking.php`, is submitted. It is passed the booking ID the user enters, and we can use this to retrieve the user's booking, and the user's details.

Open the `change_booking_details.php` page you created earlier. Add a form to the page, and name it `bookroom`. We don't need to set a form action this time, as the Update Record server behavior we are going to use adds it automatically. We are going to create the page, so that it looks similar to the screenshot overleaf:

Chapter 6

```
    Thank you, firstname surname, you can change your Booking Details below

              Arrival Date: [          ]  (yyyy-mm-dd)
            Departure Date: [          ]  (yyyy-mm-dd)
                Room Type: [Single ▼]
       In Room Extras Required: ☐ Network Connection
                                ☐ PC
          Number of Adults: [1 ▼]
        Number of Children: [0 ▼]
             Room Options: ☐ Smoking      ☐ Non Smoking

                              ┌──────────────┐
                              │              │
       Special Requirements:  │              │
                              │              │
                              └──────────────┘

                         [Change my Booking]
```

At the top of the page above the form, add the following message:

Thank you, firstname surname, you can change your booking details below.

The *firstname* and *surname* above are our placeholders, and we will replace these with the user's first name and surname from the database.

As the table with the form field above is exactly the same as the one we created on the `booking_details.php` page, we can save a lot of time by opening the `booking_details.php` page and selecting the table (just the table, make sure you don't select the form as well). You can then press *Ctrl + c*, or use *Edit -> Copy* from the main menu bar to copy the table. You can now close the `booking_details.php` page.

On the `change_booking_details.php` page, place the cursor inside the form we created, and press *Ctrl + v*, or select *Edit -> Paste* from the main menu bar. The table will now appear in the form, complete with all the form fields with their attributes intact.

Click on the hidden field named `clientID`, and look at the *Server Behaviors* tab on the *Application* panel. You will see that the Dynamic Data behavior was also copied over. This is no longer valid, so delete it by clicking the – button. We will recreate this later on, with the correct data for this page.

Create another hidden field, and name it `bookingID`. We are going to insert the booking ID number into this hidden field, so the booking number will be sent with the rest of the form fields. Hidden fields are extremely useful to pass information from page to page that you need, but don't want to display, or get from the user. Hidden fields can be inserted into the database the same as any other form fields.

Manipulating the Database

Note that the user can see hidden fields if they view the page source in their browser, so they should not be used for confidential data such as passwords etc.

Now we've created the form, we can start creating the database behaviors.

Creating the Recordsets

The first recordset we are going to create is to retrieve the booking record for the booking ID number that is passed to this page. Click on the "*Bindings*" tab, on the "*Application*" panel, and click the + button, and then select "*Recordset*". The details we are going to enter are shown here:

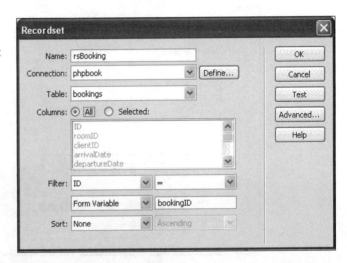

If the Recordset Dialog box appears in advanced mode, click the "*Simple...*" button, as we will be creating the recordset in the simple mode. You will often find yourself swapping between the recordset builder modes, as queries can be created quickly and easily using the simple mode, but more complicated queries require the advanced mode.

Enter rsBookings for the recordset name, and select your database connection and the bookings table. Set up the Filter so it reads:

ID = Form Variable bookingID

Finally click "*OK*". This creates our recordset containing a record where the ID field matches the bookingID sent from the previous page.

Now we need to create another recordset, to retrieves the user's details from the database table clients. Click the + button on the "*Bindings*" tab and select "*Recordset*". This time click the "*Advanced...*" Button, as we will be creating this recordset in advanced mode.

What we need to do is to open a recordset containing the record from the clients table, where the ID field matches the value stored in the clientID field of the booking record we retrieved with the previous record. In advanced mode, click the + button by the variables section, to add a new variable. The settings to enter are shown below:

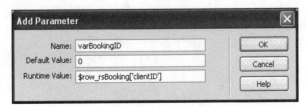

149

Enter `varBookingID` for the Parameter Name, `0` for the "*Default Value*", and `$row_rsBooking['clientID']` for the "*Run Time Value*", and click "*OK*" to add the parameter. The rest of the settings for the recordset are shown below:

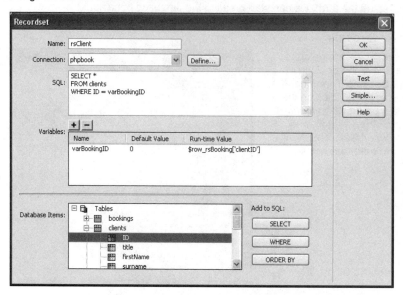

For the recordset name enter `rsClient`, and select your database connection. Click on the `clients` table, in the "*Database Items"* box, and click the "*SELECT"* button. Open the table in the tree, if it's not already open, and click on the ID field, then click the "*WHERE"* button. The SQL should now be:

```
SELECT *
FROM clients
WHERE ID =
```

Change this to

```
SELECT *
FROM clients
WHERE ID = varBookingID
```

so that the record found will be the record where ID matches the `clientID` field in the `rsBooking` recordset we created earlier. Click *OK* to create the recordset.

Adding the Dynamic Data

Now we have the two recordsets `rsBooking` and `rsClient`, we have all the fields we need to make the form fields dynamic.

First select the placeholder for firstname and insert the `firstName` field from the `rsClient` recordset as shown oppsite, then insert the surname from the `surname` field in the `rsClient` recordset.

Manipulating the Database

Select the text field that holds the arrival date, then select the `arrivalDate` field from the `rsBooking` table under the "*Bindings*" tab, and then click the "*Bind*" button. When the page is loaded in a browser, the text field will now contain the value of the `arrivalDate` field in the `rsBooking` recordset. The "*Bindings*" tab is shown in the image below:

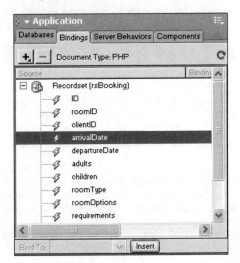

Click the text field for departure date, and bind it to the `departureDate` field in the `rsBooking` recordset. Next select the `roomType` drop-down menu, and click the "*dynamic*" button on the properties inspector panel.

Chapter 6

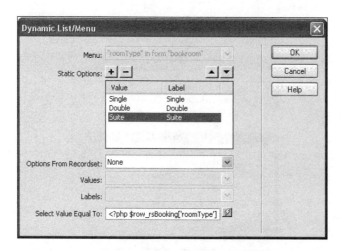

Leave "*Options from Recordset:*" set to *None*, as we only want the "*Static Options"* to be available. On the "*Select Value Equal To:"* line, click the lightning bolt icon, and select the `roomType` field from the `rsBooking` recordset. When the page is loaded in the browser, the option that is automatically selected is the same as the value of the `roomType` field in the `rsBooking` recordset.

Next we come to the two checkboxes for *Network Connection* and *PC*. First click the `networkConnection` checkbox, and click the "*dynamic*" button on the properties inspector.

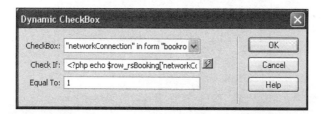

For the "*Check If:*" field, select `networkConnection` from the `rsBooking` table, and set the "*Equal To:*" Value to 1. So when the page is viewed in a browser, the `networkConnection` check box will be checked if the `networkConnection` field in the `rsBooking` recordset is equal to 1, and unchecked if the field contains 0. Click *OK*, and then click the "*dynamic*" button for the *PC* checkbox.

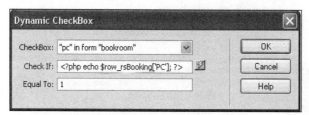

Select the *PC* field from the `rsBooking` recordset, and enter 1 in the "*Equal To:*" field. Click OK.

Manipulating the Database

Next select the `adults` drop-down menu, and click the "*dynamic*" button.

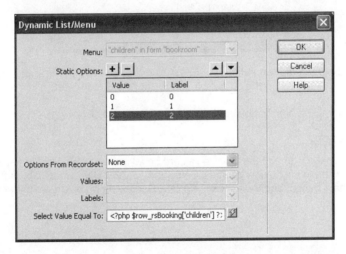

Set the "*Select Value Equal To:*" field to the `adults` field from the `rsBooking` recordset. Click "*OK*", and select the `children` drop-down.

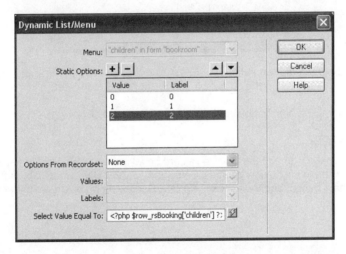

Set the "*Select Value Equal To:*" field to the `children` field in the `rsBooking` recordset. Click "*OK*". Next select one of the options in the `roomOptions` radio group, and click the "*dynamic*" button.

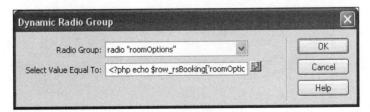

153

Chapter 6

Set the "*Select Value Equal To:*" field to the value of the `roomOptions` field in the `rsBooking recordset`, then click *OK*.

Next select the *requirements* text area, and select the `requirements` field in the `rsBooking recordset`, and click the "*Bind*" button, to bind the value in this field to the text area.

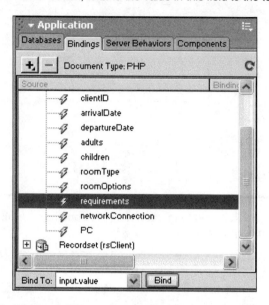

Our last job is to bind the hidden field, `clientID`, to the `clientID` in the `rsBooking` recordset, and the hidden field, `bookingID`, to the ID field in the `rsBooking` recordset.

Change the label for the submit button on the form to "*Change my Booking*".

Adding the Update Behavior

Our last job on this page is to add the Update Record behavior, to update the data stored in the `bookings` table, with the user's new choices. Select the "*Server Behaviors"* tab on the "*Application*" panel, and click the + button, and then select "*Update Record*" from the menu that appears.

Manipulating the Database

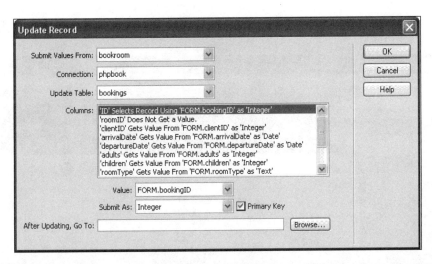

Select the `bookroom` form for "*Submit Values From:*", and `bookings` from the "*Update Table*" menu. Check the form fields are correctly matched to the fields in the database they insert into, which they should do as the form fields have the same names as the database fields.

We do need to make one change however, and that is to tell the Update Record behavior which record we want updated. It's important to make sure that this value is set correctly, as it could lead to the incorrect record being updated if it's not correct. Select the `ID` field in the `Columns` box, and then select `FORM.bookingID`, (which is our hidden field containing the booking ID number), from the *Value* menu, and make sure the "*Primary Key*" checkbox is ticked. This makes sure that the record in the `bookings` table, which is updated, has the same ID as the value in the hidden field `bookingID`.

Lastly for the "*After Updating, Go To:*" field, click browse and select `booking_updated.php` and click the *parameters* button. Add the following parameters:

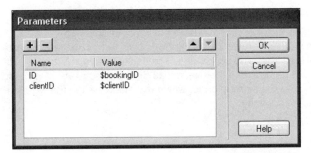

Add a parameter called `ID` with the value `$bookingID` and a parameter called `clientID` with the value `$clientID`. `$bookingID` takes the value of the `bookingID` hidden field when the form is submitted, and `$clientID` takes the value from the `clientID` field, and we pass these values to the next page `booking_updated.php` through the URL. Click *OK*, and then *OK* to close the Update Record dialog box and apply the behavior.

Chapter 6

You can now save the page, and upload to your server for testing later. The complete page when viewed in a browser is similar to the following:

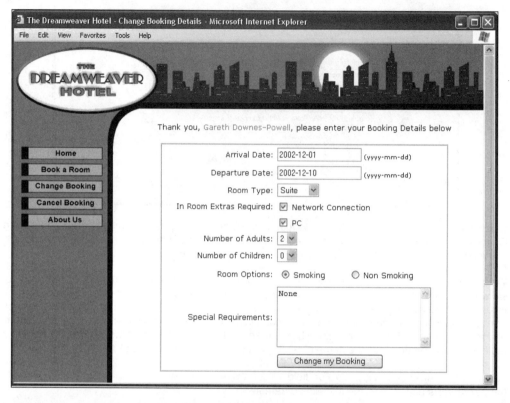

User Confirmation – booking_updated.php

This page will confirm to the user that the new booking details have been saved, and display the booking record. Again as this page is very similar to the confirm_booking.php we are going to save some time by copying the confirm_booking.php page. The easiest way to do this is to open the confirm_booking.php page, and then save it as booking_updated.php, selecting *yes* when you are prompted to overwrite the existing page, which is blank. Change the wording on the page, so it is similar to the screenshot opposite:

Manipulating the Database

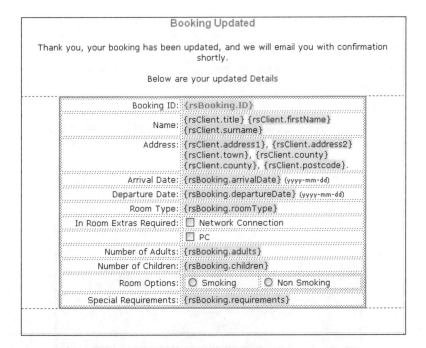

Creating the Recordsets

Before we can create our recordsets, we need to remove the two recordsets already on the page from when it was `confirm_booking.php`. On the "*Bindings*" tab, on the "*Application*" panel, click on the `rsClient` recordset and then click -. You will get a warning as we are using data from this recordset on our page, but it's ok, as we will be recreating it. Remove the `rsBooking` recordset in the same way.

We deleted the recordsets, as they took different parameters to the ones that are passed to this page, `ID` and `clientID`, which is the booking ID number and the client ID number. Click + and select *recordset*. Click the *Recordset* dialog box into simple view, if you are not already there, and set up the following options:

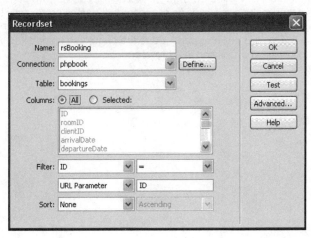

Set the name to `rsBooking`, select the `bookings` table, and set the filter as:

ID = URL Parameter ID

Click OK to create the recordset. This creates the `rsBooking` recordset which will contain a record where the ID number matches the ID parameter sent through the URL, from the previous page.

Next create another recordset to retrieve the client details:

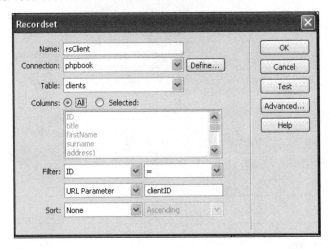

Call the recordset `rsClient`, select the `clients` table, and use the following filter:

ID = URL Parameter clientID

Click OK to create the recordset. Again this creates the `rsClient` recordset containing a record where the field `ID` is equal to the value of the URL parameter `clientID`. As we have named the two recordsets we created the same as the two we deleted, all the bindings on the page will still work, without any further intervention.

Our last job is to add a direct link to the `change_booking_details.php` page again, so the user can change their details if they make a mistake. As our recordset names are exactly the same as on the `confirm_booking.php` page, we can copy the dynamic link from that page, and then paste it into position on our `booking_updated.php` page. Save the page, and upload it to your server. The page looks similar to the following when viewed in a browser:

Manipulating the Database

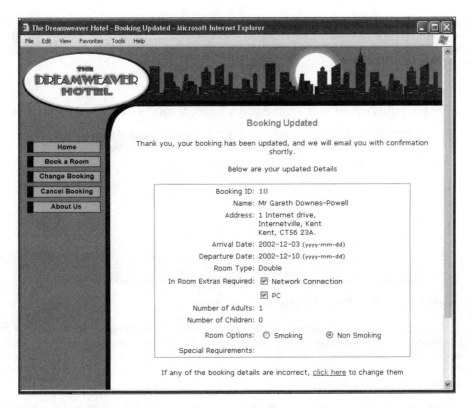

You should now be able to test this whole *Change Booking* section, and modify a booking that you previously entered.

Canceling a Booking

The last section in this chapter explains how to create the *Cancel Booking* pages, which allows a user to cancel an existing booking. To do this we use a **Delete Record** server behavior, but before we can do this we need to find out which booking to delete.

Canceling a Booking – cancel_booking.php

Open the `cancel_booking.php` page that we created at the start of the chapter. Add a form, and name it `deletebooking`. Set the form action to submit to itself, that is, `cancel_booking.php`.

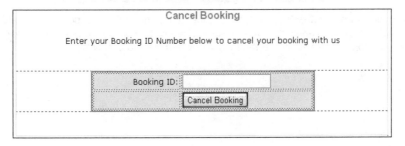

Chapter 6

Add a text field, and name it `bookingID`. Add a button to the form, and change its label to "*Cancel Booking*". The page should now look similar to the image above. Now when the form is submitted, the page will reload and the form variable `bookingID` will be set with the booking ID number the user entered.

Applying the Delete Record behavior

On the "*Server Behaviors*" tab, on the "*Applications*" panel, click the + button, and select "*Delete Record*".

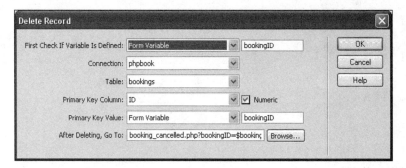

The *Delete Record* dialog box will appear as shown above.

Set "*First Check if Variable is Defined:*" as "*Form Variable*", and enter `bookingID`. Now the behavior will only delete a record if the user has entered a booking ID and submitted the form, not when the page is first loaded. Select the `bookings` table, and set the "*Primary Key Column:*" to ID, which is the field that holds the booking ID, and make sure "*Numeric*" is selected. For the "*Primary Key Value:*" select FormVariable, and again enter `bookingID`.

This means that the behavior will only delete the record where the ID field in the `bookings` table matches the booking ID entered by the user in the `bookingID` field.

Lastly set "*After Deleting, Go To:* " to `booking_canceled.php` and add the following parameter:

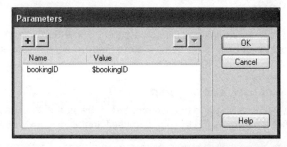

This passes the value in the `bookingID` field to the next page, as a URL parameter called `bookingID`. Click *OK*, and *OK* again to apply the Delete Record behavior. You can now save this page, and upload to your server. The page looks similar to the following when viewed in a browser:

Manipulating the Database

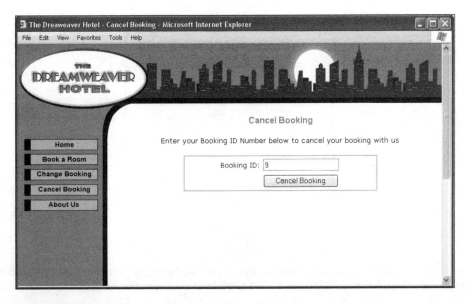

User Confirmation – booking_cancelled.php

This page is extremely simple, and simply shows a message to the user that their booking has been canceled. Create the page so it looks similar to the following:

The above is all standard text, but note we have added a placeholder for the booking ID number, which we send to the page in the URL parameter `bookingID`.

On the "*Bindings*" tab, on the "*Applications*" panel, click the + button, and select URL variable; the following dialog box appears:

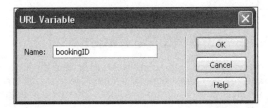

Enter `bookingID`, which is the name of the URL parameter we sent to the page, and click *OK*. The `bookingID` parameter appears in the Bindings window, and you can now insert this over your `bookingID` placeholder on the page.

161

Chapter 6

We have now finished this page, and this section. So upload the page to your browser, and test the pages we have just created. This resulting page looks similar to the screenshot below when viewed in a browser:

Editing the Template – Linking the Pages

Our final job for this chapter is to edit our template file, and update the links on the navigation menu, so that they point to our newly created pages. Open the library file that was created in the previous chapter, `NavigationBar.lbi`, which is in your Library directory. The menu appears as in the screenshot opposite:

Manipulating the Database

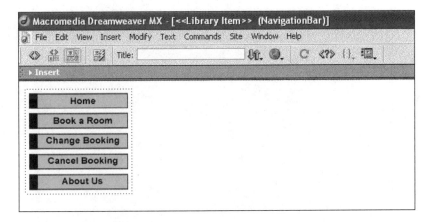

The button names, and the pages to link to are show in the table below:

Button	Page Link
Book a Room	`book_a_room.php`
Change Booking	`change_booking.php`
Cancel Booking	`cancel_booking.php`

Click on each of the buttons above, and set the link in the properties inspector to the appropriate page, as shown in the example below for the *Home* button.

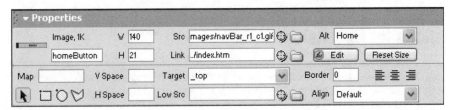

Once you have changed the link for each of the three buttons, save the file, and the following dialog box will appear:

Click "*Yes*" at the above prompt, as we want Dreamweaver MX to automatically update the links on all pages using our navigation menu.

Chapter 6

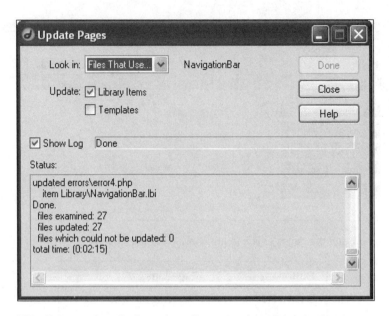

Dreamweaver MX will then automatically update all pages using our navigation menu, and the pages are shown in the dialog box as they are updated. Once the updating is complete, you can close the navigation menu library file.

You will now need to upload all the pages that have been updated to the server. The easiest way to do this is to use the Dreamweaver MX synchronize site option, which will automatically select and upload all the pages that have been updated.

Suggestions for Expansion

This has been a fairly basic example, but we have created a working system. By adding some hand coding to the pages, we could add some improvements, such as creating a login system, so the user can only change or cancel their booking if they enter a username and password.

With hand coding you also add a facility to automatically check whether the actual room is available, rather than just saving the bookings for the hotel staff to allocate, which could save both time and staff wages.

We will discuss a login system, and hand coding with Dreamweaver MX later on in the book.

Summary

In this chapter we have built a working hotel booking system, allowing users to add a booking, change an existing booking, and delete a booking.

We have used the Add Record, Update Record, and Delete Record server behaviors, to quickly and easily build database interactions into our pages, which is where Dreamweaver MX really stands out, as all the database operations can be used without any hand-coding experience.

We also used URL parameters, to pass data from page to page, so we could keep track of the user's identity, and match them to their details and booking records.

Also discussed in this chapter were recordsets, and how to use them to retrieve data from your database, in both simple and advanced modes, and creating SQL queries with dynamic parameters.

In the next chapter we will be looking at more advanced SQL usage, such as using the SQL JOIN statement to combine the results from more than one table.

7

- Advanced SQL
- Grouping
- Database Optimization

Author: Bruno Mairlot

Advanced SQL Usage

In this chapter we will look more deeply at what what makes SQL a really useful language for retrieving information.

Retrieving information is done with the `SELECT` keyword. We will analyze the syntax of `SELECT` and see how to retrieve information from multiple tables with the `JOIN` keyword. We will then look at how to order the retrieved information directly from the SQL server. Finally we will look at how to limit the result of a query.

The second part of this chapter will be dedicated to optimization. You will learn how to optimize your `SELECT` query with indexes.

Creating an Advanced Recordset

We saw in Chapter 5 the general structure of the `SELECT` statement. `SELECT` is used to retrieve rows of data selected from one or more tables. In this chapter, we will show you a lot of SQL examples. You can try them on whichever tool you prefer, but for consistency, we will show you only the SQL query and its results.

As well as retrieving data from tables, `SELECT` may also be used to retrieve rows without any reference to a table. For example:

```
SELECT 1+2;
```

will give you:

```
3
```

This example shows you one thing: even if in most of the cases where you will use the SELECT statement, you will specify at least two pieces of information – what you want to select and from where you want to select it – this is not entirely true. This example will compute the expression '1+2' and return a recordset made of one line and one row containing the value '3'.

The SELECT Statement

The Syntax of SELECT

The SELECT syntax can be summarized as follows:

```
SELECT
[DISTINCT | DISTINCTROW]
select_expression,...
[FROM table_references]
[WHERE where_definition]
[GROUP BY {unsigned_integer | col_name | formula} [ASC | DESC], ...]
[HAVING where_definition]
[ORDER BY {unsigned_integer | col_name | formula} [ASC | DESC] ,...]
[LIMIT [offset,] rows]
```

As you can see, the SELECT statement is structured in different parts that will tell the SQL server not only which rows to retrieve, but also how to show them and order them.

In the previous example, the 'select_expression' was the expression '1+2'.

As we saw on the previous example, the 'select_expression' is the only non-optional element. This is a total must and non-negotiable rule. All other parts may be omitted. But it is very unlikely that you will be in situation where you can omit the 'FROM' part, because then you can't retrieve any database information.

> Note that even though the parts of the SELECT syntax that are enclosed with [...] characters are optional, the order of these parts is mandatory. You cannot invert or reorder them; otherwise you will get a syntax error.

Using DISTINCT

The keywords DISTINCT or DISTINCTROW are shortcuts for not selecting the same row twice. It may happen that when you select some fields only once in your query, that the result contains the exact same row multiple times. Using the DISTINCT keyword will return only the rows that are different for at least one column.

Advanced SQL Usage

As an example, imagine we have the table `'exampletable'` that contains the following data:

	Var1	Var2	Var3
1	Abc	324	78
2	Dcg	65	78
3	Abc	324	78

As you can see row 1 and 3 have the exact same values. Using a `'SELECT DISTINCT …'` statement would return only rows 1 and 2.

Choosing Columns

The `SELECT` statement allows you to specify which columns you want to retrieve. You should not forget that when talking about the recordset's column we don't necessarily talk about the table's column.

In the previous example we had: `SELECT 1+2`. In this example, the `select_expression` was `'1+2'` and defined one recordset column without using a table. Suppose we have the following:

```
SELECT 1+2, 2*3;
```

The result will be:

1+2	2*3
3	6

As you see, we specified two columns.

Basically the purpose of the `select_expression` is to define the column of the recordset. It is a list of `column_expression`s separated by the "," character. We will now analyze how to build the `column_expression`.

Selecting Table Columns

To select a table column you just need to use the name of the column.

Example: We want to select the columns `ID`, `price`, `bed`, and `number` from the table `room`:

```
SELECT ID, price, bed, number FROM room
```

which will give you:

ID	price	bed	number
1	34	2	100
2	56	3	101

Note that this is pure example data.

Further in this chapter, we will see how to retrieve data from multiple tables with one query. The rule given above stays true in multiple table context except in one case: if the tables you are selecting from have a column name in common, and you are selecting one of these columns in your 'select_expression' you must precede the column name by the table's name and character.

For example, in the table 'room' and the table bookings we have the column 'ID' in common. Suppose now that we want to retrieve the room's ID and the bookings' ID. You must use the following query:

```
SELECT room.ID, bookings.ID FROM room, bookings
```

Using MySQL Functions

In the above section, we saw that the simplest form of the 'column_expression' is just the column name. In this section, we will see that 'column_expression' can be a very complex expression using many MySQL functions.

For example, suppose that the hotel stores the price of the room in pounds sterling. But, for our application, we would like to show the price of the room in a different currency. We would like to know the price of the room in Euros and Dollars. Let's say the coefficient for converting pounds in Euros is 1.61 and the coefficient to convert pounds to Dollars is 1.45. We will modify the first query as follows:

```
SELECT ID, price*1.61,price*1.45,bed, number FROM room
```

which will give you:

ID	price*1.61	price*1.45	bed	number
1	54.74	49.30	2	100
2	90.16	81.20	3	101

We could even go further. You want to make sure of the currency you're working on. And therefore, you want to add the currency symbol in your recordset. We will use the following query:

```
SELECT ID, concat(price*1.61,'•'), concat(price*1.45,'$'), bed, number FROM room
```

Advanced SQL Usage

which will give you:

ID	concat(price*1.61,'•')	concat(price*1.45,'$')	bed	number
1	54.74•	49.30$	2	100
2	90.16•	81.20$	3	101

In this example, we used the function `concat()` to concatenate a list of strings into one.

Recordset Column Aliasing

In the last example, you can see that the column names of the recordset are taken from the `select_expression`. The second column expression was `'concat(price*1.61)'` and so was the recordset column name. If your `column_expression` uses a very complex expression, the column name may grow very long. The recordset's column name can be aliased with the keyword `AS`. So we can modify the previous query to make the results look nicer:

```
SELECT ID, concat(price*1.61,'•') as priceeuro,concat(price*1.45,'$') as pricedollar,bed, number FROM room
```

which will give you:

ID	priceeuro	pricedollar	bed	number
1	54.74•	49.30$	2	100
2	90.16•	81.20$	3	101

As you can see, using the `as theprice` keyword we change the resulting column name. This is extremely important especially in our context: web application development. When you will be making reference to the different columns of your recordset it will be much easier for you if all your columns have clean and concise names.

The column name is also important when using the `HAVING` keyword, this will be covered later.

> Note : Always place the **as** keyword at the very end of the `column_expression`.

Selecting All Columns of a Table At Once

There is a shortcut in SQL that you can use to select all the columns of a table at once: the * element. The * element will return all the columns of a table. For example:

```
SELECT * FROM room
```

171

which will give you:

ID	price	bed	number
1	34	2	100
2	56	3	101

The * may seem useful at first but you cannot specify the order in which you would like the columns to appear. You also cannot specify any expression on the column, or rename the column of the recordset. The name is taken directly from the table, so be careful when using the * element.

Tables, Joining Tables, and Foreign Keys

In the previous example, we introduced the FROM keyword. When selecting the value from the table room, we used the FROM room element.

In the previous examples, we have used the FROM keyword several times. It is now time to define it thoroughly. The FROM keyword tells MySQL which table you want to take values from. The simplest usage of the FROM keyword is to define the name of the table you're working on.

In the example about the price of the room, we used the following FROM syntax:

```
SELECT ID, price, bed, number FROM room
```

The 'FROM room' tells MySQL that you want to retrieve the column ID, price, bed, and number from the table 'room'. SQL allows you to do much more powerful queries: you can use multiple tables in one query; you can also JOIN tables into virtually any new table.

Multiple Table References

In the FROM section, tables are referenced by a list of table names separated by the "," character. When using a multiple table reference, MySQL will operate what we call a scalar product of the two tables. Suppose we have the following tables:

Table 1	Table 2
Field 1	Field 2
String 1	String 2
F11 S11	F21 S21
F12 S12	F22 S22

Advanced SQL Usage

The scalar product of these two tables consists in having each row of the second table appended to each row of the first one. As an example the following query:

```
SELECT * FROM table1, table2
```

will give you:

Field1	String1	Field2	String2
F11	S11	F21	S21
F11	S11	F22	S22
F12	S12	F21	S21
F12	S12	F22	S22

As you can see the number of rows you get is the product of the number of rows of the first table and the second while the number of columns you get is the sum of the columns from each table. The values of the different columns are not multiplied or added in any way, they stay the same. Using the multiple table reference is rare and will generally not give you the result you expected, so we will focus on other forms of JOIN in this book.

Linking Tables

To explain the concept of table linking we will use the tables: room, bookings and clients. Our goal will be to have a historical list of the booking for each room.

We will know the room ID and for one specific room we will get the list of each booking, the start date, the end date, the client's name, and the price paid for this reservation. In order to achieve that goal, we will use the concept of Foreign Keys. A foreign key is a set of columns that will, for each row of a table, contain the value of the primary key of another table.

> Note: MySQL doesn't support enforced foreign keys. You will have to remember the relationship between each table and ensure yourself the correctness of your table. This is not as hard as you may think.

When looking at the table 'room' and 'bookings' you will see a special column: the room ID. In the room table it is called ID and in the table bookings it is called roomID. The following diagram shows you the table definition:

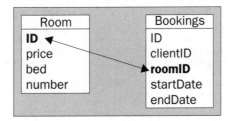

173

The diagram shows that the column `roomID` in the table `'bookings'` represents the room's `ID` to which this booking refers. In this case, we could say the column `roomID` is a foreign key to the table `'room'` because it is linked to the identifier column of the room.

In the note below we stated that MySQL doesn't enforce the foreign keys. And indeed, you have to remember that the column `roomID` in the table `'bookings'` is a foreign key to the table room. You have no way to tell MySQL explicitly about the foreign key.

The foreign key concept is what actually makes a database a relational. When using the column `'roomID'` to link to the room's ID, you are creating a relation that links these two tables and you set the meaning of the column `roomID`.

For example, if we have a booking that starts the 22nd of March 2002 and ends the 24th of March 2002 for client 1 and this client had room 2, then we will have the following row in the `bookings` table:

ID	clientID	roomID	startDate	endDate
.	.	.	.	.
23	1	2	2002-3-22	2002-3-24
.	.	.	.	.

Now suppose we want to know the list of booking for each room, we will use the following statement:

```
SELECT room.ID, bookings.ID, clientID, roomID, startDate, endDate FROM room
LEFT JOIN bookings ON room.ID = roomID
```

We will review the syntax of the `LEFT JOIN` statement later on, but here we are implementing the concept of the `roomID` foreign key in this specific statement, thanks to the `'LEFT JOIN bookings ON room.ID = roomID'` part of the query. This query will give you:

ID	ID	clientID	roomID	startDate	endDate
.	.	.	.	.	.
2	23	1	2	2002-3-22	2002-3-24
.	.	.	.	.	.

There we have something extremely interesting, even if it doesn't appear so! We have a recordset that gives us not just the room information or the bookings information, but both in one recordset.

If we wanted to have a journal of bookings for each room, then we have it. But our goal was to also have the client information. The following diagram shows another part of the relationship of our table:

Advanced SQL Usage

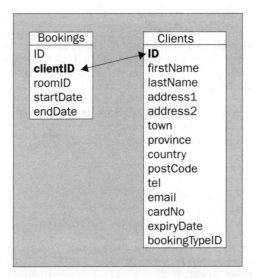

As you have probably already guessed, we have another foreign key: the `clientID` column. To get information from the table client, we will do as we did for the first query: we will use the `LEFT JOIN` keyword on the `clients` table. The new SQL query will look like this:

```
SELECT room.ID, bookings.ID, clientID, roomID, startDate, endDate, clients.firstname,
clients.lastname FROM room LEFT JOIN bookings ON room.ID = roomID LEFT JOIN
clients ON bookings.clientID=clients.ID
```

Note that this query will return the rooms that have not been booked already. This is due to the nature of the `LEFT JOIN`. Further we will see how to retrieve only rooms that have been booked at least once, with the `INNER JOIN` syntax.

In this query, we have modified two parts of the query: the `select_expression` now has the `clients.firstname` and `clients.lastname`. We have also added a new `LEFT JOIN ... ON ...` sequence. This time we are joining the table `clients` and we link the `client.ID` to the `clientID` that can be found in the bookings table. It works exactly the same way as when we linked the `bookings` table to the `room` table.

We have linked the table `bookings` to the table `room` because the meaning of the column `booking.roomID` was the room's `ID`. Therefore we do exactly the same by linking the table `bookings` to the table `clients`, because the columun `booking.clientID` was the client's `ID`.

To summarize, the `LEFT JOIN tablename ON clause` will link two tables by checking that the condition `clause` is `TRUE`. In our example,e we had the two clauses following `LEFT JOIN`:

- `LEFT JOIN bookings ON room.ID = roomID`
- `LEFT JOIN clients ON bookings.clientID = client.ID`

The interesting thing in the `LEFT JOIN` is that it allows you to construct queries with multiple tables thanks to the relationship you defined when constructing your table.

175

Joining Tables and Foreign Keys

In the previous section we introduced the concept of joining tables. In the short term, joining can be thought of as a way to retrieve information from multiple tables at once. Joining tables is the most powerful concept in SQL. You've often heard about Relational databases or relational database management system (RDBMS). The relational part comes from this very concept.

Here we will review the `JOIN` syntaxes. In the previous series of examples, we used the `LEFT JOIN` syntax to join the `room` table with the `bookings` and `clients` table. We have also reviewed multiple table references, which are also a kind of joining.

Here are the other kinds, and their syntax:

```
table_reference, table_reference
table_reference [CROSS] JOIN table_reference
table_reference INNER JOIN table_reference join_condition
table_reference STRAIGHT_JOIN table_reference
table_reference LEFT [OUTER] JOIN table_reference join_condition
table_reference LEFT [OUTER] JOIN table_reference
table_reference NATURAL [LEFT [OUTER]] JOIN table_reference
table_reference RIGHT [OUTER] JOIN table_reference join_condition
table_reference RIGHT [OUTER] JOIN table_reference
table_reference NATURAL [RIGHT [OUTER]] JOIN table_reference
```

Note that the elements enclosed with [...] are optional.

In this group of different `JOIN` syntax, the `table_reference` expression means the expression that you will construct to refer to the table you want to join. The expression `table_reference` is defined as:

```
table_name [[AS] alias] [USE INDEX (key_list)] [IGNORE INDEX (key_list)]
```

And the expression `join_condition` is defined as:

```
ON conditional_expr
OR USING (column_list)
```

We already have presented the multiple table reference as well as the `LEFT JOIN` syntax. The `LEFT JOIN` syntax is the most frequently used flavor of `JOIN`. Note that the `OUTER` keyword and the `RIGHT` keyword are syntactic keywords.

Simple Joining of Tables

At the beginning of this section we introduced the multiple table reference. The `CROSS JOIN` and the `JOIN` keywords do exactly the same type of joining. For example, the statement:

```
SELECT * FROM room, bookings
```

could be rewritten as:

```
SELECT * FROM room JOIN bookings
```

Advanced SQL Usage

INNER JOIN

The `INNER JOIN` is used when you want the conditional clause to be always `TRUE`. That may sound strange. In the previous example, we used the `LEFT JOIN` because we wanted to have a listing of **all** rooms. We therefore used the `LEFT JOIN`.

Suppose that we now want to see only the rooms that have been reserved at least once. Being reserved at least once means that we have an entry in the table bookings. By using the `INNER JOIN` we ensure not only that the `room.ID` and `bookings.roomID` are equal, but that we take only the rows of the table `bookings` for which the column `roomID` exists in the table `room` and for the column ID.

You should never have any conditions in the `ON` part that are used to restrict which rows you have in the result set. If you want to restrict which rows should be in the result, you have to do this in the `WHERE` clause.

NATURAL JOIN

The `NATURAL JOIN` or the `NATURAL LEFT JOIN` is equivalent to an `INNER JOIN` or `LEFT JOIN` where the `ON` clause would list all the existing columns in both tables. That mainly serves as a shortcut. For example, suppose we have two tables: A and B. Table A has the column C1 and C2, and table B has the column C1 and C2 also. A following `NATURAL JOIN` statement:

```
SELECT * FROM A NATURAL JOIN B
```

could be rewritten in:

```
SELECT * FROM A INNER JOIN B ON A.C1=B.C1 AND A.C2=B.C2
```

USING

There is another shortcut that is very useful: the `USING` element. The following example:

```
SELECT * FROM A LEFT JOIN B USING (C1, C2)
```

is semantically equivalent to:

```
SELECT * FROM A LEFT JOIN B ON A.C1 = B.C1 AND A.C2 = B.C2
```

To be able to use the `USING` shortcut, the column name must be the same. So if you plan to use it, you should name the column you want to have in the `USING` clause with identical names in both tables.

For example, we cannot use the `USING` keyword with the Hotel database the way it has been designed. If we wanted to do so, we should rename the column ID in the table room to be 'roomID'. Then we would have two columns named roomID: one in the room table, the other in the table bookings. Then, we would use a `LEFT JOIN` with a `USING` clause like this one:

```
SELECT * FROM room LEFT JOIN bookings USING (roomID)
```

And that would give us the equivalent statement:

```
SELECT * FROM room LEFT JOIN bookings ON room.roomID=bookings.roomID
```

Table Aliasing

Tables may be aliased for easier use. By using table aliasing you can also join the same table multiple times. The following example shows you how to do that:

```
SELECT * FROM room JOIN bookings JOIN room as room2
```

Filtering Rows

The WHERE part of a SELECT statement is used when you want to filter the recordset. The core of a search engine resides in the WHERE part of a query. It is important to note that the WHERE clause works with table columns only. If you did make some computation on the table columns and aliased them to be able to filter the recordset according to the new value, you must use the HAVING clause. The where_expression is built as a logical expression that will return either TRUE of FALSE.

The Values of TRUE and FALSE

Anything different from 0 is always TRUE. The only possible value for FALSE is 0

Building Logical Expressions

Here is a short example of a logical expression:

```
SELECT * FROM room WHERE ID > 1 AND startDate='2002-31-12'
```

The logical expression is: `ID > 1 AND startDate='2002-31-12'`

To build your logical expression you will use operators. There are four types of operators:

- The parenthesis
- The comparison operators
- The logical operators
- The flow control operators

Some of these operators will return the NULL value. This value cannot be compared to TRUE or FALSE, because it has its own meaning. If you want to know if a value is NULL or not, use the IS NULL operator or IS NOT NULL.

Parenthesis

Use the (...) to force the order of evaluation of the subexpression contained in the parenthesis, for example:

```
SELECT * FROM ROOM WHERE (3 * 2) -2
```

will give you all the rows in the table room because (3*2) - 2 evaluates to 4, therefore TRUE, while this one:

```
SELECT * FROM ROOM WHERE 3 * (2-2)
```

will return no results because 3*(2-2) evaluates to 0.

Advanced SQL Usage

Comparison Operators:

The comparison operators always return the value 0 (FALSE) or 1 (TRUE) or eventually NULL. We will talk about the NULL value in the *flow control operators* section. These functions work both for strings and numbers. Strings are automatically converted to numbers and numbers to strings as needed.

The following table shows you the list of comparison operators and their meanings as well as an example when the returned value is TRUE or FALSE. Note that the word 'expr' is an abbreviation of 'expression'.

Operator	Meaning	TRUE example	FALSE example
=	Equality Checks if both arguments are equal	'1' = 1 'ab' = 'ab'	1 = 2 'a' = 'ab'
!= <>	Different Returns TRUE if the arguments are different	'1' != 0	1 <>0
<=	Less or equal than	1 <= 2	3 <= 1
>=	Greater or equal than	2 >= 1	1 >= 3
<	Strictly less than	1 < 2	2 < 1
>	Strictly greater than	2 > 1	1 > 2
IS NULL	Returns TRUE if the value is the NULL value.	NULL IS NULL *Note that this is only case where this operator is TRUE.*	1 IS NULL
IS NOT NULL	Returns TRUE if the value is not NULL	1 IS NOT NULL	NULL IS NOT NULL. *Note that this is only case where this operator is FALSE.*
expr BETWEEN min AND max	Checks if the expr value is situated between min and max values.	2 BETWEEN 1 AND 3	4 BETWEEN 1 AND 3
expr IN (value, ...)	Checks if the expr is contained in the value list. This operator is extremely useful when used with SET and ENUM column type.	1 IN (1,2,4)	3 IN (1,2,4)

Table continued on following page

Operator	Meaning	TRUE example	FALSE example
`expr NOT IN (value, ...)`	Checks if the expression is not in the value list.	3 IN (1,2,4)	1 IN (1,2,4)
`ISNULL(expr)`	Checks if the `expr` is NULL	ISNULL(1/0)	ISNULL(0/1)
`COALESCE(list)`	Returns the first non-null item in the list.	This operator will not return a TRUE of FALSE value. Instead it will return either NULL if there is no non-NULL value or the first value of the list that is non-NULL.	
`INTERVAL(X,n1, n2, n3, ...)`	Returns 0 if X<n1, 1 if X<n2 and so on.	This operator will not return TRUE or FALSE but instead the numerical position of the first i where X<ni. Note that n1<n2<n3...is required for this function to work correctly.	

Logical Operators

There are three logical operators. They return either TRUE or FALSE or eventually NULL. For logical operators the NULL value is in most cases the same as a FALSE value.

Operator	Meaning	TRUE example	FALSE example
`! expr` `NOT expr`	This operator negates the logical value of `expr`.	! 0	! 1
`AND` `&&`	Returns TRUE only if both arguments are TRUE.	1 AND 2	0 AND 2
`OR` `||`	Returns TRUE if at least one of the two arguments is TRUE.	1 OR 0	0 OR 0

At the beginning of the filtering section, we introduced a simple query to show you a logical expression:

```
SELECT * FROM room WHERE ID > 1 AND startDate='2002-31-12'
```

There we see the AND operator, which is used to tell MySQL that we want both of the conditions: ID > 1 and startDate='2002-31-12' to be TRUE. If we want only one of these conditions, we would write the query like this:

```
SELECT * FROM room WHERE ID > 1 OR startDate='2002-31-12'
```

Advanced SQL Usage

Flow Control Operators

The flow control operators are extremely helpful when you want to build a powerful query. They act as mini branching control in your query.

- The `IFNULL(expr1, expr2)` operator returns `expr1` if `expr1` is not `NULL` otherwise it will return `expr2`.

- The `NULLIF(expr1, expr2)` operator returns `NULL` if `expr1` = `expr2`, else returns `expr1`.

- The `IF(expr1, expr2, expr3)` is the most powerful of the flow control operators. It allows you to build some tests quickly into your query. If `expr1` is `TRUE`, it will return `expr2` else it will return the `expr3`.

We have seen that the `LEFT JOIN` returns the values of the first table and each row of the second table for which the `ON` clause is `TRUE`. However, it may happen that the first table has no counterpart value in the second table. That would be the case if a room has never been booked. There wouldn't be any bookings row that would have the column `roomID` pointing at that room.

In this case a `NULL` value is used for each column value of the second table. Suppose we want to return the value 'never booked' when there is no booking value for that room, we would use the following query:

```
SELECT room.ID, IF(bookings.roomID IS NULL, ' never booked','at least once') as
booked FROM room LEFT JOIN bookings ON room.ID=bookings.roomID
```

Note that in the `IF` operator, `expr1` is evaluated as an integer value, which means that if you are testing floating-point or string values, you should do so using a comparison operation:

```
IF(0.1,1,0)
```

which will return 0 because in the `IF` context, `0.1` will be converted into an integer and then the `expr1` will be `FALSE`. When testing floating point, use:

```
IF(0.1<>0,1,0)
```

which will return 1.

Using LIKE

The `expr1 LIKE expr2` operator compares `expr1` and `expr2` and returns `TRUE` if `expr1` is like `expr2` and `FALSE` otherwise. The 'like' word means that you can use special characters in `'expr2'` to tell `MySQL` about the level of likeliness of your comparison. These characters are the following:

- %: means any string of characters of any size.

- _ (underscore): means any character, but only one.

Chapter 7

The following table will show examples of the LIKE operator and the results:

Statement	Value
SELECT 'a' LIKE 'b'	FALSE. Because there is no character % or _, and 'a' is not equal to 'b'.
SELECT 'a' LIKE '_'	TRUE. The expression '_' will match any string made of only one character.
SELECT 'a' LIKE '%'	TRUE. Note that the expression '%' will always return TRUE.
SELECT 'myroom' LIKE '%room'	TRUE. The expression '%room' matches all strings that with by the sequence 'room'.
SELECT 'myroom' LIKE 'my%'	TRUE. This is the contrary of the previous example, it matches every sequence beginning with 'my'.
SELECT 'myroom' LIKE '%theroom%'	FALSE. The sequence 'theroom' cannot be found in the value 'myroom'.

The LIKE operator is extremely useful to make a quick search of specific keywords in your database, and is therefore used often in web site design. If you are comparing case-sensitive strings with any of the standard operators (=, <>..., but not LIKE) end space will be ignored.

Grouping

The GROUP BY keyword allows you to regroup the rows of a recordset according to the recordset column names into one single row.

This means that for example, if you have a recordset that has 50 rows, but one column of this recordset can take only four different values, grouping your recordset on that column will return a new recordset containing only four rows.

The grouping is done on the recordset column name and not necessarily on the table column name. If you selected some complex expression from multiple table fields and if this expression is aliased with the AS keyword, you can group the rows by using the aliased column name.

How Grouping Works

We will illustrate the concept of grouping with the following exercise: We want to know for each table how many reservations have been registered. To do that, we will have to use the JOIN of two tables: room to get a list of each row and bookings to know about the bookings that are present in the database.

First of all, we will use an example of data contained in these two tables:

```
SELECT * FROM room
```

has:

ID	price	bed	Number
1	34	2	101
2	56	3	102

while the table bookings:

```
SELECT * FROM bookings
```

has:

ID	roomID	clientID	startDate	endDate
23	2	1	2002-3-22	2002-3-24
24	2	2	2002-3-27	2002-4-1

As you can see, in the table bookings the column `roomID` has two occurrences of the value 2. The ID of the first room is not present, which means it has never been booked. Therefore, we know the results we would like to have: room 2 has had 2 bookings while room 1 has 0 reservations.

Now we will build the query to get all this information at once:

```
SELECT room.ID as roomID,price,bed,number,bookings.ID as bookingID FROM room LEFT JOIN bookings ON room.ID=roomID
```

which will return the following:

roomID	Price	Bed	Number	bookingID
1	34	2	100	NULL
2	56	3	101	23
2	56	3	101	24

We are almost done. The important point is the recordset column `roomID`. The recordset contains the following values for this column: 1, 2, and 2. We will insert a GROUP BY sequence to group the rows of the whole recordset that have the same value for the column `roomID`. And finally we are going to introduce the `count()` function. The SQL query becomes:

```
SELECT room.ID as roomID,price, bed,number,bookings.ID as bookingID, count(roomID)
as bookCount FROM room LEFT JOIN bookings ON room.ID=roomID GROUP BY room.ID
```

This will give us the expected results:

roomID	price	bed	number	bookingID	bookCount
1	34	2	100	NULL	0
2	56	3	101	23	2

As you can see, the recordset column `bookCount` contains the number of bookings for each room. But the power of this query is that it not only requires one SQL statement, but that it also contains each piece of information about the room. So, you don't have to perform multiple queries in order to know about the room and the number of reservations.

> Note: The choice of the column on which you will group items is extremely important. We have seen that the `LEFT JOIN` allows you to retrieve results even if there is nothing in the left table. When this is the case, the column of the second table will have the value `NULL`. But if you group on a column that may have the `NULL` value, you have good chances that the result will be wrong or unexpected.

Implicit Grouping

MySQL optimizes the use of the `GROUP BY` by doing an implicit grouping if you use some grouping function in your query. If you use a group function in a statement containing no `GROUP BY` clause, it is equivalent to grouping on all rows. For example:

```
SELECT count(*) FROM room INNER JOIN bookings ON roomID=room.ID
```

will give you the number of rooms that have at least one booking. In this case, the number is 2. See the section about the `group by` function to see other examples of implicit grouping.

GROUP BY Syntax

The following syntax shows you the syntax for the `GROUP BY` structure:

```
GROUP BY {unsigned_integer | col_name | formula} [ASC | DESC], ...
```

This syntax above shows you that the `GROUP BY` expression can be made of a list of grouping elements. It means that you can group the column successively with different column names. For example, the following query:

```
SELECT * FROM room GROUP BY number, price
```

will group your recordset first by the number of the room, and then with the price column.

The `unsigned_integer` expression is the column number of your recordset section starting from 1. The `col_name` expression represents one of the recordset column names. If your recordset column is made of a complex subexpression you must alias it with the `AS` keyword and use that alias as the column name. The `formula` expression means a formula computed from anything that is valid SQL.

Advanced SQL Usage

For example, you could use the following:

```
SELECT * FROM room INNER JOIN bookings ON roomID=room.ID GROUP BY room.ID/2
```

Be careful that if your formula is an unsigned integer it will be used like a column number. If you really want to group rows by an integer, then use a formula: 0+19 for example.

This example will show you the difference between the types of grouping. Note that we supposed that the data in the table `bookings` are the same as for the previous example:

```
SELECT * FROM bookings GROUP BY 2
```

which will give you:

ID	roomID	clientID	startDate	endDate
23	2	1	2002-3-22	2002-3-24

Because the groupment has been made on an unsigned integer, which means the second column of your recordset. As the table bookings has the value '2' for the `roomID` in all the rows, the result is only one row.

```
SELECT * FROM bookings GROUP by clientID
```

which will give you:

ID	roomID	clientID	startDate	endDate
23	2	1	2002-3-22	2002-3-24
24	2	2	2002-3-27	2002-4-1

Because the column `clientID` has two different values, the grouping doesn't do anything, and you get the whole content of your table `room`. Now the following query:

```
SELECT * FROM bookings GROUP BY 0+1
```

which will give you:

ID	roomID	clientID	startDate	endDate
23	2	1	2002-3-22	2002-3-24

because the group by expression, '0+1', is a formula and always evaluates to the same value: 1, therefore, all the rows of your recordset are grouped together.

Functions To Use in GROUP BY

In the previous part we introduced the function count(). We will now review a number of functions that imply the use of a GROUP BY clause.

185

count(expr)

The `count(expr)` returns a count of the number of non-NULL values in the rows retrieved by a SELECT statement. Note that it doesn't return the sum of the values, just the number of rows. In the example about the reservation of a table, we introduced the function `count()`.

```
SELECT room.ID as roomID,price, bed,number,bookings.ID as bookingID, count(roomID)
    as bookCount FROM room LEFT JOIN bookings ON room.ID=roomID GROUP BY room.ID
```

As you can see on this statement, the `count(roomID)` will return the number of rows that have the same `roomID`, thanks to the grouping made on `room.ID`.

The expression COUNT(*) is somewhat different in that it returns a count of the number of rows retrieved, whether or not they contain NULL values. COUNT(*) is optimized to return very quickly if the SELECT retrieves from one table, no other columns are retrieved, and there is no WHERE clause. For example:

```
select COUNT(*) from room
```

will return the number of rows contained in the table room.

count(DISTINCT ...)

The `count(DISTINCT expr1, ...)` function returns a count of the number of **different** non-NULL values.

avg(expr)

The `avg(expr)` returns the average value of the grouped column value. For example, if we want to know the average price of the room, we will use the following query:

```
SELECT avg(price) FROM room
```

which will give you the average price of the rooms. You may notice that we computed the average value on the column price, but did not specify any groupment clause. This is an example of the implicit grouping that we saw above. The implicit grouping will group all the rows into one single row. Therefore, the average will be computed on all rows, which is exactly what we want.

min(expr) and max(expr)

The `min(expr)` and `max(expr)` returns the minimum and the maximum value of the grouped value. For example, if we want to know the lowest priced room as well as the highest priced room, we will do as follows:

```
SELECT min(price),max(price) FROM room
```

which will give you the following result:

min(price)	max(price)
34	56

Advanced SQL Usage

sum(expr)

The `sum(expr)` function is used to compute the sum of all grouped values. This could let us know, for example, the amount of money the hotel could make, if all the rooms are booked.

```
SELECT sum(price) FROM room
```

Will give you 90 as the result.

Filtering Using HAVING

With the `WHERE` clause, we have already had a chance to look at how to filter a recordset, but the `WHERE` clause can only work on the table column level. If you use a complex expression as a recordset column, you won't be able to use a `WHERE` clause on that column.

SQL provides a second mechanism to address this issue: the `HAVING` clause. `HAVING` works almost the same way as the `WHERE` clause, except that it works on the recordset column while `WHERE` works at the table columns level. To illustrate the `HAVING` clause, try to execute the following query:

```
SELECT year(startDate) as startyear ,year(endDate) as endyear FROM bookings WHERE
startyear=2002
```

Executing this query will result in a syntax error telling you that the column `'startyear'` is unknown in the `WHERE` clause. Now try to execute this query:

```
SELECT year(startDate) as startyear ,year(endDate) as endyear FROM bookings HAVING
startyear=2002
```

This will return the correct recordset. The `HAVING` expression is built with the exact same syntax as the `WHERE` clause. You can use the entire `WHERE` operators and functions.

Sorting the Recordset

The `ORDER BY` clause is used for ordering the rows retrieved in a specific order. The syntax for the `ORDER BY` is as follows:

```
[ORDER BY {unsigned_integer | col_name | formula} [ASC | DESC] ,...]
```

The `unsigned_integer` expression is, like in the `GROUP BY`, relative to the recordset column and starts from 1. The following example shows you how to order a recordset by the second column:

```
SELECT * FROM room ORDER by 2 DESC
```

which will give you:

ID	price	bed	Number
2	56	3	102
1	34	2	101

Note that the DESC keyword has been used to reverse the order of the sort. The ASC keyword is used to order the recordset in normal order. It is optional and you can omit it. The col_name expression represents the name of one of the recordset columns. We could have written the previous example as:

```
SELECT * FROM room ORDER by price DESC
```

If you want to order by the number of beds, use the following query:

```
SELECT * FROM room ORDER by bed
```

The formula expression represents a formula computed from anything that is valid SQL. For example, you could use the following:

```
SELECT * FROM room ORDER BY rand()
```

This example will return a recordset ordered by random values. Another example: In the GROUP BY part we have learned how to group the room to retrieve the bookings. The following query will show you how to order the result by the room number.

```
SELECT room.ID as roomID,price, bed,number,bookings.ID as bookingID, count(roomID)
as count FROM room LEFT JOIN bookings ON room.ID=roomID GROUP BY room.ID ORDER BY
room.number
```

which will give you:

roomID	price	bed	number	bookingID	count
1	34	2	100	NULL	0
2	56	3	101	23	2

Limiting the Number of Rows

Sometimes the number of rows you will get from a SELECT statement will be huge and you will want to limit the amount of rows. Other times you will just be interested in the first 10 rows. You may even want to implement recordset navigation by selecting small portions of a larger recordset. To do this, we will use the LIMIT clause. The syntax of the LIMIT clause is shown below:

```
[LIMIT [offset,] rows]
```

The offset is the first row that you want to limit, and the rows element is the number of rows you want to limit. To illustrate the LIMIT concept, we will use a table with the following content:

Advanced SQL Usage

Table: example

ID	Value
1	10
2	3
3	5
4	78
5	82
6	9

The following queries will show you the result of the `LIMIT` clause:

```
SELECT * FROM EXAMPLE LIMIT 2
```

which will give you:

ID	Value
1	10
2	3

```
SELECT * FROM EXAMPLE LIMIT 2,3
```

which will give you:

ID	Value
3	5
4	78
5	82

A Lottery Example

An interesting application of the `LIMIT` clause is when you want to pick a random row. Suppose that in our hotel, each month a room is picked randomly and its current occupant is given a free day.

To select the room, we will use the following query:

```
SELECT * from room ORDER BY rand() limit 1
```

This query will select all rows from the table `room`, sort them in a random order, then will just output the first row.

Modifying the Structure of Existing Tables

Very often you will need to change your application. The database for our hotel application is rather simple. If we want to turn it into a real application we might want to add a description of a room. You may also like to remove a field from a table because you no longer need it. The modification of an existing table is done using the ALTER TABLE command.

While ALTER TABLE is executing, the original table is readable by other clients. Updates and writes to the table are stalled until the new table is ready.

The ALTER TABLE Syntax

The following table will show you the complete syntax of the ALTER TABLE SQL command. The indexes part will be reviewed in the following section.

```
ALTER [IGNORE] TABLE tbl_name alter_spec [, alter_spec ...]

alter_specification:
        ADD [COLUMN] create_definition [FIRST | AFTER column_name ]
  or    ADD [COLUMN] (create_definition, create_definition,...)
  or    ADD INDEX [index_name] (index_col_name,...)
  or    ADD PRIMARY KEY (index_col_name,...)
  or    ADD UNIQUE [index_name] (index_col_name,...)
  or    ADD FULLTEXT [index_name] (index_col_name,...)
  or    ADD [CONSTRAINT symbol] FOREIGN KEY index_name (index_col_name,...)
            [reference_definition]
  or    ALTER [COLUMN] col_name {SET DEFAULT literal | DROP DEFAULT}
  or    CHANGE [COLUMN] old_col_name create_definition
  or    MODIFY [COLUMN] create_definition
  or    DROP [COLUMN] col_name
  or    DROP PRIMARY KEY
  or    DROP INDEX index_name
  or    RENAME [TO] new_tbl_name
  or    ORDER BY col
  or    table_options
```

IGNORE

The IGNORE expression controls how the ALTER works if there are duplicates on unique keys in the new table. If IGNORE isn't specified, the copy is aborted and rolled back. If IGNORE is specified, then for rows with duplicates on a unique key, only the first row is used; the others are deleted.

ADD

The ADD column expression allows you to create a new column on the existing table. It allows you to specify the position of the new column in the table. The keyword COLUMN is optional, as is the position clause. If not specified MySQL will create the new column at the end of the table.

Example: We want to add the column 'description' for the table room. We want the new column to be placed after the column 'bed'. Here is the SQL command:

```
ALTER TABLE room ADD description varchar(255) AFTER bed
```

Advanced SQL Usage

create_definition

In the ADD column expression we have the create_definition expression. This is supposed to be replaced with a column definition. The syntax used is the same as when you create a new table. Refer to Chapter 2 for the syntax of table creation.

ALTER

The ALTER column expression is used only when you want to change the default value for a column. When we added the field 'description' we did not mention any default value. For example, in our web application we would like to have at least the value 'no description yet' instead of a blank empty value. To change the default value of the column 'description' the following SQL command is used:

```
ALTER TABLE room ALTER description SET DEFAULT "no description yet"
```

CHANGE

The CHANGE expression will allow you to modify the definition of a field without losing all the table's values for this field. We have defined the description field as a varchar of 255 bytes in size. This may look a bit short if you want to have a big description. We will now change it into a text type:

```
ALTER TABLE room CHANGE description description text
```

Note: When changing the definition of a field, you must specify first the current name of the field, then its new name, even if you don't change the name.

If we wanted to change the name of the field 'description' into 'roomdescription', we would use the following SQL command:

```
ALTER TABLE room CHANGE description roomdescription text
```

DROP

The DROP column expression allows you to remove a column from your table. If we want to remove the column 'description' from the table room we will use:

```
ALTER TABLE room DROP description
```

RENAME

The RENAME expression allows you rename an existing table. To rename the table 'room' into 'newroom', use the following SQL command:

```
ALTER TABLE room RENAME TO newroom
```

Optimization

When you want to look up an old friend's telephone number in a telephone directory, how do you do it? Would you go to the first page and start reading all names until you find your friend's name? That would take a very long time and you would get hungry quickly before even reaching the letter 'B'.

Instead you take the index part of the directory, look up your friend's name first letter, read the starting page and go there. Next you will look up the second letter and so on. It takes less than a minute to find a person in a book that may contains thousands of names.

In this example we have introduced the concept of optimization. Just think about it: instead of hours, if not days, you took a minute to find the information you were looking for.

Now apply this concept to a query where you would look up one row of information between thousands. Using the index would speed up the search tremendously. The second part of this chapter is about optimization. We will look at how to optimize your database to get the best performance out of it.

Indexes

In this section we will briefly cover what an index is, and how it can help you, before moving on to adding indexes to existing tables.

What Is an Index?

An index is a collection of data that is hidden from the user, and is organized in a way that allows a search to be executed extremely quickly. This data is actually a part of the real data it works with. When you define an index, you specifically define it to work on one table. An index cannot be spanned across multiple tables, and furthermore across multiple databases.

You will not be able to query against an index. All you can know about indexes is that they exist, the size in bytes they represent and how they are organized. The data is organized to allow quick searching; MySQL references the index when you execute a query on the relevant table.

Consider the directory example. You found your friend's name in less than a minute. How did you do that? You implicitly used the fact that the names are sorted in an alphabetical order. It is easy to know that the name "Doe" is placed way before the name "Smith". So if you are at the page containing the name "Gill" and you search the name "Doe" you know you must look at the earlier pages.

But the data in the table is not automatically organized in alphabetical order. It is stored in the exact same order that you inserted it. In the case of the directory, it is obvious that it will be sorted by name, but how would MySQL know which row it should use? Suppose that you have to look up a telephone number now, and not a name.

To address this issue, the database designers introduced the index concept. In our directory example, an index could be a list of letters with the page the names start at. You can have many indexes on a table. We could define a second index that would know the telephone number and the associated page.

MySQL Indexes

MySQL supports four types of index:

- Primary key
- Unique index
- Multiple index (also called a classic index, or just index)
- The Full-Text index.

All these indexes make use of the techniques described above.

Advanced SQL Usage

Primary Keys

The primary key is a core concept in SQL. We have already encountered some use of a primary key. The table `room` of our hotel reservation application has a primary key made of the field 'ID'. To illustrate the concept of a primary key, we will compare it to a simplified postal address system.

In your house's street, if you want to identify your house, you will, in most cases, use the number of your house. The house that has the number 1 is obviously different from the house that has number 10. But there is certainly not only one house in your city that has the number 1.

So what do we do if we want to identify a house in a city? We would use the street and the house's number. A street name and a number are sufficient to find a house in a city, but what if we are speaking about the whole country? We need to specify the city also.

This way, we can identify a house anywhere in the country. If we want to find a house anywhere in the world, all we have to do is to add the country on the address, and we are done.

What have we done in this example? We started by defining the house number, and then we noticed that it is just enough for one street. Then we added the street, then the city and finally the country. By doing this, we have ensured a group of data that identify one and only one house in the world.

We could therefore say that we have a primary key for identifying a house. A more rigorous definition of a primary key is:

> A primary key is a set of fields in a table that identifies in a unique manner each and every row of a table.

How to choose the fields of the primary key? It is not that difficult to get the fields that will fulfill the requirements of the primary key definition. Either you precisely know them, or you can create a new unique numeric field.

auto_increment

In the table `room`, how did we choose the primary key? Well, no fields could exactly represent a room in a unique manner. Therefore we add a field named 'ID'. The field ID is numeric and has the extra features `auto_increment`. The `auto_increment` attribute is a specific feature made specifically for the primary key. That way, we don't need to make sure the 'ID' value of a row is unique, MySQL will find the unique value for you.

You may then ask: why not always use a 'ID' field for each table we create in MySQL? First, because it is not always required: Sometimes you will build a very short table where the primary key will not be a numeric type. My suggestion is to use it whenever you don't know what to use as the primary key. This happens in 99% of the tables you will create.

The Unique Index

With an UNIQUE index, you ensure that there are no two rows in the table that have the same value. If you create a unique index on the field 'number' of the table `room`, you are sure that there won't be two rooms that will have the same number in your table.

MySQL itself enforces these constraints. MySQL won't let you insert the same value twice in a column that has been indexed as unique.

> Note that if you do not specify a primary key, but have a unique index, MySQL will silently convert it into a primary key.

The Multiple Index

The multiple index is the most common type of index. It provides the basic functionality of an index. It doesn't have any specific features. In MySQL you will see it called `'index'`. You may refer to a normal index with the keyword `index`. See the section about creating an index to see examples of the normal index.

The Full-Text Index

The full-text index type is a special index type. It provides the functionality for searching through long text values (and thus will only index `VARCHAR` and `TEXT` columns). The lookup on a full-text index has been designed to search on human language. More information on full-text searching can be found at *http://www.mysql.com/doc/*

Handling Indexes On Existing Tables

To create an index, you will use the `ALTER TABLE` SQL command. We will review here the part of the `ALTER table` syntax that allows you to create, change, and delete indexes on a table. Normally you would create indexes at the table creation time, but it may happen that you want to add an index on an existing table. The following table shows you the syntax of the `ALTER TABLE` for the `INDEX` part:

```
ALTER TABLE table_name alter_spec [, alter_spec ...]
```

The `alter_spec` explains to MySQL how you want to alter the table. Here is the syntax for the `alter_spec` expression:

```
ADD INDEX [index_name] (index_col_name,...)
OR ADD PRIMARY KEY (index_col_name,...)
OR ADD UNIQUE [index_name] (index_col_name,...)
OR ADD FULLTEXT [index_name] (index_col_name,...)
OR DROP PRIMARY KEY
OR DROP INDEX index_name
```

Creating an Index

To create a new index on an existing table, you will use the `ADD index_type index_name (index_col_name,...)` command. For example, if we want to index the column `'number'` of the table `room` we would do the following:

```
ALTER TABLE room ADD INDEX (number)
```

This SQL command will create an `INDEX` named number containing the field `'number'`. It is called automatically by MySQL according to the first column in the column list and the first available index name for this column. So if the table `room` already has an index named `'number'` the second one will be called `'number_2'`

Advanced SQL Usage

The name of indexes exists only to reference them when using the `JOIN` keyword, where you can specify that you specifically want to use an index. This index is a normal index type. If we wanted to create a unique index the SQL query would have been:

```
ALTER TABLE room ADD UNIQUE (number)
```

And in the case of a full-text index type:

```
ALTER TABLE room ADD FULLTEXT (number)
```

Altering an Index

In MySQL, it is not possible to alter an index. If you want to change something on an existing index, you first have to delete this index and creating a new one with the new structure. If you don't care about the index name, you can create the new index first and then delete the old one.

Deleting an Index

To delete an index, the `alter_expression` will be `'DROP INDEX index_name'`. If you want to delete the previously created index on the `number` column of the table `room`, you will use the following SQL command:

```
ALTER TABLE room DROP INDEX number
```

A Note On Indexes

Indexes are very powerful, but they have their drawbacks. They are very efficient when doing a `SELECT` on an indexed table. But they need to be accurate. That means that each time you insert a new row into your database the index must be updated. If you have many indexes or if your table contains a lot of records it can slow down the insert time.

You should not create an index on each field of a table. Instead, my suggestion is to design completely your application and the tables. Then review your `SELECT` query and check for those that are executed many times and that could benefit from using an index.

Summary

In this chapter we have had a in-depth review of most of the SQL syntax that will help you in producing recordsets for your web application.

We reviewed the `SELECT` statement, which is made of multiple clauses that could change radically the information you want to retrieve. A `SELECT` statement is primarily made up of a `select_expression` that will contain the definition of the column of your recordset. The column definition is basically constructed around a column name and eventually completed with expressions made of functions in order to get more comprehensive data. This column name expression can be aliased with the keyword `AS` to have a nice column definition for your recordset.

In a `SELECT` statement, the data comes from tables, and these tables are specified within the `FROM` clause. You can use multiple tables in a query, either simply by listing them, or by using the keywords `LEFT JOIN` or `INNER JOIN`. These tables can be joined with relations that are constructed with foreign keys. You will specify the relation with which you want to link tables in a `JOIN ... ON ...` clause.

The data retrieved from a `SELECT` statement can be filtered with the keyword `WHERE`. The `WHERE` clause is made up of a logical expression; this expression may be built with logical operators and other expressions.

Some rows of a recordset can be grouped into a single row with the keyword `GROUP BY`. The `GROUP BY` function can be implicitly called by using the group functions without telling on which column you want to group. In this case MySQL will automatically group all rows into a single one. You can use the `GROUP BY` functions to know about the elements that have been grouped together: `count()`, `avg()`, `max()`, `min()`, `sum()`.

There is a second keyword to filter rows from a recordset: `HAVING`. The `HAVING` keyword is different from the `WHERE` keyword, in that `WHERE` works at the table column name level while `HAVING` works at the recordset column name level.

You can sort the results of a `SELECT` statement by using the `ORDER BY` keyword. The keyword `ASC` or `DESC` can set the way the sorting is done.

The final clause that you can add in a `SELECT` statement is the `LIMIT` clause. This clause will select a portion of the global recordset by specifying an offset and a number of rows.

To change the structure of an existing table, you can use the `ALTER TABLE` sql command. With this command you can add a column in your table, change an existing column definition, remove a column from your table and rename your table.

A key concept in SQL is the primary key. A primary key is a set of fields in a table that identifies in a unique manner each and every row of a table.

Finally we looked at the concept of indexes. An index is a data structure that will make the `SELECT` a lot faster. The index data are hidden to the user. The creation, modification, and deletion of indexes is performed with the `ALTER TABLE` statement.

If you want to learn more about MySQL syntax, can find the complete MySQL documentation at *http://www.mysql.com/doc/*.

8

- Designing the interface
- Building the query
- Displaying the results

Author: Bruno Mairlot

Creating a Search System

In the previous chapter, we reviewed some elements of the SQL language in depth. In this chapter, we'll to use it to perform a real-world task, a simple search system (or "search engine") for the Dreamweaver Hotel site.

First, we will take a look at what kind of search engine we can build with SQL and the advantages and limitations of such a system. Then we will look at how to build the user interface to the engine. This step will lead us to the last step of building a search engine: building a dynamic query that will search through the information in the database and then present the results to the user.

Search Engines

The term "search engine" groups a large category of tools. As their name tends to indicate, they all have one thing in common: they search for information from a set of data. There are a wide variety of search engines, ranging from massively powerful ones like Google to the smaller system we'll be creating in this chapter. Google uses around 10,000 computers all linked together. Our search engine will be made of some lines of HTML and PHP code running on our server. The set of data used is also not very comparable: Google has more than 2 billion entries, whereas a hotel with a hundred rooms is a pretty large hotel.

Despite their differences, both of these systems implement the following common functionality:

1. They both have a user interface. Google's basic user interface consists of a single text field while the hotel's user interface may be very complex.

2. They both search through a set of data, and return a subset of that data that matches the user input.

3. And finally, they serve no other purpose than to find information. They provide a gateway to more detailed and accurate information.

How Does a SQL Search Engine Work?

Here's a diagram showing how SQL search engines typically work, and this is the system we'll be following for our application:

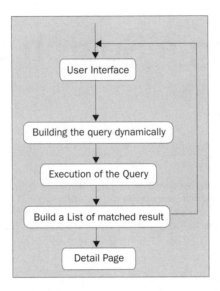

The User Interface

The user interface (sometimes called UI) design is a very important part of the search engine design. Often web site designers focus on the query building, which is great, but the UI deserves special attention. The more complex you make it, the more information the user will be able to enter to feed the search engine, which might help them find a better result. However, an interface design that is too complex may make it harder to use.

The UI part of the search engine is made up of an HTML page, which can either be a pure HTML page with no dynamically generated code or it can be HTML generated by some PHP code on the server.

Building the Query Dynamically

By "building the query dynamically", I mean that the SQL query is never completely written in the PHP file. Instead, it is constructed "on the fly" each time a search is requested by the user. The code will analyze the input given by the user and insert it into the query.

Execution of the Query

Once the query string has been built it needs to be executed, just like any other SQL query. We will use the PHP MySQL functions to send the query to the MySQL server for execution.

Building a List of the Matched Results

This stage is exactly the same as returning the results from a standard database query. We need to present a nicely formatted display of the results to the user.

Designing the User Interface

We'll design the user interface in pure HTML using Dreamweaver.

Building Your Page

The search system interface is made primarily of HTML input tags, all grouped into a special HTML tag, which is named <form>. You can have multiple <form> tags on your page. When the user clicks on the submit button, the browser will only send the values of the input elements that are inside the <form>...</form> tag that contains the button to the server.

Dreamweaver MX Interface Tools

Dreamweaver MX provides a series of tools to build the user interface. Most of these tools are located in the *Forms* tab in the *Insert* panel:

This panel will let you insert the following standard HTML input elements:

- The main <form>...</form> tag
- text input element
- hidden input element
- textarea input element
- checkbox input element
- radio button
- select input element
- image input element
- file input element
- button element

The User Interface for Our Search Engine

For the user interface of our search engine, let's build a page that will let the user search for rooms in our hotel using two criteria: the number of beds and a price range. The user interface we'll be using on our system looks like this:

Chapter 8

The interface is composed of the following elements:

- A drop-down menu (a select menu), allowing the user to specify a range of number of beds to search for. The name of the element is `bed_option`. The possible values of the `bed_option` are: *More than*, *Less than*, or *Equal to*.

- The number of beds that the user wishes to search for. Here we're using a textbox as the input element. The name of the element is `bed`, with any value permitted.

- A drop-down menu asking whether the price searched should be above or below the stated value. The name of the menu is `price_option`. The possible values are: *above* and *below*.

- The textbox where user can enter a price that they wish to search. The input element used is a text input. The name of the element is `price`.

- A submit button, to confirm the search request.

The HTML code used for the user interface is the following (it's in the code download for the book in the file `form.html`, or you can build it yourself using Dreamweaver – just make sure that the names of all the input elements are correct):

```
<form name="form1" method="post" action="search.php">
  <table width="400" border="0">
    <tr align="center">
      <td colspan="3">Search for a room</td>
    </tr>
    <tr>
      <td width="152" align="right">Number of beds :</td>
      <td width="38"><select name="bed_option" id="bed_option">
          <option value="more" selected>More than</option>
          <option value="less">Less than</option>
          <option value="equal">Equal to</option>
        </select></td>
      <td width="196">
      <input name="bed" type="text" id="bed" value="1" size="2"
          maxlength="2">bed(s)</td>
    </tr>
    <tr>
      <td align="right">Price Range :</td>
      <td><select name="price_option" id="price_option">
          <option value="above" selected>Above</option>
          <option value="below">Below</option>
        </select></td>
```

202

Creating a Search System

```
            <td>$<input name="price" type="text" id="price" value="25" size="5"
                   maxlength="5"></td>
        </tr>
        <tr>
            <td align="right"> </td>
            <td colspan="2" align="center">
            <input type="submit" name="Submit" value="Search"></td>
        </tr>
    </table>
</form>
```

Retrieving the Value Entered By the User

OK, so we've got our user interface. How does our code know what values the user has entered and submitted to the server? Luckily, PHP provides a very easy way to get those values.

Let's say we have the following HTML code:

```
<form name="form1" action="search.php" method="post">
    <input type="text" name="number">
</form>
```

This HTML code has a `<form>` tag named `form1` and one input element of type `text`, named `number`. That piece of code will insert an input box in the browser window, which could be used to search for information about a room number, for instance. But how are we going to retrieve the numbers the user entered in their browser?

We can use the predefined PHP array: `$HTTP_POST_VARS`. This PHP array is automatically defined at the start of our script and all values posted from the user's browser are put into this array. If the form's `method` is `get` instead of `post`, we can use the array `$HTTP_GET_VARS` instead.

The difference between a `get` and a `post` method resides in the way the browser will send information to the server. In case of a `get`, all information will be passed through the URL variable. The user will be able to see all of the data in the location bar of their browser. In the case of a `post`, everything is passed silently without any notice to the user. In this chapter, we will be using the `post` method.

> *In the newest versions of PHP, 4.1 and above, these arrays have been deprecated in favour of the following arrays: $_POST and $_GET.*
>
> *However, this syntax is not available on servers with older versions of the PHP scripting engine, so we won't use it.*

So, to access the value the user has entered into our `number` box, we can use the following code:

```
$HTTP_POST_VARS['number']
```

Let's have a look at a fuller example. Suppose we have the following HTML code in a page called `index.html`:

203

```
<html>
   <body>
      <form action="print.php" method="post">
         Enter a number : <input type="text" name="myinput">
      </form>
   </body>
</html>
```

This example will show like this in a browser :

The file `print.php`, looks like this:

```
<html>
   <body>
      You typed : <?php echo $HTTP_POST_VARS["myinput"]?>
   </body>
</html>
```

You can find these two HTML pages in the code download for the book. If the user types *789* into the input box and presses return, their browser will display the following result:

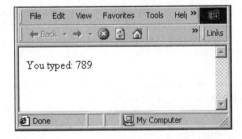

Building the Query

We've built the simple user interface for our query and examined how we can get the values that the user enters into our PHP code. So let's move on to take a look at building the query that will get the data that the user requires out of our database.

The Base Query

We'll build our query with two parts. There's the unchanging part, or base query, and then a dynamic part which we will generate using PHP code. Let's start off by looking at the base query.

The first step is to create the correct SELECT statement, without filtering any values. To do that, we will create a normal recordset that will select the ID of the room, its number, the bed number, and the price:

```
SELECT ID,bed,price,number FROM room
```

Executing this query on the MySQL server will return all the rooms in the room table of our database.

Creating the Recordset in Dreamweaver

Open the Application panel and select the *Bindings* tab. Click on the '+' button, and select the *recordset* menu item.

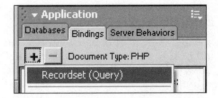

This will pop up the window to design the recordset:

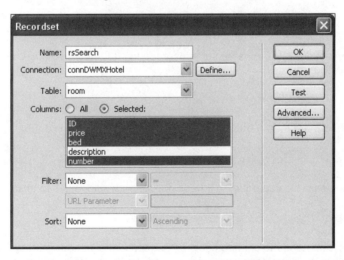

Set the name of the recordset to *rsSearch*. Select the connection you set up for the hotel application, and select the room table. On the *Columns* option, click on the *Selected:* radio button, and then select the following fields: *ID*, *price*, *bed*, and *number*. Leave all the other options at their default values. *Filter* and *Sort* should be set to *None*. You can check to make sure that everything's OK by clicking on the *Test* button, which should give a list of the rows contained in the room table. Click on *OK* to finish the recordset.

Dreamweaver will now insert the following code in your page, above the `<html>` tag:

```
<?php
    mysql_select_db($database_connDWMXHotel, $connDWMXHotel);
    $query_rsSearch = "SELECT ID, price, bed, number FROM room";
    $rsSearch = mysql_query($query_rsSearch, $connDWMXHotel) or
die(mysql_error());
    $row_rsSearch = mysql_fetch_assoc($rsSearch);
    $totalRows_rsSearch = mysql_num_rows($rsSearch);
?>
```

As you can see the third line contains our "base" query. We'll filter the results of this query, depending upon the values that the user has entered by manipulating the query itself.

Creating the Dynamic Query

Now that we have a working recordset, we will modify the recordset to integrate a WHERE statement.

Which Options Have Been Selected?

The user has two choices to make: the number of beds they're searching for, and the price range. The values of `bed_option` and `price_option` can be obtained in PHP with the following code:

```
$HTTP_POST_VARS['bed_option']
```

and:

```
$HTTP_POST_VARS['price_option']
```

Let's look at some example queries for some user inputs. If the user selected less than 3 beds, the query should look like this:

```
SELECT ID,price,bed, number FROM room WHERE bed < 3
```

If the user selected more than 5 beds, the query should instead look like this:

```
SELECT ID,price,bed, number FROM room WHERE bed > 5
```

And finally, if the user selected equal to 2 beds, the query would look like this:

```
SELECT ID,price,bed,number FROM room WHERE bed = 5
```

So the only thing that needs to change between queries is the symbol used for comparison and the number to compare to. Therefore, we need to design a mechanism to add these two factors into the query dynamically, depending upon what the user has entered.

Creating a Search System

We're going to have to do a little hand coding here, because the possible values in $HTTP_POST_VARS["bed_option"] are less, more, or equal, but we need to insert the symbol <, >, or = into our query. To do that we will define a new variable, called $bComp. This variable will hold the symbol that we need depending upon the user input: >, <, or =.

We will use the following code in our page:

```php
<?php
   if($HTTP_POST_VARS["bed_option"] == "less")
   {
       $bComp = "<";
   }
   else if($HTTP_POST_VARS["bed_option"] == "more")
   {
       $bComp = ">";
   }
   else
   {
       $bComp = "=";
   }
?>
```

It is important that you place this piece of code just before the recordset code in your document.

Now we have a variable named $bComp that contains the value <, >, or = depending upon whether the user has selected the *more than* or *less than* option. We are now ready to modify the base query.

Building the New Query

To build the new query, open the Bindings panel. You should see the recordset rsSearch in the list of data sources:

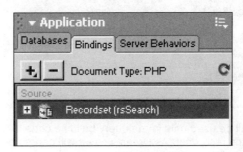

Double-click on the recordset, and click on the *Advanced* button, which will bring up the following window:

207

Chapter 8

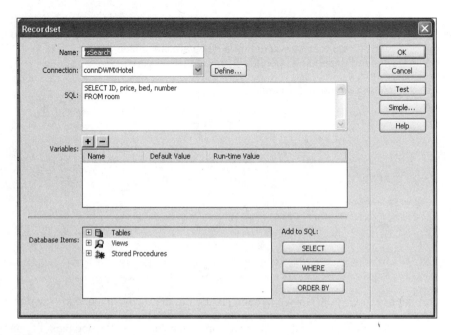

Recordset Parameters

Click on the + button above the *Variables* box. This will open the *Add Parameter* dialog box which will help us to create a new recordset variable for your query. Enter the values as shown in the following window:

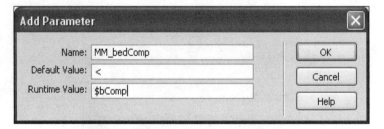

The parameter's *Name* will be used only in the query building code that Dreamweaver generates when you finish creating the recordset. As Dreamweaver will generate the recordset code automatically, it's best to prefix the name with 'MM_'.

The *Default Value* is a string value that the PHP script will use if the *Runtime Value* is not defined, so here we're going to make the default value the less than operator, <. Note that Dreamweaver will enclose the default value with double quotes when it generates the code. So, you can use anything as your *Default Value*, but don't use PHP code. This is because it won't be executed correctly, and the results are sometimes unpredictable.

The *Runtime Value* is the part of code that the recordset variable should take if everything goes all right, which is the value of the variable $bComp that we defined in our code earlier.

Creating a Search System

We can use the same process to add a parameter for the number of beds. Use the following values:

- Name: `MM_bedNum`
- Default: `0`
- Runtime Value: `$HTTP_POST_VARS["bed"]`

The *Variables* table should now look like this:

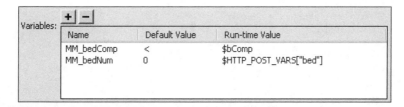

Inserting the Parameter Into the Recordset

To insert the newly created parameters, `MM_bedComp` and `MM_bedNum`, into the query, we just have to modify the SQL in the Recordset window:

```
SELECT ID, price, bed, number FROM room WHERE bed MM_bedComp MM_bedNum
```

Your complete Recordset dialog box should look like this:

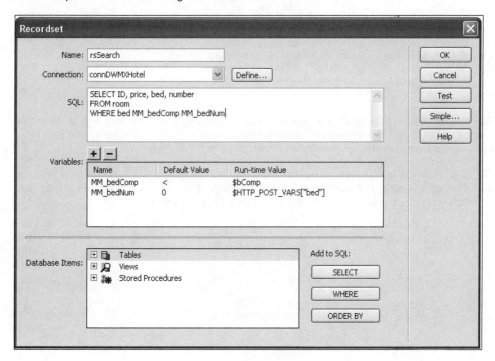

Chapter 8

Click *OK* to confirm the changes to your recordset.

Your PHP code should now look like the following:

```php
<?php require_once('Connections/connDWMXHotel.php'); ?>
<?php
   if($HTTP_POST_VARS["bed_option"] == "less")
   {
      $bComp = "<";
   }
   else if($HTTP_POST_VARS["bed_option"] == "more"
   {
      $bComp = ">";
   }
   else
   {
      $bComp = "=";
   }
?>
<?php
$MM_bedComp_rsSearch = "<";
if (isset($bComp)) {
  $MM_bedComp_rsSearch = (get_magic_quotes_gpc()) ? $bComp : addslashes($bComp);
}
$MM_bedNum_rsSearch = "0";
if (isset($HTTP_POST_VARS["bed"])) {
  $MM_bedNum_rsSearch = (get_magic_quotes_gpc()) ? $HTTP_POST_VARS["bed"] : addslashes($HTTP_POST_VARS["bed"]);
}
mysql_select_db($database_connDWMXHotel, $connDWMXHotel);
$query_rsSearch = sprintf("SELECT ID, price, bed, number FROM room WHERE bed %s %s", $MM_bedComp_rsSearch,$MM_bedNum_rsSearch);
$rsSearch = mysql_query($query_rsSearch, $connDWMXHotel) or die(mysql_error());
$row_rsSearch = mysql_fetch_assoc($rsSearch);
$totalRows_rsSearch = mysql_num_rows($rsSearch);
?>
```

Note that, except for the little bit of code we wrote at the top, Dreamweaver has written all the rest of the code for us. If you want to change something in the recordset, it's much easier and less error-prone to use Dreamweaver rather than trying to manually edit this code.

Now, we need to generate the code to modify the query for the price range that the user entered. The methodology is exactly the same as for the bed options. First we need to do a little bit of hand coding, which we'll place just after the hand coding that we did before:

```php
<?php
   if($HTTP_POST_VARS["price_option"] == "above")
   {
      $pComp = ">";
   }
   else
   {
      $pComp = "<=";
   }
?>
```

Creating a Search System

This bit of code has a very similar function to the code that we have had before. `$HTTP_POST_VARS["price_option"]` will contain either `above` or `below`, depending upon user input. We've defined another variable, `$pComp` that will have the value `>` if `$HTTP_POST_VARS["price_option"]` contains `above`, otherwise it will have the value `<=`. Now we need to go back into the recordset and edit it so that it has two new parameters, `MM_pComp` and `MM_pNum`, exactly as we did for the beds. Change the SQL for the recordset as follows:

```
SELECT ID ,price,bed, number FROM room WHERE bed MM_bComp MM_bedNum AND MM_pComp
MM_priceNum
```

This will mean that the search system will only return rooms that match both the user's price and bed criteria. If we wanted to make a search system that returned rooms that matched either of the user's criteria, we could use the following:

```
SELECT ID ,price,bed, number FROM room WHERE bed MM_bComp MM_bedNum OR MM_pComp
MM_priceNum
```

The final code looks like this:

```php
<?php require_once('Connections/connDWMXHotel.php'); ?>
<?php
    if($HTTP_POST_VARS["bed_option"] == "less")
    {
        $bComp = "<";
    }
    else if($HTTP_POST_VARS["bed_option"] == "more")
    {
        $bComp = ">";
    }
    else
    {
        $bComp = "=";
    }
?>
<?php
    if($HTTP_POST_VARS["price_option"] == "above")
    {
        $pComp = ">";
    }
    else
    {
        $pComp = "<=";
    }
?>
<?php
$MM_bedComp_rsSearch = "<";
if (isset($bComp)) {
  $MM_bedComp_rsSearch = (get_magic_quotes_gpc()) ? $bComp : addslashes($bComp);
}
$MM_bedNum_rsSearch = "0";
if (isset($HTTP_POST_VARS["bed"])) {
  $MM_bedNum_rsSearch = (get_magic_quotes_gpc()) ? $HTTP_POST_VARS["bed"] :
addslashes($HTTP_POST_VARS["bed"]);
```

```
}
$MM_pComp_rsSearch = "<=";
if (isset($pComp)) {
   $MM_pComp_rsSearch = (get_magic_quotes_gpc()) ? $pComp : addslashes($pComp);
}
$MM_pNum_rsSearch = "0";
if (isset($HTTP_POST_VARS["price"])) {
   $MM_pNum_rsSearch = (get_magic_quotes_gpc()) ? $HTTP_POST_VARS["price"] :
addslashes($HTTP_POST_VARS["price"]);
}
mysql_select_db($database_connDWMXHotel, $connDWMXHotel);
$query_rsSearch = sprintf("SELECT ID, price, bed, number FROM room WHERE bed %s %s
AND price %s %s",
$MM_bedComp_rsSearch,$MM_bedNum_rsSearch,$MM_pComp_rsSearch,$MM_pNum_rsSearch);
$rsSearch = mysql_query($query_rsSearch, $connDWMXHotel) or die(mysql_error());
$row_rsSearch = mysql_fetch_assoc($rsSearch);
$totalRows_rsSearch = mysql_num_rows($rsSearch);
?>
```

Displaying the Results

OK, so we've generated the code that searches through the database, but we still need to display those results to the user. Select the *Bindings* tab in the Application panel. You should find your recordset `rsSearch`:

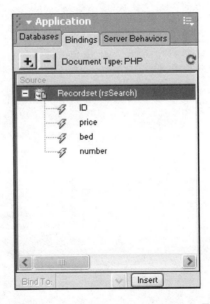

If the recordset tree is not expanded, click on the + icon next to it. This will expand the recordset to show the column names.

Inserting Dynamic Values into the Page

We're going to display the results to our users in a table, with the cells populated by the values contained in the recordset. Create a new table in your document with two rows and four columns. The first row contains the column headings, so fill those in as per the screenshot below.

To make the rest of the cells display the values in the recordset, select the *ID* column of the `rsSearch` recordset in the Bindings panel. Make sure your document cursor is place in the second row, first column, and then click the *Insert* button at the bottom of your Bindings panel. This will insert the dynamic value *rsSearch.ID* in your page. Repeat the same operation with the other values of the recordset in the other cells of the second row.

The page should look like this when you've finished:

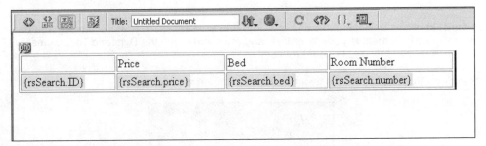

Repeating a Region

Now, all you have on your page is a single row of dynamic values, but it's likely that sometimes more than one result will be returned from the search system.

The very last step is to use the **Repeat Region** Server Behavior. First we need to select the region we want to repeat. To do that, place your cursor in one of the dynamic rows of your table. Then, at the bottom of the page, you have the Tag Selector list. Click on the tag *<tr>* that is at the most right position. This way you will select the whole row.

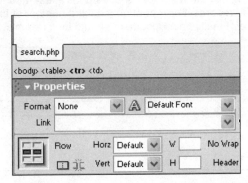

Now, click on the *Server Behaviors* tab in the Application panel group.

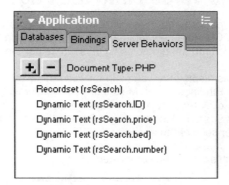

This panel shows you all the dynamic behaviors that are present in your document. You can see that the first dynamic element is your recordset, and after that come the Dynamic Text elements. These are those you have inserted in your table cell.

Now click on the + button, and select the *Repeat Region* menu item.

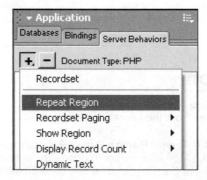

You will then be asked to select the recordset you want to repeat, and to choose the option to either repeat all the values of the recordset or repeat only a fixed number of times. Choose to repeat all of the values of the recordset. Finally your document should look like this:

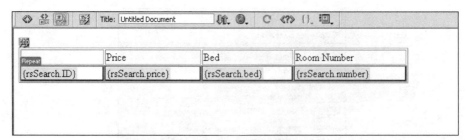

You can see the little *Repeat* box above the cell that contains *{rsSearch.ID}* indicating that this part of your document is inside a Repeat Region.

Summary

In this chapter we have had a look at how to design a search system for our application. We've seen how to edit the recordset within Dreamweaver so that the query is dynamic; that is, it varies depending upon input from the user. We've also had a look at the user interface design for our system, and how we present the results to the user.

In the next chapter, we're going to be taking a more detailed look at hand coding within Dreamweaver.

9

- PHP syntax primer
- Hand coding features in Dreamweaver MX
- Snippets
- Login example

Author: Gareth Downes-Powell

Hand Coding within Dreamweaver MX

So far in this book, we've been using features of Dreamweaver MX to introduce PHP code into our pages. However, in this chapter, we'll take a look at hand coding within the Dreamweaver MX environment – that is, typing in and amending PHP code and HTML.

We'll start with an overview of PHP code syntax. We won't go into too much depth, but will give enough explanation to give you a step up towards writing your own PHP code and understanding the examples in this chapter.

We'll then discuss the benefits of hand coding, setting up the code-editing environment, and explain the new features of Dreamweaver MX that make hand coding easier.

There are various good coding practices, which will be explained along with details of the functions in Dreamweaver MX that can help you to achieve them. You'll be able to ensure that your code is readable, and easy to edit if you need to change it in the future.

We finish the chapter with a practical example, in which we add a user login system to our Dreamweaver Hotel project, so that staff can log in and view bookings. We look at validating data, reading and writing to a database table, and using sessions to create a secure area for the hotel staff that outsiders cannot access.

PHP Code Syntax

As we said above, we'll start with an overview of PHP syntax. So far in this book, you'll have seen many examples of PHP code, as added by Dreamweaver MX into your pages. However, you haven't really had to write any yourself, or understand exactly what the code does. While you can do a lot using Dreamweaver MX in this way, it is also useful to have a basic knowledge of PHP syntax in order to edit the PHP code that Dreamweaver MX adds or to write your own.

PHP is similar to other server-side technologies, in that the PHP code has to be placed between special tags, to delimit it from the rest of the HTML markup in the page. There are four types of PHP tag you can use for delimiting the code. These are:

Tag Type	Opening Tag	Closing Tag
Standard PHP syntax	`<?php`	`?>`
Shorthand style	`<?`	`?>`
ASP Style	`<%`	`%>`
Script style	`<script language="PHP">`	`</script>`

Anything between the above PHP tags will be interpreted as PHP code by the PHP compiler. You can use any of the above styles of tag syntax, although we will be sticking with the standard style throughout this chapter.

Statements

Now to the PHP code itself. Much of the code consists of single statements. These are written on a single line, and are followed by a semicolon, ;, as shown in the example below:

```
<?php
   echo "This is a test line showing PHP syntax" ;
?>
```

This statement prints the text *This is a test line showing PHP syntax* to the page.

Variables

In the above section, we mentioned the use of **variables**. These are ways of storing pieces of information for future use. They consist of a name and a value.

Variable Names

Variable names in PHP always start with the $ character, and can be any combination of letters or numbers, as long as the rules below are followed.

- The variable name must always start with either a letter, or an underscore character (_).

- The first character can be followed by any combination of letters, numbers, or underscore characters.

Examples of valid variable names are:

```
$total
$_cell1
$length_of_string
```

Examples of invalid variable names are:

```
total
$1_total
$2_length
$!total
```

Variable Values

PHP is what is known as a "**loosely typed**" language. This means that a variable can hold any type of data (for example a number or a string of characters) – you don't have to specifically assign a **data type** to a variable. You can change the data type for a variable at any time.

For example, a variable called `$myVariable` could contain the string value `"hello"` at one point in the code, and could store the number `10` later on, without having to tell PHP that you're changing the data type of the variable.

Note that strings are always surrounded by quote marks, so `"123"` and `'123'` are string values, but `123` is a numeric value.

Assigning Variables

In PHP, to assign a value to a variable, you use the `=` operator. For example, to assign the integer value 10 to a variable called `$total`, you would use:

```
<?php
  $total = 10;
?>
```

Assigning Strings To Variables

To assign a string to a variable, you can use double quotes (`"`) or single quotes (`'`), as shown in the example below:

```
<?php
  $example1 = 'This is a single quoted string';
  $example2 = "This is a double quoted string";
?>
```

So what's the difference between single- and double-quoted strings?

Take a look at the next example:

```
<php
  $total = 10;

  $example1 = 'The total is $total';
  $example2 = "The total is $total";
?>
```

The contents of the variables will now be:

Variable	Value
$example1	The total is $total
$example2	The total is 10

As you can see, text enclosed between single quotes is taken literally by PHP, and is put straight in the string without processing.

For `$example2`, where the text is enclosed in double quotes, the value of `$total` is substituted into the text.

Appending Strings To Strings

PHP has a handy way of appending one string to another using the concatenation operator ".", for example:

```
<php
$a = 'apples';
$b = 'bananas';
$c = '';

$c = $a . ' and ' . $b;
?>
```

In this example, `$c` would have the value "`apples and bananas`".

You can also quickly append one string to another using ".=", for example:

```
<php
$a = 'apples';

$a .= ' and bananas';
?>
```

`$a` would now have the value "`apples and bananas`".

Escaping Characters

Escaping a character tells PHP to ignore it. Why would we want to do this? Imagine we want to print the following text to the screen:

This is an example showing double quotes (" ")

If we try and insert this into a variable, and print it to the screen, as in the following example, we will get an error:

```
<?php
  $example = "This is an example showing double quotes (" ")";
  echo "$example";
?>
```

This causes an error, because the PHP parser gets confused where the string starts and finishes – there are too many quote marks in the string. To stop this from happening, we have to escape the quotes we want to write to the screen using the backslash character (\). Change the example to the following:

```
<?php
    $example = "This is an example showing double quotes (\" \")";
    echo "$example";
?>
```

As we have preceded the quotes in the string with the backslash, they are ignored by the PHP engine and printed to the screen, as we intended. This method should also be used if you want to include some quotes in a string that is to be inserted into a database.

Below is a list of the characters that need to be escaped in this way.

Character	Escaped Character	Description
not applicable	\n	Adds a linefeed
not applicable	\r	Adds a carriage return
not applicable	\t	Adds a tab
\	\\	Backslash
$	\$	Dollar Sign
"	\"	Double Quote

Arrays

Arrays are similar to variables, in that they are used to store pieces of data. However, unlike variables, arrays are useful because they can hold more than one piece of data at a time. For example, imagine that you wanted to store all the items in a shopping list. You could use an array to store these items. To create an array in PHP you use the `array()` function. Each item in the array is identified by a **key**. So to create an array for our shopping list, we could use the following code:

```
$shoppingList = array( 1 => "toothpaste", 2 => "sun cream", 3 => "band-aids");
```

To retrieve an element (a specific bit of data) from the array, we use the name of the array followed by the key in square brackets. So, to get the third item from our array, we can use the following piece of code:

```
echo "The third item in the shopping list is $shoppingList[3];"
```

This would display "*The third item in the shopping list is band-aids*" on the screen.

Control Structures

PHP uses a variety of control structures to affect which code is executed, when, and for how long. We'll cover two types here, `if` and `foreach`. There are other statements, like `do..while`, which we won't cover here. More details and useful examples can be found in the online PHP manual.

if

If you've used any other programming language, then you'll be familiar with the `if` statement. It's used to conditionally execute some code: if a condition is met, then run a section of code.

For example, if we have two variables, `$apples` and `$bananas`, and we want to print a message on the screen if the value of `$apples` is greater than `$bananas`, we could use the following code:

```
if ($apples > $bananas)
    echo "You have more apples than bananas!";
```

Here the code checks to see whether a condition is met: whether `$apples` is greater than `$bananas`, using the `>` operator. If so, then the second line is executed, and the message is displayed. There are several conditional operators that you can use in your code:

Operator	Meaning
==	Equal to
!=	Not equal to
<>	Not equal to
<	Less than
>	Greater than
<=	Less than or equal to
>=	Greater than or equal to

Be careful when comparing two variables for equality. The correct operator to use is `==` (two equals signs). This is because `=` (one equals sign) is the assignment operator, for setting the value of variables.

If you want the `if` statement to conditionally execute more than one line of code, then you can enclose the block of code that you want to execute with curly braces, `{}`. So, for example, you could make the example we used above set the number of bananas to zero as well as displaying the message by using the following code:

```
if ($apples > $bananas)
{
    echo "You have more apples than bananas, so I'm taking away your bananas!";
    $bananas = 0;
}
```

foreach

The `foreach` statement is used to loop through an array, looking at all of the elements in the array in turn. For example, if I wanted to display all the contents of an array:

```
<?php
$numbers = array(2,3,4,2);
foreach ( $numbers as $v )
{
```

```
      echo "Current value of \$v: $v <BR>";
   }
?>
```

this would produce the following result:

Current value of $v: 2
Current value of $v: 3
Current value of $v: 4
Current value of $v: 2

Functions

You may have noticed the use of some of PHP's own functions in the code produced by Dreamweaver in previous chapters. They encapsulate a task that can then be called and run from elsewhere in your code.

It's possible to write your own functions in PHP and use them in a similar manner, allowing you to reuse a piece of useful code without constantly retyping it. For example, you could write the following function that checks the length of a certain piece of data:

```
<?php
   function check_length($data)
   {
      if (strlen($data) < 6)
         return "The data was too small";
      else
         return "That data was fine";
   }
?>
```

If the length of the data passed to the function as a parameter between its parentheses is less than 6, then the string `"The data was too small"` is returned by the function to wherever it was called from. If the length of the string wasn't less than 6, then the string `"That data was fine"` is returned.

The function can then be called anywhere in your code. For example:

```
<?php
$example = "qwertyuiop";
echo check_length($example);
?>
```

In this case, *the data was fine* is printed to the page, since the value `"qwertyuiop"` has more than 6 characters.

PHP Resources

If you find that you need more information about the PHP commands we use in the hand coding examples in this chapter, you may find the following two web sites useful.

First, there is PHP.net – *http://www.php.net/*. This is the home of PHP and contains a huge amount of useful information, including online PHP manuals, searchable by function.

Second, there is Zend – *http://www.zend.com/*. The Zend founders created PHP 4 and the Zend Engine, on which all PHP site and applications are run. Their web site contains many articles, code fragments, and tutorials, which can help you to learn and use PHP 4.

When you're hand coding in PHP, it's very useful to have a browser open at the above web sites, so you can quickly check PHP syntax, for example the parameters for a function. It's definitely worth adding them to your browser's bookmarks.

If you prefer to learn from a book, we recommend *Professional PHP4* (Harish Rawat et al., Wrox Press, ISBN 1-861006-91-8). This is an excellent PHP resource, and covers the whole PHP 4 language in detail.

Why Hand Code within Dreamweaver MX?

Although Dreamweaver MX contains a range of built-in PHP server behaviors to perform various operations, if you're building a complex site, you'll soon find that you want to do something for which there isn't a built-in server behavior.

Since PHP is an open-source product, it is widely supported by a range of open-source developers and a huge user community. As a result PHP evolves much faster than other commercial languages, and the code is continuously updated with bug fixes, enhancements, and language extensions, which extend its capabilities.

Hand coding allows you to implement the latest PHP developments in your code as soon as they are released. It offers you total freedom to ensure that your web site does exactly what you want it to, and you are not just limited to the built-in code generated by your development program.

Code that you've written yourself can also interact with the Dreamweaver MX-generated code, so you can create standard code quickly using the Dreamweaver MX server behaviors, and then modify it yourself to perform extra functions.

Coding Options in Dreamweaver MX

We're now going to look at the many ways you can create and edit code (both PHP and HTML) in Dreamweaver MX.

Code View and Code Inspector

There are a number of different ways to view your code within Dreamweaver MX. You can display your code in the Document window by turning on Code view, you can use the Code inspector to view and edit your code in a separate window, or you can split your Document window in two, and see both the page and its underlying code.

- **To View Code in the Document window**:
  From the main menu bar, select *View -> Code*. The Document window will now show the underlying page code.

Hand Coding within Dreamweaver MX

- **To View Code in a Separate Window:**
  From the main menu bar, select *Window -> Others -> Code Inspector*, or alternatively press *F10*.

- **To View Both the Page and Code in the Document window:**
  From the main menu bar, select *View -> Code and Design.* This view is extremely useful when working on the underlying page HTML, as you can instantly see the effects your changes have made.

It's also worth noting that there are shortcuts for the three views of the Document window (Code, Page and Code, and Page) on the *Documents* toolbar, which are shown here. You can turn on the *Documents* toolbar by selecting *View -> Toolbars -> Document* from the main menu bar.

Code Options in Preferences Window

There are a number of options for how code is displayed that can be set in the Preferences window. To open the Preferences window, select *Edit -> Preferences* from the main menu bar, or use the shortcut keys *Ctrl + U*.

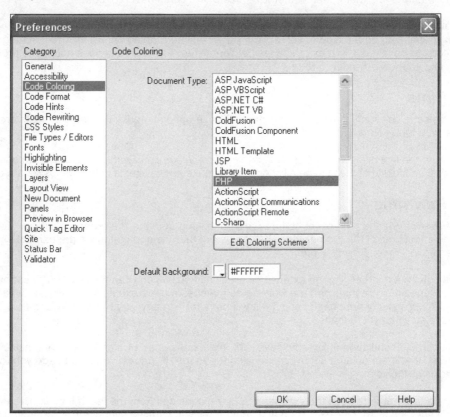

225

Code Coloring Options

The first option we'll look at is Code Coloring, so click on *Code Coloring* in the *Category* menu. From the list of languages that appears, select *PHP*, and then click on *Edit Coloring Scheme*.

If you scroll down the "*styles for*" menu in the new window that appears, you will see a number of PHP options. You can select the text color and background color, as well as bold, underline, and italic for each of these options. This is particularly useful if you are migrating from another development program, and you are used to a particular set of colors representing different sections of code.

The effects of the changes you make can be seen immediately in the preview area. When you have finished making any changes, click *OK* to continue.

Code Format Options

The next category we'll look at is Code Format. This presents a new set of options, which are used to determine how the code is formatted in Code view.

You can set whether spaces or tabs are used to indent the code, and how many, and set the case of your HTML tags to either uppercase or lowercase, or a combination of both.

One important selection is the Line Break type. This should be set to either *CR LF (Windows)* or *LF (Linux)* depending on the type of server your pages will be running on. An incorrect setting can cause your code to be laid out with extra spaces between lines. Although this does not cause problems, it can make your code harder to read.

Code Hints

Next, select *Code Hints* in the *Category* menu. These options modify the way that hints are given to you as you type your code.

Make sure the first two options, *Enable Auto Tag Completion* and *Enable Code Hints* are both turned on – we'll be looking at these in detail shortly. Also make sure all items in the *Menus* list are checked.

Code Rewriting

Code Rewriting is the next set of options we'll be looking at in the Preferences window. Most of the options affect your HTML, rather than PHP code, but there is one option we are particularly interested in: *Never Rewrite Code*.

In this option, a number of page extensions are specified, which Dreamweaver MX recognizes. If the page extension of the page you are working on matches a page extension in this list, Dreamweaver MX will ignore any of your hand coding – it will not alter it in any way, which guarantees the code will appear exactly as you intended.

With a default installation of Dreamweaver MX, the extensions `.php` and `.php3` are included already in the list. If you are using a different extension for your PHP pages, you should add your page extension to the list.

It is important not to remove the `.php` and `.php3` extensions from the list. If you do, Dreamweaver MX will not recognize your PHP code and could modify it, causing syntax errors when you run the page on your server.

Fonts

The last set of options we will be looking at in this section is *Fonts*. Here you can set the fonts and sizes for different parts of the Dreamweaver MX interface.

The particular option we are interested in is *Code View*, which by default is set to Courier New, and is usually 9pt or 10pt. If you are using a high monitor resolution, you may find the text in the Code view is too small to read comfortably with these settings, in which case you should increase its size here.

To close the Preferences window and save your changes, click the *OK* button.

New Hand Coding Features in MX

In this section, we'll be taking a look at the new hand coding features included in Dreamweaver MX. In each Dreamweaver release the coding environment has been improved, and this release is no exception – there are a number of new features to make life easier when hand coding.

Code Hints

One of the major new features of Dreamweaver MX is the Code Hints system. This system monitors the code that you type, so that when you type certain characters, it can pop up a list of suggested options to complete the code you're typing.

You can use Code Hints to:

- Insert or edit code
- See all available attributes for the tag you're currently using
- See all available parameters for a function
- See all available methods for an object you're working on

Let's play with this feature to see how it works. Open a new PHP page in Dreamweaver MX: choose *File -> New* from the main menu bar, click on the *General* tab in the dialog box that appears, select *Dynamic* for the page category, and then select *PHP*.

Open the Code inspector by pressing *F10*, and place the cursor between the `<body>` and `</body>` tags. Type `<`, and you will notice a pop-up list containing all the available HTML tags. We'll insert a simple horizontal rule onto our page, so from the pop-up list double-click on `<>` *hr*. You will see that `hr` is added to the `<` you typed initially. Press the space bar once, and another list pops up, this time containing all of the different attributes for the `<hr>` element. Scroll down the list, double-click on *width*, and you will see that it adds the attribute `width = ""`, with the insertion point between the two double quotes. Enter `200` for the width value, and then close the tag with a `>`.

You should now have:

```
<hr width="200">
```

Go back into Design view, and you'll see the horizontal rule, 200 pixels long, displayed in the center of the screen.

Chapter 9

Next, go back into the Code view, and position the cursor to the left of the closing > of our tag. Press the space bar, and the attributes list pops up again. This time, double-click on *align* – `align=""` will be automatically inserted into the code, and a new pop-up menu appears listing the available alignment options: *left*, *right*, or *center*. Double-click on *left* and it will be inserted between the quotation marks.

Your inserted tag will now read:

```
<hr width="200" align="left">
```

Once again, go back to the Design view. As expected, our horizontal line is now on the left of the screen.

Many hand coders may not wish to change between using the keyboard and the mouse, so there are other options for selecting an item from the lists that pop up. You can scroll to the item using the arrow keys, and then press the Return key to add it to your code. Alternatively, you can type the first few letters of an item until it becomes selected and then press the *Tab* key to add the chosen item.

This system makes entering HTML code by hand a much quicker and easier process, and also means that you have all the tag attributes instantly at hand without having to consult a reference.

> Note that if the code you type is not recognized, you can still carry on with your code but no pop-up list will be displayed.

Code Hints also has various PHP tag and function references built in. For example, in Code view type the following:

```
<?php
$mySQL = mysql_connect(
```

After you have typed the opening parenthesis of the function, a Code Hints box pops up, showing the protocol for the `mysql_connect()` function, as shown in the screenshot below.

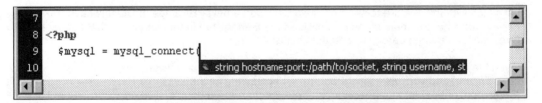

This makes entering PHP code much easier, as there is an instant reference for the function you are using, showing the parameters and data format the function expects. As you add the various parameters for the function, they are removed from the Code Hints box, so you can see which parameters have not yet been filled in.

PHP default variables, such as `$HTTP_POST_VARS`, are also recognized – after typing the first few characters, you can add the desired variable by double-clicking on it in the list that appears.

If you don't wish to use the Code Hints system, you can turn it off in the *Code Hints* section of the Preferences window, which we talked about earlier in this chapter.

The Insert Panel

The Insert panel normally sits at the top of the screen, although it can be dragged to a different location, if required. If the panel is closed, you will see a white arrow pointing to the right, and the word *Insert*. Click on the arrow or the word *Insert*, and the panel will open revealing a number of different tabs.

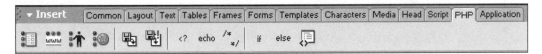

Click on the *PHP* tab. (If this is not displayed, it means that Dreamweaver MX does not recognize your page as a PHP page. Save your page with a `.php` extension, and the *PHP* tab will appear.)

Under the *PHP* tab, there are a number of buttons – when clicked, they will automatically add their respective PHP code into the Code window. To see what code a particular button will insert, hold your mouse cursor over the button. After a short delay, its description will be displayed.

Point the mouse at each button in turn, and you will see all the built-in PHP functions that can be inserted. If you click on the button with the description *More Tags...*, the Tag Chooser window will open. Click on *PHP Tags*, and extra PHP tags that can be automatically inserted are displayed.

All tags are inserted at the current location of the text cursor. For example, in Code view, click the *<?* button (with the description *Code Block*), and you will see that Dreamweaver MX automatically inserts the code below at the current cursor position:

```
<?php ?>
```

If you select some text and then click a button, the inserted code will be wrapped around the selected text. For example, if you select some text and click the */* */* button (with the description *Comment*), comment syntax will be wrapped around the selected text.

The code available from the Insert panel can also be inserted by selecting *Insert -> PHP Objects* from the main menu bar.

The Tag Editor

Another new feature is the tag editor, and the best way to view it in action is with a demonstration.

On a new page, insert a table, with three rows and three columns. Once the table has been inserted, select it in Code view by clicking on the `<table>` element, and then click the right mouse button. From the pop-up menu that appears, select *Edit Tag <table>*. Alternatively, you can use the tag editor keyboard shortcut, *Ctrl + F5*.

The tag editor window appears, which offers an easy way to change all available attributes for the `<table>` tag.

Chapter 9

For the selected `<table>` tag, the tag editor displays five sets of options. These are:

- *General*
- *Browser Specific*
- *Style Sheet/Accessibility*
- *Language*
- *Events*

The tag editor is shown below, showing the *Browser Specific* options:

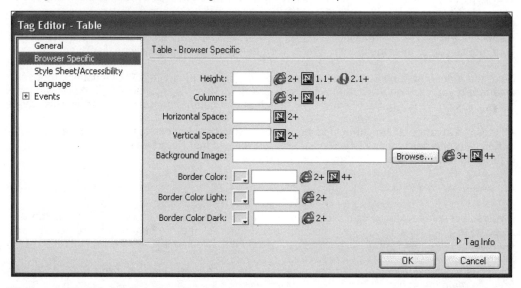

We'll now take a quick look through all the options, as there are a number of new features.

General

The *General* menu offers the standard options for the `<table>` tag, such as `alignment`, `width`, `border`, `cell padding`, etc.

Browser Specific

The *Browser Specific* menu contains options that only apply to certain browsers. Next to each option you'll see browser icons and numbers, which represent the versions of browsers that support that particular option. Details are included for Internet Explorer, Netscape Navigator, and Opera.

Style Sheet/Accessibility

This set of options allows you to assign CSS style settings to the table.

Language

The *Language* menu allows you to set various international language options to the table.

Events

The *Events* options are one of the most convenient features of the tag editor. When you click on the + icon to expand the *Events* menu, you'll see a list of all the applicable JavaScript events that can be applied.

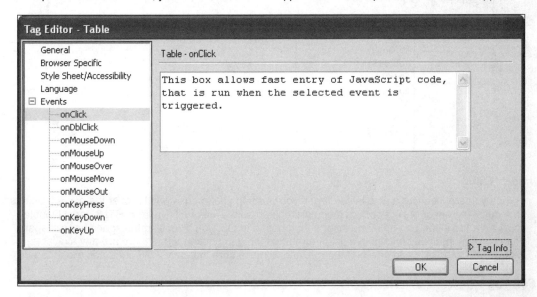

You can click on an event, and then enter JavaScript code directly into the textbox. All relevant code is then inserted for you automatically. This makes adding and editing code for the events a much easier process, and by removing all excess code and leaving just the code you want to see, it also makes debugging easier.

Tag Info

Tag Info isn't a menu option, but can be activated by clicking on *Tag Info* at the bottom right of the tag editor, just above the *Cancel* button. The dialog box then expands, and a tag reference is displayed for the tag you're currently editing. This is an extremely helpful feature as you constantly have an HTML reference available for any given HTML tag.

Finally, click *OK* to apply your changes.

Quick Tag Editor

The quick tag editor allows you to quickly insert an HTML tag in the Design view. It is activated by pressing *Ctrl + T*, and has three modes:

- *Insert HTML*
- *Edit Tag*
- *Wrap Tag*

It opens in the most appropriate view for the selected tag or cursor position. However, once open, you can cycle through the available modes by pressing the *Ctrl + T* key combination.

The next figure shows the quick tag editor in *Insert HTML* mode:

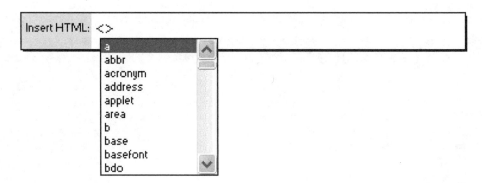

Insert HTML

When you are inserting a new HTML tag, if you position your mouse pointer over the angle brackets in the quick tag editor (<>), a pop-up menu will appear with a list of all available HTML tags. Double-clicking a tag in the pop-up menu inserts the chosen tag for you. Pressing the space bar will again open a pop-up menu containing a list of attributes for your chosen tag (if there are any available). This allows you to quickly add new HTML tags, and to make sure that only valid attributes are entered.

Edit Tag

You can edit an existing HTML tag by selecting the object in Design view and opening the quick tag editor with *Ctrl + T*. The quick tag editor will display the HTML tag for the selected object only – you can then add, edit, or delete the tag attributes. Placing the cursor after an attribute in the quick tag editor and pressing the space bar, will open a new pop-up menu with all available attributes for the tag being edited. Simply double-click on an attribute, and it will be automatically inserted. You can easily move between attributes in the quick tag editor by pressing the *Tab* key to move forwards and *Shift + Tab* to move backwards. Press *Return* at the end of the line to apply your changes.

If you enter any invalid HTML, Dreamweaver MX will attempt to correct the code for you automatically. It does this by automatically closing any open quotation marks, or adding missing end angle brackets.

Wrap Tag

By selecting an object or unformatted text in Design view, you can easily wrap the selection with a set of HTML tags – pressing *Ctrl + T* opens the quick tag editor in *Wrap Tag* mode. Simply enter an opening tag, for example, <b>, and press *Return*. Your tag is inserted at the start of your selection, and the appropriate closing tag is automatically added to the end of the selection.

PHP Tags

In Design view, if you invoke the quick tag editor, by selecting a PHP icon and pressing *Ctrl + T*, the PHP code will be shown, and can be edited, without having to switch to Code view.

The Tag Inspector

The next feature we'll examine in this section is the Tag inspector, which is located in the Code panel, by clicking on the relevant tab. The Tag inspector shows a hierarchical view of all tags in the current document.

Hand Coding within Dreamweaver MX

At any time you can select an object on the page, or click on a tag in the Tag inspector, to get a list of the tag's attributes, which you can add to, edit, or delete.

The Tag Library Editor

The Tag Library editor allows you to add to and edit the built-in Tag Libraries at the core of Dreamweaver MX, which are used in all the various tag editing features.

To call up the Tag Library editor, you need to select *Edit -> Tag Libraries* from the main menu bar. The dialog box that appears is shown in the figure below.

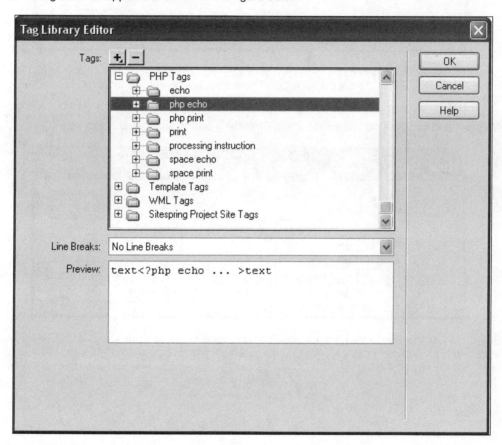

The dialog box contains all the tag categories and subcategories, and allows you to add new tags or attributes to the library, or edit existing ones.

Adding New Tags

To add a new tag to the library, click the + button and select *New Tags*. You can now select the category the tag will appear under, and give the tag a name.

As an example, we'll add a new custom HTML tag, `<content>`, which could be used in a content management system to hold details of the page content.

233

Chapter 9

In the Tag Library editor, click + and select *New Tag Library*. The following window will appear:

Enter Custom for the library name, and then click *OK*. You will now see a new folder called *Custom* in the Tag Library editor. Select the folder, and from the *Used in* options in the box underneath, select *HTML*.

We now need to create our <content> tag. Click the + button again, and select *New Tags*.

Select the *Custom* Tag Library we just created, and enter content for the tag name. Select *Have Matching End Tags*, so Dreamweaver MX will automatically include a closing tag for our <content> tag. Click *OK* to add the tag.

Hand Coding within Dreamweaver MX

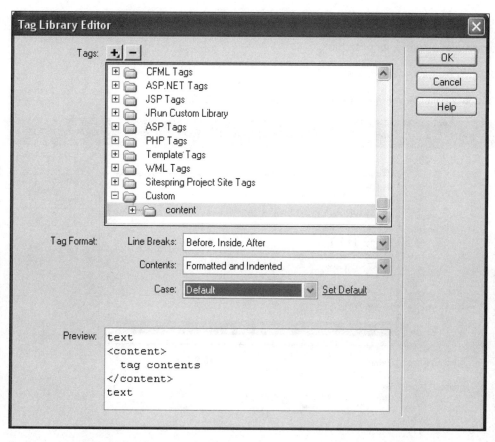

The tag will now be inserted into the *Custom* folder, and you will see some new options to format the tag. Run through the various options to see the effects. We used line breaks before, inside, and after the tag, and set the contents to be formatted and indented.

Once you have added a tag, you can click the + button again and select *New Attributes* to add extra attributes for that tag. We're going to create a new attribute for our `<content>` tag called `title`.

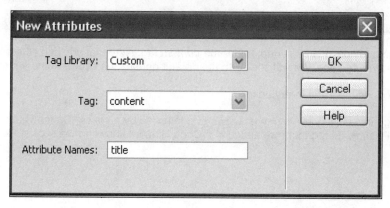

Select *Custom* for the Tag Library, the *content* tag we just created, and enter `title` for the attribute name. You can enter more than one attribute at once by entering the attributes separated by a comma and a space, for example:

`title, length, keywords`

For now we'll stick with just a single attribute, so select *OK*.

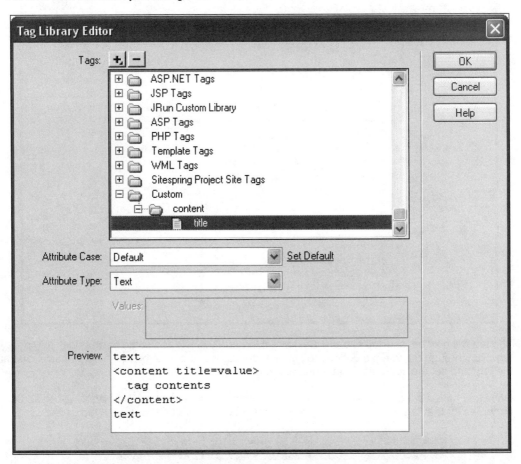

Our attribute has now been inserted, under the *content* tag. Note that you can select the *Attribute Case*, and *Attribute Type*. We will stick with the default options, as shown in the figure above.

Click *OK* to close the Tag Library editor.

If you now go into Code view and type `<content`, followed by a space, Dreamweaver MX will automatically show the attribute we added in a Code Hint, as shown in the screenshot opposite.

Hand Coding within Dreamweaver MX

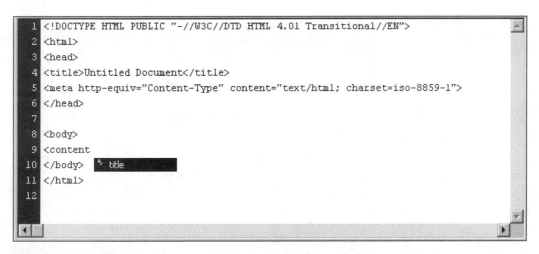

The new tag information for our `<content>` tag is also available in other places, such as the Tag Inspector.

Editing Existing Tags

If you want to edit an existing tag, select the relevant category in the Tag Library editor, and then click on the tag or attribute you wish to change. As soon as you click on an item, you can select and change the various options available for that particular tag.

Deleting a Tag

To delete a tag, or one of its attributes, click on the item in the tree view of the Tag Library editor and click on the - button. (Alternatively, press the *Backspace* or *Delete* key.)

> Be extremely careful when you delete tags, as removing any of the built-in Dreamweaver MX tag libraries may cause problems in the future, and you'll lose the ability to add and edit these tags. If you do delete any of the built-in tag libraries, you will have to reinstall Dreamweaver MX to correct this.

The Snippets Panel

Although small, the Snippets panel is well worth a mention, and is one of the most useful features to have been added.

237

Chapter 9

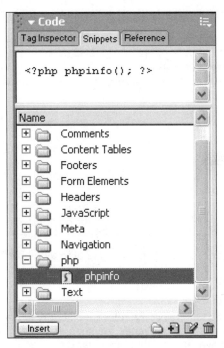

The Snippets tab is located in the Code panel, and is a library for small snippets of code that you frequently use. The code can be HTML, JavaScript, ASP, PHP, etc. It can be a straight block of code, or it can wrap around an existing piece of code. If you take a look at the Snippets panel, you will find it already contains a large number of useful functions, which you can insert straight into your code.

As well as the predefined Snippets, and snippets you add yourself, there are a number of web sites which offer snippets of code that you can add to your personal snippets library. You can also easily share your snippets with other developers.

Adding a New Snippet

To demonstrate how easy the Snippets panel is to use, we are going to add the simple `phpinfo()` function, to the Snippets panel.

Open the Code panel, if it's not already open, and then click on the Snippets tab, to bring the Snippets panel into view. Click the *New Snippet* button, which is one of those located at the bottom right of the Snippets panel.

A new dialog box is displayed, where we can enter the details to create our snippet. For the name, enter `phpinfo`. If you want to enter an optional description for the snippet, you can. This is well worth filling in to explain complex functions, especially if you are going to be sharing the snippet with other developers.

As this is only a very simple example, we just want the snippet to insert our line of code, so for *Snippet Type* select *Insert Block*. The other option, *Wrap Selection*, lets you wrap your code around an existing object or tag.

If you had an object or piece of code selected when you clicked on *New Snippet*, you will see that the code for selection is automatically entered in the *Insert Code* box. This makes adding a block of code a very quick process. However, in this case, we want to enter our own function, so delete anything that is already written in the *Insert Code* box. Instead, enter:

```
<?php phpinfo(); ?>
```

The last option to select is whether the code to insert is active in Design view or Code view. For this example, choose *Code*.

Click *OK* to store the snippet.

Your snippet will now be shown in the snippets directory tree. Since it's one of our own custom snippets, we'll make our own folder for it.

Right-click at the root of the directory (next to *Name*), and choose *New Folder*. Call the folder PHP, and then drag your *phpinfo* snippet into the new *PHP* folder.

We can just as easily create a new snippet that wraps around a block of code. Imagine that we have two PHP functions that print the HTML for the page header and page footer. We want to be able to create the body of the page, and then apply a snippet that adds the `print_header()` function at the top, above the body, and the `print_footer()` function below the body.

Create a new snippet, by pressing the *New Snippet* button. Use `Format Page` for its name, and select *Wrap Selection*. Enter the following in the *Insert Before* box:

```
<?php print_header(); ?>
```

and this in the *Insert After* box:

```
<?php print_footer(); ?>
```

The Snippet dialog box should look similar to the one below.

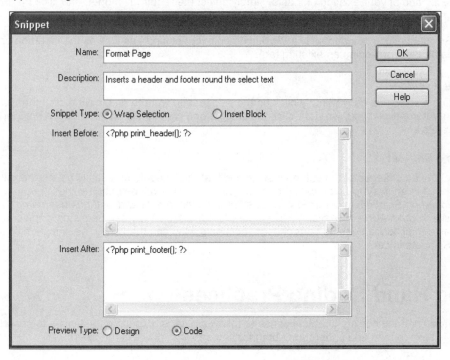

Click *OK* to add the snippet.

Now you can select your page body, and insert this *Format Page* snippet. It will automatically wrap the code above, around your selection.

Inserting your New Snippet

We're now going to insert our snippet into our code.

Switch into Code view, and place the insertion point between the `<body></body>` tags.

Double-click *phpinfo* in the *PHP* folder and the code snippet will be inserted. Alternatively you can click *phpinfo* once to select it, and then click the *Insert* button on the Snippets panel.

You will see that your code snippet:

```
<?php phpinfo(); ?>
```

has been inserted into the code.

Obviously this is only a very simple example, but larger and more complicated code blocks can be inserted just as easily.

Over time, the Snippets panel will become more and more useful as you build up a library of all your frequently used blocks of code.

Editing an Existing Snippet

To modify one of your existing snippets, simply select the required snippet, and click the *Edit Snippet* button which is one of those at the bottom right of the Snippets panel.

The Snippets dialog box appears, and you can edit your snippet, as well as the insertion options (as a code block, or wrapping an existing tag).

Deleting a Snippet

Deleting a snippet is easy. Simply click on the snippet you want to delete, and click the *Remove* button. Alternatively, you can right-click the snippet and choose *Delete*, or select a snippet and press the *Delete* key.

Sharing a Snippet

One of the advantages of the snippets system is that the snippets can easily be shared. All snippets are stored in an easy-to-find location on your hard disk. This will be either in the *Configuration\Snippets* folder or in Windows 2000 in *Documents and Settings\username\Application Data\Macromedia\Dreamweaver MX\Configuration\Snippets*. They can be simply copied to disk, or sent as e-mail attachments to your chosen recipients, who can then copy the snippet files into their own Snippets folder.

Good Hand Coding Practices

When you're hand coding, it makes sense to follow a number of simple guidelines to ensure your code is easy to read and understand, both for yourself and others in the future.

Hand Coding within Dreamweaver MX

It's worth spending a little extra time laying your code out neatly and adding comments – you'll really appreciate it when you have to go through the code again to add a function in the future.

In this section we'll be looking at how the built-in features of Dreamweaver MX can help you to create nicely laid out and easily readable code.

Code Options

When you are in Code view, or using the Code inspector, at the top of the Code window is the *View Options* button. If you are unsure which button it is, hold your mouse cursor over each button in turn, and their names will be displayed.

This menu contains the following options:

- **Word Wrap** – Turns on word wrapping within the Code window. It's useful for viewing long lines of code.

- **Line Numbers** – This option shows line numbers next to your code. This makes debugging much easier, as the line number is usually displayed in the error message, and you can go straight to it in Dreamweaver MX.

- **Highlight Invalid HTML** – Turning on this option shows any invalid HTML with a highlight, so you can quickly see any problems in your HTML code.

- **Syntax Coloring** – This feature changes the text color of different objects within your code, and is useful for debugging. The object colors are determined by the options set in the Preferences menu, which we talked about earlier in this chapter.

- **Auto Indent** – This turns on auto indenting of the code that Dreamweaver MX inserts, and makes the code easier to read and better laid out.

Indenting Code

Indenting code makes it more readable, and easier to see the code structure. For example, look at the code below without indentation:

```
<?php
if($myresult > 1)
{
if ($myresult < 5)
echo ("small");
if ($myresult > 5 AND $myresult < 10)
echo ("medium");
if ($mtresult >= 10)
echo ("large");
}
?>
```

The same code, with indentation, is easier to read:

```php
<?php
  if($myresult > 1)
  {
    if ($myresult < 5)
      echo ("small");
    if ($myresult > 5 AND $myresult < 10)
      echo ("medium");
    if ($mtresult >= 10)
      echo ("large");
  }
?>
```

You can now see that the code is one `if` statement, the contents of which are run if the variable `$myresult` has a value greater than 1. In that case, the value of `$myresult` is checked to see if it is less than 5, between 5 and 10, or greater than or equal to 10, in which case the text *small*, *medium*, or *large* is printed to the page. It's much easier to understand the program flow.

You can either indent code yourself, using the *Tab* key, or can use the Dreamweaver MX Indent command, by selecting *Edit -> Indent Code* from the main menu bar. (Alternatively, you can use the keyboard shortcut *Ctrl + Shift + >*.)

To outdent code (which is the opposite of indenting – it moves the line to the left instead of the right), you should select *Edit -> Outdent Code* from the main menu bar. Again there is a keyboard shortcut: *Ctrl + Shift + <*.

Commenting Your Code

When you are typing your code, it's always best to add comments here and there, to explain how the code works. If someone else has to work on the code in the future, or indeed if you have to add a function to the code in six months' time, it makes the code much easier to go back to and understand. You don't have to go into minute detail, but write a short accurate description of what the code is doing, or what type of data a function expects, for example.

Comments are ignored by the PHP engine – they are only there to make the code easier to understand for the programmer, and anyone else who has to work on the code in the future.

In PHP, there are three types of comments you can use in your code.

These are:

- Hash marks (#)

- Double forward slashes (//)

- Multi-line comments (/* */)

Hash Marks

Hash marks are usually used to head sections of code, as they are very visible and easy to find in your code. The PHP engine ignores everything in the code from the hash mark to the end of the line, or the closing PHP tag, whichever happens first.

For example:

```
###############################
# Send Email confirming login details
###############################
```

Double Forward Slashes

Double forward slashes are used in exactly the same way as the hash marks above. For example:

```
///////////////////////////////////////////////////////
// Send Email confirming login details
///////////////////////////////////////////////////////
```

or to comment a single line of code:

```
// This is an example of a simple comment
```

Multi-Line Comments (/* */)

The /* and */ marks are used to delimit a comment when it spans more than one line. For example:

```
/*
    This is a comment spanning
    multiple lines.

    It makes the code easier to read, and can
    be as long as you like.
*/
```

When the page is run, everything between the opening tag (/*) and closing tag (*/) is ignored, including valid PHP code.

Naming Variables

It's worth mentioning the way you name variables here. It's handy when you're starting some PHP coding to create some rules for variable names, and then to use that convention all the way through the site.

For example, prefix the name of all variables that should contain text with `str`:

```
$strMessage
$strErrorDescription
```

For variables that should only hold numbers, use the prefix `val`:

```
$valAmount
$valDiscount
```

For all recordset parameters, use the prefix `rs`:

```
$rsName
$rsAge
```

Chapter 9

Sticking to such a naming convention makes the code much easier to follow and understand, and is extremely useful when debugging. When you're designing a site with others, make sure you all agree on your naming conventions before you start, so everyone uses the same method.

You will then be able to swap code with the other developers, and will all be able to understand the way the code functions.

Balancing Braces

Dreamweaver MX's *Balance Braces* option is extremely useful for checking your code. This option is available by either selecting *Edit > Balance Braces* on the main menu bar, or using the key combination *Ctrl + '*.

As the name suggests, this option scans your code, and checks that all tags or braces ({ }) are balanced. This is extremely useful when your code is complex and has many opening and closing braces.

Take the following code for example:

```php
<?php
function example()
{
    if($x==2)
    {
        if($y>3)
        {
            echo "Value added";
        }
    }
}
?>
```

This has three sets of braces, nested into one block of code.

If we are in Code view, and place the cursor to the right of the first brace, {, and then select the *Balance Braces option*, the code is highlighted as shown below:

```
 9
10  <?php
11  function example()
12  {
13      if($x==2)
14      {
15          if($y>3)
16          {
17              echo "Value added";
18          }
19      }
20  }
21  ?>
22
```

Notice that all the code between the opening brace and its closing brace is highlighted – this shows that all the opening and closing braces within those braces are balanced.

What happens if we missed a brace, as in the code below?

```php
<?php
function example()
{
  if($x==2)
  {
    if($y>3)
    {
      echo "Value added";
    }

}
?>
```

Again, place the cursor to the right of the first brace, and select *Balance Braces*. The area will be shown without highlighting, as shown below, indicating that the braces aren't balanced.

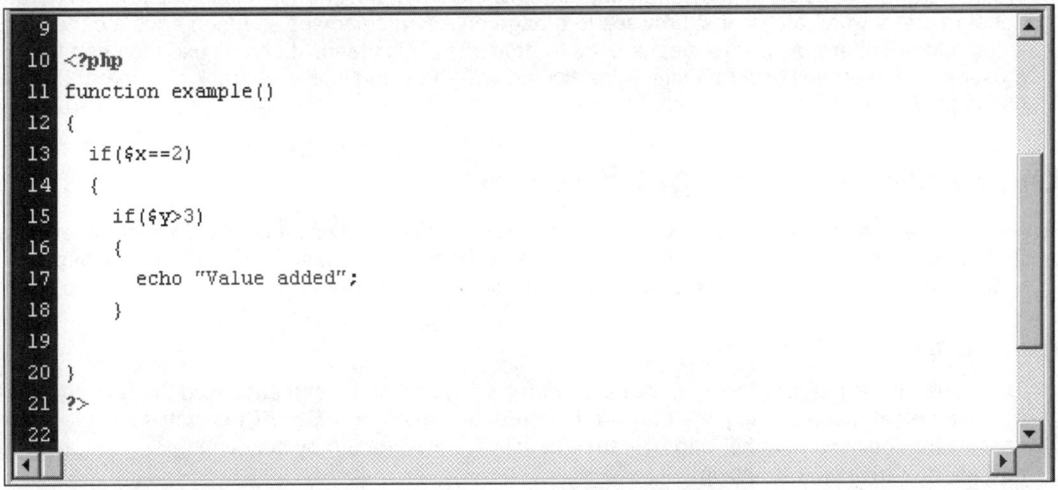

```
 9
10 <?php
11 function example()
12 {
13   if($x==2)
14   {
15     if($y>3)
16     {
17       echo "Value added";
18     }
19
20 }
21 ?>
22
```

If you now start with the cursor to the right of the innermost brace, after `if($y>3)`, you can work outwards quickly by repeatedly using the key combination *Ctrl + '*, until you come to the unbalanced brace. You can then correct the problem, by adding a closing brace. This is extremely useful, as it saves all the time you would have spent manually reading through the code, trying to find out the braces that were unbalanced.

Chapter 9

Practical Example – Login System for Dreamweaver Hotel

Now that we've looked at the new hand-coding features of Dreamweaver MX, we're going to create a login system, so that the staff at the Dreamweaver Hotel can log in and view client bookings.

In this example, we're going to hand code some PHP to perform the following actions:

- Read in the values from a custom-made login form.
- Verify the correct type of data is contained in the form values.
- Encrypt the password.
- Verify the username and encrypted password against the values stored in the database.
- Display either a failure notice or a success notice to the user, and set a session containing the user's status.

We'll be using the idea of a session throughout this example, so it needs a little explanation here. A **session** starts when a user first browses to a page on a particular web site, and ends a certain length of time after they last request a page for that site. This means it can be used to keep track of a user throughout their visit to a site. In particular, we'll be using it to keep track of whether the user has logged in or not.

Overview of Our Login System

Listed below are the login pages we are going to be creating, and how they link to each other. The first three pages are to be stored in a folder called *admin* in the root site directory. The final page is to be stored in a folder called *include*, also in the root site directory.

login.php

This page allows users to log in. Only users with a valid username and password that are checked against the database can log in – they are then redirected to menu.php. Their status is saved in a session for checking on other pages. If their details are incorrect, they stay on the login.php page, and an error message is shown.

menu.php

This page shows a menu of options to users who have successfully logged in, and who have either "Staff" or "Admin" status. It redirects any non-logged in users back to the login.php page.

create_user.php

This page is linked to by menu.php, but can only be accessed by managers who have "Admin" status. It can be used to add a new user to the database, after validating the data and encrypting the user's password. It redirects any users with "Staff" status back to the menu.php page.

dreamweaver_hotel_admin.php

This is purely a PHP file; there is no HTML code. It contains our generic functions, which can be used on any page which has an include statement pointing to this file.

The Database Users Table

Our first step is to create a `users` table in the database, to hold the user details for the Dreamweaver Hotel staff.

Below is the structure for the `users` table:

Field Name	Field Type	Notes
ID	integer(8)	Primary Key, Auto increment
username	varchar(20)	Stores staff member's username
password	varchar(20)	Stores staff member's password
firstName	varchar(30)	Stores staff member's first name
lastName	varchar(30)	Stores staff member's last name
status	varchar(10)	Stores staff member's admin status

The SQL Query below will create this table when executed:

```
CREATE TABLE 'users' (
'ID' INT(8) NOT NULL AUTO_INCREMENT PRIMARY KEY,
'username' VARCHAR(20) NOT NULL,
'password' VARCHAR(20) NOT NULL,
'firstName' VARCHAR(30) NOT NULL,
'lastName' VARCHAR(30) NOT NULL,
'status' VARCHAR(10) NOT NULL
);
```

You can create the table through the MySQL command line, or with your favorite MySQL Administration tool.

Create Users Page – The Layout

The first page we'll create is a page to add users to the `users` table, which we'll call `create_users.php`. It contains the following form fields:

```
<form name="createuser" method="post" action="<?php echo($PHP_SELF) ?>">
   <input name="firstName" type="text" id="firstName" maxlength="30">
   <input name="lastName" type="text" id="lastName" maxlength="30">
   <input name="username" type="text" id="username" maxlength="20">
   <input name="password" type="password" id="password" maxlength="20">
   <input name="confirmpassword" type="password" id="confirmpassword"
          maxlength="20">
```

```
    <select name="status" id="status">
      <option value="Admin">Admin</option>
      <option value="Staff" selected>Staff</option>
    </select>
    <input type="submit" name="Submit" value="Create User">
</form>
```

Look at the `action` attribute for the `<form>` element above, and you'll see it's set to:

```
<?php echo($PHP_SELF) ?>
```

`$PHP_SELF` is one of the built-in PHP variables. When the code is run, it is replaced with the location of the current page. We use this because we want the form to submit the data back to the same page. If in future we change the location of this page, the code will still work with no changes necessary.

Lay the form out in a similar manner to the form below, using the template for the Dreamweaver Hotel developed in Chapter 5:

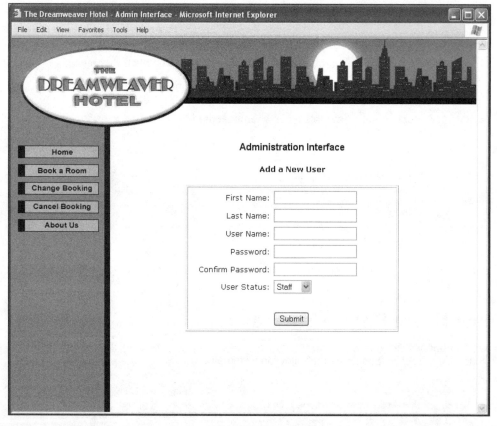

Save the page as `create_users.php`, and place it in a directory called *admin*, off the site root.

We now need to add the PHP code, which will make the page dynamic.

At first, we'll ignore the security checks so that we can use our `create_users.php` page to add our main admin record. We'll add security checks to it later.

Our first task is to create our PHP include file (`dreamweaver_hotel_admin.php`) containing custom functions we are going to use to validate various aspects of the form data.

These are all generic functions that can be used on any site, rather than being specially written for our Hotel Admin system. This is an area where the Snippets panel really becomes useful, as over time you can build a library of such PHP functions, and then just insert the snippets you're going to need into your include file.

Using an include file containing generic functions keeps your page neater, and easier to read and debug. All specific functions, which are hard coded to do a specific job on that page only, can be stored in the page code, keeping them separate from the generic functions.

The PHP Include File

Our include file will be called `dreamweaver_hotel_admin.php`, and will be stored in a directory called *include*, which is in the site root.

The include file contains many functions, each listed one after the other. We'll discuss each of these functions separately to avoid confusion.

trim_data()

```
function trim_data($formdata)
{
  // Trim any leading or trailing spaces
  // $formdata = Form Data Array
  foreach($formdata as $key => $value)
  {
    $key = trim($key);
    $value = trim($value);
  }
  return $formdata;
}
```

This function is passed an array of form data. It works through this array, and trims any leading or trailing spaces from both the key to the array and the value stored at that key. The function returns the trimmed array.

check_form()

```
function check_form($formdata)
{
  // Check all fields are filled in
  // $formdata = Form Data Array
  foreach ($formdata as $key => $value)
  {
    if (!isset($key) || $value == "" )
    return false;
  }
  return true;
}
```

When passed an array of the form data, this function works through each form field checking that the value in the array is not empty for every key in the array that has been set.

If any fields are left blank, the function returns `false`, otherwise the function returns `true`.

check_password_length()

```
function check_password_length($formdata, $password, $minlen)
{
  // Check that password is required length
  // $formdata = Form Data Array
  // $password = Name of password field
  // $minlen = Minimum number of password characters
  if (strlen($formdata[$password]) < $minlen)
    return false;
  else
    return true;
}
```

This function is passed an array containing the form data, the name of the password field, and the minimum number of password characters allowed. If the password is less than the minimum number of characters allowed, then the function returns `false`, otherwise it returns `true`.

confirm_password()

```
function confirm_password($formdata, $password1, $password2)
{
  // Check that two passwords given match
  // $formdata = Form Data Array
  // $password1 = Name of first password field
  // $password2 = Name of second password field

  if ($formdata[$password1] === $formdata[$password2])
    return true;
  else
    return false;
}
```

This function is passed an array of form data, and the names of both the password, and the confirm password field. It then checks that both password fields are identical, and returns `true` if they are, and `false` if they are not.

check_unique()

```
function check_unique($formvalue, $db, $dbhost, $dbuser, $dbpassword, $table, $field)
{
  // Checks a table in a database, to see if passed value already exists
  // $formvalue = Value you are checking to see whether it is unique
  // $db = mySQL Database Name
  // $dbhost = mySQL Server address, for example localhost
  // $dbuser = mySQL user name
  // $dbpassword = mySQL password
  // $table = mySQL Table to search
  // $field = mySQL Field to search
```

```php
    $error = "";
    
    // Connect to the mySQL Server
    $mysql = mysql_connect($dbhost, $dbuser, $dbpassword);
    if(!$mysql)
    {
      $error = "Cannot connect to Database Host";
      return($error);
    }
    
    // Open the mySQL Database
    $mysqldb = mysql_select_db($db);
    if(!$mysqldb)
    {
      $error = "Cannot open Database";
      return($error);
    }
    
    // Query Table to see if $formvalue is unique
    $myquery = "SELECT * FROM $table WHERE $field = '$formvalue'";
    $result = mysql_query($myquery);
    if (!$result)
    {
      $error = "Cannot run Query";
      return($error);
    }
    
    // Get number of Records found, should be 0 if $formvalue is unique
    $unique = mysql_num_rows($result);
    if ($unique > 0)
    {
      $error = $formvalue. " already in use";
      return($error);
    }
    
    // Return true if $formvalue is unique
    return("true");
}
```

This is the last, and the longest, function in our include file. The purpose of the function is to take the form value that is passed to it and check it against a field in a table in the database, to see if the value already exists or not. For example, we'll be using this function to check whether an entered username already exists in the database.

The function is passed the form value, the database name, the database host, the database username and password, and the field and table names you wish to check. The function then connects to the database, and opens the table with a WHERE clause that searches for the passed form value in the passed field. It then checks to see if any records are returned from the database.

If there are no records returned, the function returns true, and the value will be unique when added to the database. If a record is returned, the value will not be unique, so the function returns an error message. If there are any errors connecting to the database, these are also returned by the function.

You can see that any of the functions we've described above could be used in any site without changes. It's a good idea to make your functions generic, because you'll soon end up with a library of code, which will save you from having to waste time rewriting code in the future. A good idea would be to add the functions to the Snippets panel (as detailed earlier in the chapter), allowing you to quickly insert them into a PHP include file in the future.

Create Users Page – Adding the Code

We're now going to add the PHP code to the create users page (`create_users.php`) we started earlier, to make the page validate the form data and insert the new user into the `users` table.

Switch to Code view, and scroll to the top of the page. The first line to add goes before the `<HTML>` tag – it includes our file `dreamweaver_hotel_admin.php`.

```
<?php include("../include/dreamweaver_hotel_admin.php"); ?>
```

We'll now create three more pieces of PHP code, that are added after this include line.

insert_data()

First, we create a function that inserts our form data into the `users` table.

```
<?php
function insert_data($formdata)
{
  // Insert Data into users table
  // $formdata = form array

  // set up database connection variables
  $error = "";
  $myhost = "localhost";
  $myuser = "php";
  $mypass = "password";
  $mydb = "php";

  // set up data to insert
  $firstName = $formdata['firstName'];
  $lastName = $formdata['lastName'];
  $username = $formdata['username'];
  $password = $formdata['password'];
  $status = $formdata['status'];

  // encrypt the password using the key "DWMXPHP"
  $password = crypt($password,"DWMXPHP");

  // connect to mySQL server
  $mysql = mysql_connect($myhost, $myuser, $mypass);
  if (!$mysql)
  {
    $error = "Cannot connect to mySQL server";
    return($error);
  }

  // Connect to Database
  $mysqldb = mysql_select_db($mydb, $mysql);
```

```
    if (!$mysqldb)
    {
      $error = "Cannot open database";
      return($error);
    }

    // Insert Data
    $myquery = "INSERT INTO users ( firstName, lastName, username, password, "
    $myquery .= "status) VALUES ('$firstName', '$lastName', '$username', "
    $myquery .= "'$password', '$status')";
    $result = mysql_query($myquery, $mysql);
    if (!$result)
    {
      $error = "Cannot run Query";
      return $error;
    }

    // Return True if record written successfully
    return("true");
}
?>
```

This function takes the data from the form array that's passed to it, and puts the values into variables. It then encrypts the password, using the key "DWMXPHP", and this encrypted value is stored in the database. crypt() is a one-way hash function built into PHP, which means that once the data is encrypted, it can never be unencrypted again. To check against it, we encrypt the value to test with the same key, and if the two encrypted values match, we know the value is correct.

Next, we connect to the MySQL database, and insert the user data into the users table. The query returns true if the record is inserted correctly, otherwise it returns a relevant error message.

verify_data($formdata)

This next function validates the user data entered in the form on the page. If it is validated successfully, it calls the insert_data() function described above.

```
<?php
function verify_data($formdata)
{
  // This function uses the functions in the include file,
  // and uses them to validate various aspects of the form.
  // If validation fails, it returns $error, the appropriate error message
  // If validation suceeds, return true
  $error = "";
  $form_data = trim_data($formdata);
  $user = $form_data['username'];

  // check all form fields are filled in
  if (!check_form($form_data))
```

```php
  {
    $error="All Form Fields must be filled in";
    return($error);
  }

  // check password and confirmation password match
  if (!confirm_password($form_data, 'password', 'confirmpassword'))
  {
    $error = "Password and Confirm Password do not match";
    return($error);
  }

  // check length of password
  if (!check_password_length($form_data, 'password', 5))
  {
    $error = "Password should be 5 characters or more";
    return($error);
  }

  // check that username is unique
  $check = check_unique($user, 'php', 'localhost' , 'php', '20012001', 'users', 'username');
  if ($check != "true")
  {
    $error = "Username is already in use, select another";
    return($error);
  }

  // if validated successfully, insert data into table
  $insert_check = insert_data($formdata);

  // if error with insertion, return error
  if ($insert_check != "true")
    return($insert_check);

  // form validated and record inserted successfully
  return("");
}
?>
```

This function uses the validation functions defined in our include file to verify that all the fields are filled in, that the password and confirmation password match, that the length of the password is correct, and that the chosen username is unique.

If all these validations are successful, the function calls the `insert_data()` function defined above, which inserts our user record into the `users` table. If everything is successful, the function returns nothing; otherwise the function returns the relevant error message.

Using the Functions

The last piece of code for this section is as follows:

```php
<?php
  // Main Code - Verifies the form data, and inserts into
  // the users table in the Database
  if($Submit=="Create User"){
    $error = verify_data($HTTP_POST_VARS);
    if ($error == "")
      $success = "User inserted successfully";
  }
?>
```

This code is run every time the page is loaded. First, it checks to see if the variable `$Submit` is equal to "Create User". If it is, the form data in the variable `$HTTP_POST_VARS` is passed to our `verify_data()` function, as defined above.

The variable `$Submit` will only equal "Create User" if the form has been submitted – Submit is the name of the submit button, and "Create User" is the label for the button. If you have changed either of these, you will need to change them in the code here as well.

If the form has been submitted, it will run the `verify_data()` function, which if successful, will call the `insert_data()` function to insert the user details into the database.

The values of two variables, `$error` and `$success`, are now set in such a way that one has a value and one is empty. If an error is returned by the `verify_data()` function, then `$error` has a value, and `$success` is empty. If no errors are returned, `$error` will be empty, and `$success` will be set to "User inserted successfully".

We can place the two variables onto the page above the form using:

```php
<?php echo($error); ?>
<?php echo($success); ?>
```

When a user first visits the page, nothing will be displayed, since both variables are empty. However, once the form has been submitted and the page is redisplayed, one of the two messages will be shown – either an error message or the success message.

Using the Page

We're now going to use this page, to create an "Admin"-level user. Upload the page to your server (along with the include file), and then load the page in your web browser. Enter your name, a username, and password. Select *Admin* from the status dropdown, and click *Submit*.

You should get a success message returned. If not, you will have to go back and check over your code. View the `users` table, and you should be able to see your new record. Look at the password field, and you will see it has been encrypted.

At the moment, anybody can access the page and create a new user. Obviously, this isn't something we want, so we will return to this page later, and add some more code, so that only "Admin"-level users can use the page.

Chapter 9

The Login Page

The login page is a simple page that contains a table with a username and password field.

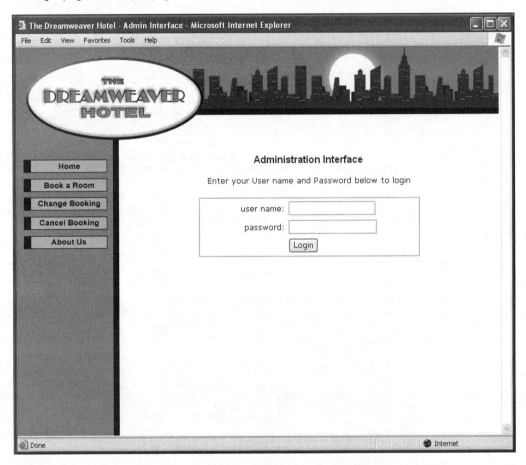

The details for the form are as follows:

```
<form name="form1" method="post" action="<?php echo($PHP_SELF) ?>">
   <input name="username" type="text" id="username" maxlength="20">
   <input name="password" type="password" id="password" maxlength="20">
   <input type="submit" name="Submit" value="Login">
</form>
```

Note that, like the `create_user.php` page, this page submits back to itself using the `$PHP_SELF` variable.

Layout the page as above using the template for the Dreamweaver Hotel site, and save the page as `login.php` in the *admin* folder.

Hand Coding within Dreamweaver MX

Next we'll add the code that checks the login details against the database. Change into Code view, and scroll to the top of the page. On the first line, before the `<HTML>` tag, we include the PHP file `dreamweaver_hotel_admin.php`, which we created earlier.

```php
<?php include("../include/dreamweaver_hotel_admin.php"); ?>
```

Again, we'll create two more pieces of PHP code to be added below this include file line.

check_login()

We'll first add a function to check the user details entered against those stored in the table.

```php
<?php
function check_login($formdata)
{
  // This section queries the users table, and searches for
  // the username and password that were supplied. If the
  // user is not found, an error is returned. If the user
  // details are correct the users status is returned.

  // Set up MySQL Connection variables (change these to your own)
  $dbhost = "localhost";
  $dbuser = "username";
  $dbpassword = "password";
  $db = "databasename";

  // Get Form Data
  $form_data = trim_data($formdata);
  $user = $form_data['username'];
  $password = $form_data['password'];

  // Connect to the mySQL Server
  $mysql = mysql_connect($dbhost, $dbuser, $dbpassword);
  if(!$mysql)
  {
    $error = "Cannot connect to Database Host";
    return($error);
  }

  // Open the mySQL Database
  $mysqldb = mysql_select_db($db);
  if(!$mysqldb)
  {
    $error = "Cannot open Database";
    return($error);
  }

  // Query Database with username and encrypted password
  $myquery = "SELECT * FROM users WHERE username = '" . $user;
  $myquery .= "' AND password = '" . crypt($password,"DWMXPHP") . "'";
```

```
  $result = mysql_query($myquery);
  if (!$result)
  {
    $error = "Cannot run Query";
    return($error);
  }

  // Check that we have a record returned
  $numRows = mysql_num_rows($result);
  if ($numRows < 1)
  {
    $error = "User name or password not recognised";
    return($error);
  }

  // Get user status from returned record
  $userRecord = mysql_fetch_array($result);
  $status = $userRecord["status"];
  return($status);
}
?>
```

The first section of this function sets up the database connection variables. Next, the form data array, which is passed to the function, is run though the `trim_data()` function we created earlier in the include file `dreamweaver_hotel_admin.php`.

The function then connects to the MySQL server, and opens the database. It then queries the database with the following SQL statement:

```
SELECT * FROM users WHERE username = ' " . $user . " ' AND
password = ' " . crypt($password,"DWMXPHP") . " ' "
```

Recall that when we create a user, we use the PHP `crypt()` function to encrypt the password with the key `"DWMXPHP"`, and it was the encrypted password that we stored in the database.

As we mentioned earlier, `crypt()` is a one-way hash function – once the original data is encrypted it is lost. This doesn't cause us a problem, because encrypting data with the same key will produce the same result. By encrypting the provided password with the key `"DWMXPHP"`, if the two passwords are the same, the encrypted user password will match the encrypted password stored in the database.

Next, we check the query has returned a record. If it hasn't, it means that the username or password are invalid, and we return this error.

If a record has been found, then the username and password provided were correct, and the user's status (either "Admin" or "Staff") is returned.

Using the Functions

The main code for the page is shown below:

```php
<?php
// This section is only run when the form has been submitted
if($Submit=="Login")
{
  session_start();

  // Check whether the login details are correct, and put
  // the user status into a session variable.
  $statusCheck = check_login($HTTP_POST_VARS);
  if ($statusCheck == "Admin" || $statusCheck == "Staff")
  {
    session_register("statusCheck");
    header("Location: menu.php");
  }
}
?>
```

This code is only run if the form has been submitted, in which case the variable `$Submit` has the value `"Login"`.

We then use the PHP function `session_start()` to begin a session, which we can use to store the user's status.

We next run the `check_login()` function we created earlier in this page, and pass it the form values, using the PHP variable `$HTTP_POST_VARS`. This function returns the user status (Admin or Staff) if their username and password are correct; otherwise an error message is returned. We store the result of the function in the variable `$statusCheck`.

Next, we check to see if `$statusCheck` contains `"Admin"` or `"Staff"`, which means the login was successful. If so, we put the user's status into a session, which will allow their status to be saved and checked against as they change pages. Then we use the PHP `header()` function to redirect the user to the administration menu page, `menu.php`. Note, you can only use the PHP `header()` function if the header hasn't already been written by the browser. Keeping this code above the `<HTML>` tag ensures that the `header()` function can be used successfully, as the headers haven't been written yet.

If the `check_login()` function returns an error, then the session won't be set, and the page continues to load as normal.

You can now add the following code to your page, above the login form:

```php
<?php echo($statusCheck) ?>
```

When the user first goes to the login page, this will show nothing since the `$statusCheck` variable will be empty. `$statusCheck` will only have a value once the user has submitted the login form, and the `check_login()` function has run. As this is not yet the case `$statusCheck` will contain the error message.

The Menu Page

The menu page is called `menu.php`. It is this page that users are redirected to once they have successfully logged in. For this example, it will contain three links, as shown in the screenshot below:

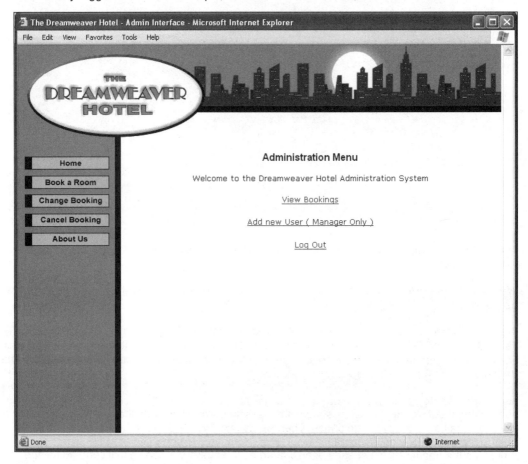

- **View Bookings**

    View Bookings should link to a page that will allow the user to view the various bookings that have been made. We will not actually be creating this page in this example.

- **Add New User (Manager Only)**

    This link will point to the `create_user.php` page we created earlier.

- **Log Out**

    This link takes the user back to the `menu.php` page, but with a query string parameter to tell the `menu.php` page that the user wants to log out. The `href` of the link is:
    `menu.php?action=logout`

Hand Coding within Dreamweaver MX

Lay out a page with such links using the Dreamweaver Hotel template. Save it as menu.php in the *admin* folder.

The Menu PHP Code

Switch into Code view, and go to the top of the menu.php code, above the <HTML> tag.

The first segment of code we need to add is to start session support for the page. We then need to check the user has a session set, which can only happen if they have logged in correctly. If the user hasn't got a valid session, they are redirected back to the login page.

```
<?php
  session_start();
  // If no session is set, redirect to login.php
  if (!session_is_registered("statusCheck"))
    header("Location: login.php");
?>
```

This segment of code needs to be inserted at the top of every page you wish to protect with the login system. Because the session is checked, it means that people who know the name of the page cannot bypass the protection by pointing the browser manually to that page.

We have one more segment of code to add to this page, and that is to log the user out. When the *Log Out* link is clicked, it sends the browser to the URL menu.php?action=logout. We modify the code block above, and add some code to handle the logout. Change the code above to read:

```
<?php
  session_start();
  // If the user logs out, destroy their session
  if($action=="logout"){
    session_unregister("statusCheck");
    session_destroy();
  }
  // If no session is set, redirect to login.php
  if (!session_is_registered("statusCheck"))
    header("Location: login.php");
?>
```

When the extra code we inserted above is run, it checks to see if the $action variable contains the value "logout", that is if the page is called through the *Log Out* link. It then deregisters and destroys the statusCheck session.

The original code is then run, and because a session is no longer set the user is redirected to the login.php page – effectively, they are logged out.

Create Users Page – Security

We now need to go back to the create users page, create_users.php. Open the page, and switch into Code view.

Earlier in this chapter, when we created this page, we didn't set any security, which meant that any user could log in and create a user. Obviously, we don't want this happening: we need to restrict ordinary staff (who have "Staff" status) from entering the page, but allow all managers (who have "Admin" status) to enter.

We're going to add some code to check the status value in the session variable `statusCheck`, and redirect the user back to the menu page if they only have "Staff" status. The page will load normally if the user has "Admin" status.

Go the top of the code, and you'll see the following line, which adds our extra functions stored in `dreamweaver_hotel_admin.php` to the code.

```
<?php include("../include/dreamweaver_hotel_admin.php"); ?>
```

Just after this line add the following block of code:

```
<?php
  session_start();
  // Check the Users status, if not Admin level
  // redirect back to the menu.php page
  if ($statusCheck != "Admin")
    header("Location: menu.php");
?>
```

This code can be placed on any page that needs protecting so that only "Admin" status users can use it. As the code uses the PHP `header()` function to redirect the user's browser, it is important that there is no "whitespace" (spaces or line breaks) sent to the browser before the code is executed. Make sure there are no spaces between your blocks of PHP code.

We've now completed the login section, so upload it to your server and you can see the pages in action.

Obviously, this is a very basic system, but it can be expanded on and used as a skeleton to make more complicated login systems, with more levels of authorization. This system can protect a large number of pages easily, simply by adding the relevant block of code to the top of the page, depending on which level of access is required.

Summary

In this chapter we've taken a brief look at PHP hand coding. This should make the code that Dreamweaver MX produces easier to understand, and help you along the way to create your own PHP code.

We also looked at why you might need to hand code within Dreamweaver MX, and how to switch to Code view or open the Code inspector. We've discussed the Preferences, which affect the way your code is displayed, and the new hand coding tools, which make their debut in Dreamweaver MX.

We next looked at good code practices for hand coding, to make your code neater and easier to follow, and discussed the various features, like indenting and commenting, that you can use.

In the last section, we created a user login system using hand coding, which verified a username and encrypted password against those stored in a database and set the user's status to one of two levels. We looked at putting generic functions in an include file, and how to add different levels of protection to your pages, by inserting a small code block at the top of the page.

In the next chapter, we're going to look at how to construct our own server behaviors, to make automating common tasks in Dreamweaver MX easier.

Hand Coding within Dreamweaver MX

10

- Predefined server behaviors
- Building your own server behaviors
- Designing an interface for your server behaviors

Author: Bruno Mairlot

The Server Behavior Builder

In the previous chapter, we discovered that even with all the powerful tools that Dreamweaver provides, you might be confronted with a situation where the code you need is not available in the Server Behavior menu items. What can we do in this situation? The quick solution is to go for hand coding the part of the script you need. However, if you were to find yourself writing hand-written code often to carry out a task, wouldn't it be great if we could build our own server behaviors to automate that task? Luckily, Dreamweaver MX allows us to do just that with a tool called the **Server Behavior Builder**.

The Server Behavior Builder is an interface that will let you write some code, add some **parameters** to make the code flexible, and build a user interface for those parameters quickly. In this chapter, we'll look at how to use it to create your own server behaviors. With a little work these server behaviors can be packaged in a file format that will allow you to share them with other Dreamweaver users to help them make Dreamweaver more useful.

What Is the Server Behavior Builder?

The Server Behavior Builder, also called **SBB**, is a tool that will let you design your own Server Behavior. It was first introduced in Dreamweaver UltraDev 4 and has been improved within Dreamweaver MX.

The Server Behavior Builder allows you to create brand-new server behaviors, and also allows you to edit existing ones.

> A large amount of documentation available for the Server Behavior Builder uses the following abbreviations: **SB** for server behavior and **SBB** for Server Behavior Builder.

The Predefined Server Behaviors

Dreamweaver MX comes with a series of predefined server behaviors. In the previous chapters we've already had a look at some of them.

The Server Behavior interface can be found in the Application panel group, under the *Server Behaviors* tab:

Recordset

We've already had a look at this server behavior in the previous chapters. It is one of the most important server behaviors, as it's the one that runs queries on our databases and allows us to retrieve information from them.

Repeat Region

The Repeat Region server behavior is used for repeating selected regions in your document. We saw an example of this in action at the end of Chapter 8.

Recordset Paging

Under *Recordset Paging* is a set of server behaviors for placing navigation elements in your document. They are mainly used in conjunction with a Repeat Region server behavior when we haven't specified to repeat all records, so we can split the results up into pages and move between them using this server behavior.

The following are the Recordset Paging server behaviors:

- Move to first page
- Move to last page
- Move to previous page
- Move to next page

The Server Behavior Builder

Show Region

Under *Show Region* is a set of server behaviors that will let you hide or show some part of the document, depending on the values contained in the recordset. Note that these predefined server behaviors will only work if we have a recordset defined for the document.

The following are the Show Region server behaviors:

- SHOW IF RECORDSET IS EMPTY
- SHOW IF RECORDSET IS NOT EMPTY
- SHOW IF FIRST PAGE
- SHOW IF NOT FIRST PAGE
- SHOW IF LAST PAGE
- SHOW IF NOT LAST PAGE

These server behaviors can be used in conjunction with the Recordset Paging and Display Record Count behaviors to create a fully featured way for the user to navigate around the recordset.

Display Record Count

Under *Display Record Count* is a set of server behaviors that will allow you to give the user an indication of where they are in the recordset when used with the Recordset Paging server behavior.

The Display Record Count server behaviors are as follows:

- Display Starting Record Number
- Display Ending Record Number
- Display Total Record Count

Dynamic Text

Dynamic Text is the second most useful server behavior after the Recordset behavior, but generally we don't use it from the Server Behaviors menu. The Bindings panel contains all of the dynamic elements that you can place into your document. When you place a dynamic element from the Bindings panel into your document, Dreamweaver will create a Dynamic Text server behavior that will be added into the Server Behavior panel.

Insert, Update, and Delete Record

These server behaviors allow you to modify the data in your recordset. See Chapter 6 for an in-depth explanation of these server behaviors.

Dynamic Form Elements

Dynamic Form elements allow you to construct a user interface dynamically with data from the recordset, as well as with Bindings variables.

When To Use the Server Behavior Builder

Generally, it's a good idea to create your own server behavior if the following two criteria are met:

- The goal you want to achieve with a piece of PHP code is not present on the predefined list of server behaviors.
- You find that you are often writing the same kind of PHP code, with only a few things that change each time.

How To Build a Server Behavior

Building a simple server behavior is usually a pretty straightforward process. Building a very complex server behavior may require a different approach, but the Server Behavior Builder is very often a great step to begin with. After creating your server behavior, you will be able to modify it and make it more complex as you wish.

Here's the process we use to create a server behavior:

1. Start up the Server Behaviour Builder
2. Give a name to your server behavior
3. Create the code blocks and set up the parameters
4. Tell Dreamweaver where to position the code blocks in the page
5. Define the interface for the server behavior

If you remember from Chapter 8, where we created a search system, we introduced a little piece of code that gets the value of one variable, and then sets the value of another depending on some conditions. Let's create a server behavior that will do that for us.

Here's the code again:

```
<?php
    if($HTTP_POST_VARS["price_option"] == "above")
    {
        $pComp = ">";
    }
    else
    {
        $pComp = "<=";
    }
?>
```

This bit of code looks at what the user has selected from the drop-down menu for the price range (the possible values are `above` and `below`) and then sets the value of `$pComp` accordingly (either `>` or `<=`). In this chapter, we'll build a server behavior that will place that piece of code in our document, but make it flexible so we can change some parts of it.

The Server Behavior Builder

Starting the Server Behavior Builder

To start the Server Behavior Builder, select the Application panel group and open the *Server Behavior* tab. Click on the + button, and select the menu entry *New Server Behavior...*

This will pop up the following window:

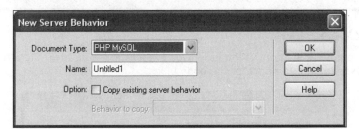

You will notice that the server behavior is dependent on the server model that you're currently working on. Make sure that the *Document Type* is *PHP MySQL*. When using the Server Behavior Builder, you must define the correct Document Type because Dreamweaver will only show the Server Behaviors available for that type of document.

This window will also ask you for a name for your server behavior. Let's call it "*Set Variable on Form Value*". On this interface you can also choose to create your server behavior by copying an already existing server behavior. For now, leave that checkbox unchecked – we'll take a look at it later. Click *OK* to proceed to the main window of the Server Behavior Builder.

The Code Blocks

The main window of the Server Behavior Builder is where you are going to specify almost all features of our new server behavior. The first thing you should do is to switch on the *Advanced* button to be able to design our server behavior with the advanced interface. This is because we need to see some of the options that would otherwise be hidden. The window should now look like this:

Chapter 10

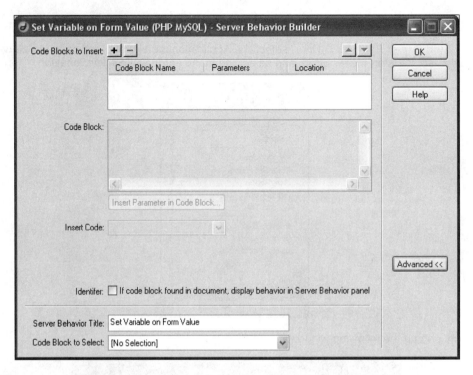

Inserting a Code Block

Click on the + button at the right of the label *Code Blocks to Insert:* to create a new code block. You will be asked to enter a name for the code block.

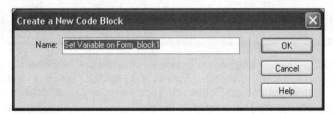

Dreamweaver will suggest a code block name that is made from your server behavior's name and a block number. It's usually best to go with Dreamweaver's suggestion. Click *OK* and we're taken back to the main window:

The Server Behavior Builder

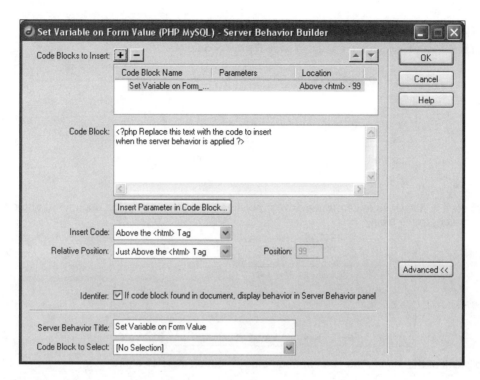

The Server Behavior Builder Interface Explained

You can now see that some parts of the interface that were previously grayed out are now available for us to use. Let's have a look at what they do before we continue with our example.

Code Block List

A code block is a piece of code that you want to be inserted by the server behavior into the document. A server behavior can be made of multiple code blocks, because you might want different bits of code to be placed at different locations in the document. In our example, however, we'll only be using one code block

The code block list displays all of the code blocks present in your server behavior. Clicking on a code block enables us to edit its parameters and where it will be positioned in the document:

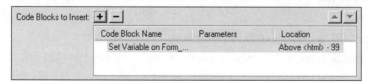

271

Code Block Area

This is where we can input the actual code for the code block:

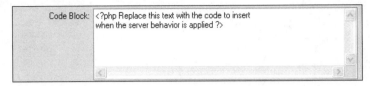

As you can see, all we have to do is replace the text with our own code.

Code Behavior

This section allows us to determine how to position the code block in the document, and add parameters to the block.

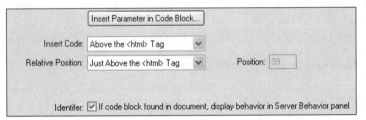

We'll look at the *Insert Parameter in Code Block...* button in detail shortly.

Below the button are drop-down menus that allow us to specify where the code block will be inserted in the document. The first menu gives us the following options:

- *Above the <html> tag*
- *Below the <html> tag*
- *Relative to a specific tag*
- *Relative to the selection*

Depending on which option you select, Dreamweaver will ask you to specify a relative position. This means, for example, that if we select the *Above the <html> tag* option, we will specify in the second drop-down menu that we want our code block to be placed at the beginning of the file, just before the recordsets, just after the recordsets, just above the `<html>` tag, or in a custom position.

Server Behavior Title and Code Block Selection

The server behavior title and Selection element are only shown when you are in advanced mode.

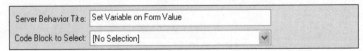

They will let you specify the title of your server behavior, which is what will be displayed in the server behavior list.

The Server Behavior Builder

Creating a Parameter for Your Server Behavior

The *Insert Parameter in Code Block...* button is fairly self-explanatory: it inserts a parameter into our code block! A parameter in the code block is simply a placeholder for a value that can vary each time the server behavior is applied to the document. In our example, we are trying to set the value of a variable value depending on the value of the `price_option` variable. Using a parameter instead of having the word `price_option` hard coded in the code block allows us to specify the variable we want to check for each time we use the server behavior on your document. In the code block, a parameter is represented by its name enclosed with the characters @@. This will be replaced by the value that you've given the parameter when the server behavior is applied to the document.

The power of a server behavior resides in its ability to have one or more parameters that are inserted into the PHP code. It's a very rare occurrence to have a server behavior with no parameters; a server behavior without parameters would probably be better as a snippet (refer back to Chapter 9 for more information about snippets).

To create a parameter in your code block, click on the *Insert Parameter in Code Block...* button, which will bring up the following window:

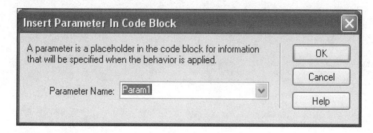

The term 'information' in the window is not really accurate, as the information that is inserted is a piece of valid PHP code.

Let's look at our example code again:

```
<?php
    if($HTTP_POST_VARS["price_option"] == "above")
    {
        $pComp = ">";
    }
    else
    {
        $pComp = "<=";
    }
?>
```

To make this code flexible, there are several elements that we'll replace with parameters:

- The form variable, which is `$HTTP_POST_VARS["price_option"]`

Chapter 10

- The value which is to be compared against the form variable, which is `above`
- The name of the variable that we want to contain the result, `$pComp`
- The values that this variable will take if the test is `true`, `>`
- The other value the variable can take if the test is `false`, `<=`

Click on *Cancel* to go back to the main Server Behavior Builder window, so that we can continue building our server behavior.

Continuing the Server Behavior Example

Now that we understand the Server Behavior Builder interface, let's continue with our example.

The Code Block

Select the first code block in the Code Block list, *Set Variable on Form_block1*, and enter the following code in the code content area:

```
<?php
    if(@@Form Variable@@ == "@@Form Value@@")
    {
        $@@New Variable Name@@ = "@@If Value@@";
    }
    else
    {
        $@@New Variable Name@@ = "@@Else Value@@";
    }
?>
```

This will create our code block. As you can see, we've used five different parameters to replace certain elements of the original code:

- `@@Form Variable@@`
- `@@Form Value@@`
- `@@New Variable Name@@`
- `@@If Value@@`
- `@@Else Value@@`

> A parameter in the code block is identified by the enclosing `@@` characters.

The Server Behavior Builder interface should now look like this:

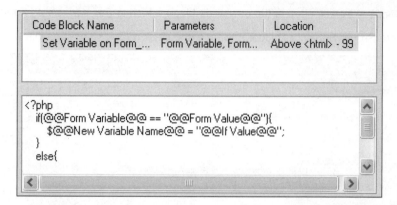

As you can see in the *Parameters* column, the server behavior builder has automatically noticed that we've added parameters to the code, even though we didn't use the *Insert Parameter in Code Block...* button. As long as they are enclosed by @@...@@ in the code, the Server Behavior Builder will recognize them as valid parameter names.

Code Block Positioning

Now, we still have to tell the Server Behavior Builder where to insert our code block into the document. As we want to be able to use the new variable in the recordset code, we will select as the position *Above the <html>* tag (because the recordsets are always positioned before the <html> tag in the PHP page) with the relative position *Just before the recordsets*.

Check the *Identifier* option. We want this option to be checked because we only have one code block in our server behavior. This option will let Dreamweaver know that if it finds that code block in your document, it will add the title of the server behavior to the Server Behavior panel.

Server Behavior Title

To set the server behavior's title, enter the following value into the *Server Behavior Title* box:

```
Set Variable on Form Value (@@New Variable Name@@,@@If Value@@,@@Else Value@@)
```

When the title is shown in the server behavior list for your document, it will be displayed with the values of the parameters. You can put in as many parameters as you like, but too many might make the name too long!

The Code Block to Select

For *Code Block to Select*, choose the only code block, which is *Set Variable on Form_block1*.

The complete Server Behavior Builder interface should now look something like this:

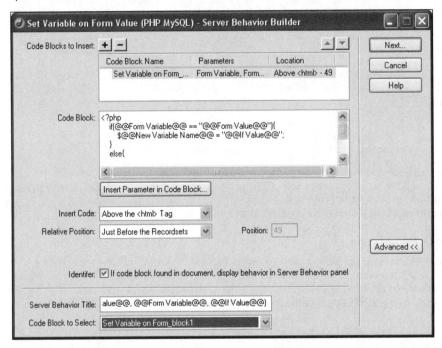

We've now finished building most of the server behavior. Click *Next...* to proceed to the final step: building the interface.

Building an Interface for Our Server Behavior

The interface of our server behavior will be displayed when the user of our server behavior uses it on their document. Dreamweaver provides an easy way for us to generate a user interface: the Generate Behavior Dialog Box, which looks like this:

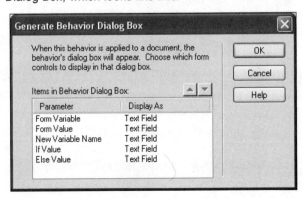

The Server Behavior Builder

You will notice that the SBB presents you with all of the parameters that we created in the code block. If we had more than one code block, each with its own parameters, they would all appear in this list.

Click on the first item in the list, the *Form Variable* parameter, and click on the down arrow button that appears. You will be presented with the different types of interface controls that you can use.

Interface Controls

There are many different interface controls that you can use in your server behaviors to allow the user to enter parameters.

Recordset Menu and Recordset Field Menu

These two controls let the user of your server behavior choose values for the parameters from the recordsets defined for the document. Recordset Menus display a list of all of the recordsets defined for the site, while Recordset Field Menus will automatically contain a list of the fields contained in the recordset selected in the Recordset Menu. If you use the Recordset Field Menu without a Recordset Menu control, it will not be populated correctly and Dreamweaver will generate an error when the user tries to launch the server behavior interface.

For example, if we had a behavior where we wanted the user of the behavior to be able to select fields from the `rsSearch` recordset that we used in Chapter 8, we could present them with an interface like this:

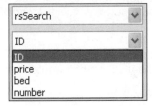

The top menu is a Recordset Menu and the second menu is a Recordset Field menu.

Editable Recordset Menu and Editable Recordset Field Menu

These two controls work the same way as Recordset Menus and Recordset Field Menus, but the user can edit the values that they've chosen.

CF Data Source Menu

The ColdFusion Data Source Menu provides the user with a menu populated with items from a ColdFusion Data Source. There's no reason to use it when designing a PHP server behavior.

Connection Menu, Connection Table Menu, Connection Column Menu

Connection Menus, Connection Table Menus, and Connection Column Menus are populated with the Connection data for the site. This is a convenient way to present the user with the different values from a Connection. They work in a similar way to Recordset Menus, in that they automatically populate depending upon user choice.

Dreamweaver will generate an error if you try to use one of them without having the parent UI control in your interface. For example, you cannot add a Connection Column Menu if you have no Connection Table Menu, and you cannot have a Connection Table Menu if you have no Connection Menu.

The following picture shows you an example of these three elements in action:

Text Field

A Text Field is the common text box. Text-Fields are useful when you want the server behavior's user to be able to enter anything that they like as a parameter.

Dynamic Text Field

Dynamic Text Fields work in almost the same way as Text Fields, but add a little button that will invoke a `DataSource` dialog where the user can select a value from the dynamic data defined for the document.

You may think that if it works the same way as a Text Field but adds a feature, why not always use it instead of a Text Field? Well, if the user has an icon telling them that they can use dynamic data, they will be tempted to use it, which is not always what you want. For example, in our server behavior, in the case of the `Form Value` parameter, we don't want the user to enter a dynamic variable because we enclosed the parameter `Form Value` with quotes in our code block. If the user entered dynamic data as a parameter, it wouldn't work correctly.

URL Text Field

A URL Text Field is a control that allows the user to specify a URL as one of the parameters. The user will be able to browse to find a file that they want the server behavior to interact with.

Here's what the user is presented with:

Numeric Text Field

The Numeric Text Field will allow you to get a smaller Text Field that requires a numeric entry from the user.

Unfortunately, however, you will have to edit the `.htm` file generated by the Server Behavior Builder in order to get this functionality working. We will not cover the modification of this file, as it would go beyond the scope of this book.

Recordset Fields Ordered List

As for the Numeric Text Field, this UI control requires some modification on the generated files. We will therefore not cover it here.

Text Field Comma Separated List

A Text Field Comma Separated List presents the user with an input area where they can enter multiple values. When passed to the server behavior, these values are concatenated together as a comma-separated list.

The Server Behavior Builder

List Menu, Checkbox and Radio Group

The List Menu, Checkbox, and Radio Group are familiar ways for the user to select options from your interface.

Here's some radio buttons:

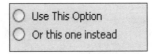

The value of a checkbox or radio button is either nothing if it is unchecked or `true` if checked. Checkboxes and radio buttons are mainly used with conditional code blocks, which are code blocks that are inserted by the server behavior into the document only if a condition is `true`.

The use of conditional code blocks is outside the scope of this book, but there's more information about it in the Dreamweaver documentation.

The Interface of Our Example

Getting back to our example server behavior, we have the following parameters:

- `Form Variable`
- `Form Value`
- `New Variable Name`
- `If Value`
- `Else Value`

We will use the Text Field UI control for each of our parameters, except the first, `Form Variable`, which will be a Dynamic Text Field instead. This is because the value for `Form Variable` is defined in the Bindings panel, and therefore can be retrieved with a Dynamic Text Field, which is much easier and less error-prone than trying to type something like *$HTTP_POST_VARS["price_option"]* into a textbox!

Your Generate Behavior Dialog Box should now look like this:

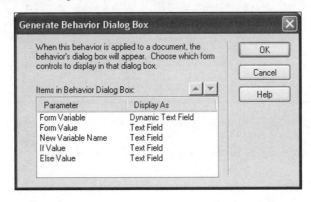

Chapter 10

Finishing the Server Behavior

Once you have all your Interface controls set up, click on *OK* to finalize your server behavior.

If you click on the + button in the Server Behavior panel, you will see your new server behavior menu item.

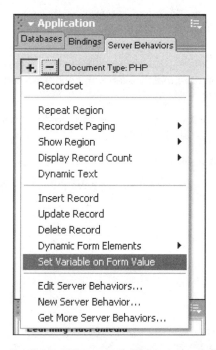

Click on the Set Variable on the Form Value menu item to see what your server behavior's interface looks like:

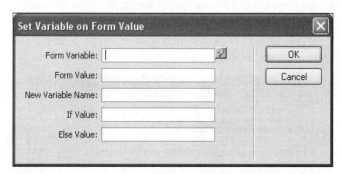

Let's fill it in with the values that we used for the search engine in Chapter 8:

- *Form Variable: $HTTP_POST_VARS["bed_option"]*

- *Form Value: less*

- *New Variable Name: pComp*
- *If Value: >*
- *Else Value: <=*

When you click on *OK* the server behavior will generate the following code, placed above the recordsets definition in the document:

```php
<?php
   if($HTTP_POST_VARS["price_option"] == "above")
   {
      $pComp = ">";
   }
   else
   {
      $pComp = "<=";
   }
?>
```

How To Copy a Server Behavior

It's tempting to try and design one server behavior that can handle all the tasks that you throw at it. Don't fall into the easy trap, which is to make your server behavior more and more complex, just to be able to handle every case you may encounter. Instead, I would recommend that you design multiple server behaviors, and group them with a common prefix name. An easy way to produce similar behaviors based on a common one is to copy an existing behavior and modify it.

In the example we built, we used the following code:

```php
<?php
   if(@@Form Variable@@ == "@@Form Value@@")
   {
      $@@New Variable Name@@ = "@@If Value@@";
   }
   else
   {
      $@@New Variable Name@@ = "@@Else Value@@";
   }
?>
```

and that forced us to use a Text Field control for the Form Value parameter. We could have removed the quotes surrounding the parameter and been able to use a Dynamic Text Field instead.

But we can also create a new Server Behavior that will do that specifically for us. To copy a server behavior, click on *New Server Behavior...* in the Server Behavior panel in the Application panel group.

Enter the name of the new server behavior, and check the option to copy an existing server behavior. Now select the *Set Variable on Form* value behavior that we want to copy. The rest of the operation is exactly the same as for a brand-new server behavior, so just modify the code block.

```php
<?php
    if(@@Form Variable@@ == "@@Form Value@@")
    {
        $@@New Variable Name@@ = "@@If Value@@";
    }
    else
    {
        $@@New Variable Name@@ = "@@Else Value@@";
    }
?>
```

Give the new behavior a new name, and we're done!

Summary

We have seen how Dreamweaver MX lets us create our own server behaviors to automate tasks to make Dreamweaver easier to use and more efficient. We started by having a look at the built-in server behaviors, and then went on to see how to build our own. We looked at how to position the code on the page, and how to add parameters to make our server behaviors flexible. We finished up by looking at how we make a user interface so that the user of our behavior can provide the server behavior with values for our parameters.

In the next chapter we'll be looking at debugging your code. No matter how good you are at PHP or Dreamweaver, this is a very useful chapter.

The Server Behavior Builder

11

- PHP error types
- Debugging techniques
- Where to get help

Author: Gareth Downes-Powell

Debugging Your Code

This chapter explains ways of debugging, or finding errors, in your code. We start by discussing error handling in PHP, looking at the types of errors that can occur. We then create a custom error handler, so that we can present a professional and helpful message to the user if an error occurs, instead of showing the default PHP error message.

We then look at how to view your server settings, and see which libraries, etc. have been installed. Next, we create a custom debug function, which can print details of your variables, so you can track them through your code.

In the last section of this chapter, we look at the ways of getting help that are available on the Internet, giving details of web sites, newsgroups, and forums that can help you to quickly solve your problems.

If you've been following the examples from the book so far in Dreamweaver MX, it's more than likely that you've already had to debug your code. In this chapter we're going to be looking at various ways to make finding errors in your code easier.

PHP in general is quite good at giving an accurate error message, giving you the precise line number of the code that contains the error. Unfortunately this isn't always totally reliable, as we'll explain later, and we look at ways of tracking down different errors.

Programming Errors

Understanding the various error types and error messages is essential to debugging your PHP code. In this section we are going to look at the various types of errors that can occur.

The first types of errors we are going to look at are programming errors. These can be broken down into three main categories, and we'll look at each of these separately, and how to avoid them.

- Syntax errors
- Run-time errors
- Logic errors

Syntax Errors

Syntax errors are caused by an error in your code, and are probably one of the commonest errors you'll see. Common examples of syntax errors are misspelling a function, missing a semicolon from the end of a statement, or missing a closing bracket.

As an example, if we try and open a web page with the following code:

```
6   <?php
7      echo("Debugging your Code")
8      echo("Part 1");
9   ?>
```

We will get an error message similar to the following:

Parse error: parse error, expecting `,'" or `;'" in /home/sites/site17/web/errors/error1.php on line 8

We can see that the error isn't actually on line 8; it's because of the missing semicolon at the end of line 7.

When you get an error message similar to the one above, it's always worth looking backwards through the code a couple of lines, as often an error lies there, instead of on the line shown by the error message. This occurs because the PHP parser recognizes that a semicolon is missing, but keeps parsing to the end of the code block trying to find it. As a result when the PHP parser has got to the last line of the code block, and has still not found the missing semicolon, it shows the error message, but the line number shown is the line the PHP parser is currently on, which is the last line of the code block.

If you haven't already, it's a good idea to turn on the *Line Numbers* option for *Code view* or the *Code inspector,* which you can do by clicking the *View Options* button, which is on the Dreamweaver MX *Document* toolbar.

If you haven't got the *Document* toolbar turned on, then select *View -> Toolbars -> Document.* You can see the *Document* toolbar, and the *View Options* button in the screenshot opposite.

Debugging Your Code

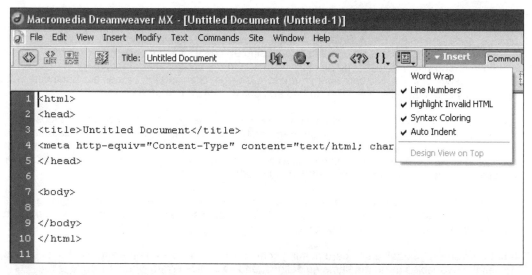

You now have the line numbers printed alongside the code, and it makes it much easier to track down the line the error applies to.

Another syntax error which is common, but can be harder to track, is a missing } (a curly brace) at the end of a code block. If we take a look at the code below:

```
1   <html>
2     <head>
3       <title>Untitled Document</title>
4       <meta http-equiv="Content-Type" content="text/html; charset=iso-8859-1">
5     </head>
6     <?php
7       if($Submit == "Submit") {
8         echo("Debugging your Code");
9         echo("Part 1");
10    ?>
11    <body>
12    </body>
13  </html>
```

When this page is viewed in a browser, it can lead to an error message similar to the following:

Parse error: parse error in /home/sites/site17/web/errors/error1.php on line 13

We can see straight away that the problem is actually caused by a missing } , which should be at the end of line 9. So why does the missing bracket on line 9 give a parse error on line 13? Again, the reason behind this is because PHP knows that a closing bracket should be there, and so it checks all the way to the end of the code trying to find it. When it reaches the end of the code (line 13 in our example), it shows the error message, giving the last line as the line with the error in the error report. These errors can be tricky to find, as the line number in the error message no longer corresponds to the actual line giving the error.

In cases like this you need to manually work through the code, and check that for each { there is a closing }. This is made a lot easier if you have indented your code, as it's easier to see the program flow, and where code blocks start and end.

287

The *Balance Braces* function in Dreamweaver MX also makes this process much easier. We covered the *Balance Braces* in detail in Chapter 9 on Hand Coding, but to recap you can place the cursor in a block of code and select *Edit > Balance Braces*, or use the key combination *Ctrl* + ' . If the braces are balanced, that is there is an opening and closing brace ({ }), the code block will be highlighted, showing you that code block is correct, and the braces are balanced. By starting on the innermost block of code, you can work your way outwards, checking the braces are balanced, which significantly cuts down the time taken to find and correct the source of the error.

Another common cause of errors when writing PHP is variable type. PHP is known as a loosely typed language, as variables can change from one type to another during run-time. This means that you can for example place a string in a variable, which previously held a numerical value. Although this is convenient, it means that you can have a situation where you assume one type of data is in a variable, whereas it's actually a different type altogether.

Another easy mistake to make is forgetting the case of a variable name, for example, $myvariable is a totally separate variable to $myVariable. This can cause you problems if you're working on a lot of code, and you switch from one to the other.

It helps if you set yourself a standard naming convention when working on a site, so that everybody names their variables using the same guidelines, and so avoids errors when the code is run. For example, if you have a variable name consisting of two words for example $showtotal, it is easier to understand if you capitalize the first letter of the second word, for example $showTotal. This way you can clearly see where one word ends and the next word starts.

Run-time Errors

Run-time errors occur when the program is actually running, and can be caused by outside events, rather than errors in your code. For example, your code could work fine for months, but as soon as the server's hard disk becomes full, it crashes when it tries to output a file. Another example is when you're pulling data from another site. Although your code works the way it was intended, the other site's server could be down, causing your code to crash if there is no error checking. Perhaps your site uses an include file. If that include file is deleted, any code calling a function in that file will return an error when the script tries to load it.

Scenarios like these should be thought of in advance. You need to add relevant error trapping to your code, so that if a problem does arise, your web site returns a professional and easy-to-understand message telling the user what's gone wrong, rather than stopping in the middle of a page and displaying a standard error message.

Another example of run-time errors occurring is when a user enters text into a box meant for a numerical value. It's amazing what people will enter into your forms either accidentally, or even maliciously, trying to crash your code and / or reveal internal data. On an e-commerce site, for example, what would your script do it the user entered a negative rather than a positive quantity for an item in their cart, would it end up refunding the card instead of charging it?

Don't leave anything to chance, and always check the user input is valid, and is the same type of data that you are expecting. Set up form fields with a character maximum the same as the character maximum of the field in the database you're inserting them into.

We'll be talking about ways of trapping and dealing with run-time errors later in this chapter, so that the page carries on functioning and displays a friendly error message, rather than just crashing.

Logic Errors

Logic errors occur when your code is technically correct, but doesn't do what you intended it to do. If you look at the following piece of code:

```
1   <html>
2     <head>
3       <title>Untitled Document</title>
4       <meta http-equiv="Content-Type" content="text/html; charset=iso-8859-1">
5     </head>
6     <body>
7       <table width="50%" height="8" border="1" align="center"
            cellpadding="0" cellspacing="0">
8         <tr align="center">
9         <?php
10          for($myCount=0; $myCount < 5; $myCount++);
11            echo("<td>" . $myCount . "</td>");
12        ?>
13        </tr>
14    </table>
15    </body>
16  </html>
```

When we run this code, we would expect the output to be:

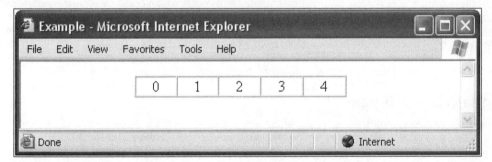

Instead the page appears as follows:

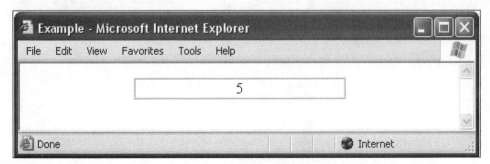

Why is this happening? If you look at lines 10 and 11 which read:

```
10          for($myCount=0; $myCount < 5; $myCount++);
11            echo("<td>" . $myCount . "</td>");
```

You can see that at the end of line 10 there is a semicolon added by mistake. This means that the loop runs as it should, but because of the extra semicolon, line 11 is only executed when the count is completed, rather than for each stage of the count.

Notice that the code still executes and runs without any error messages, as the code is perfectly valid, even though it didn't do what we wanted it to do. As a result of this, these errors can sometimes be hard to track down.

This is much less likely to occur if you use braces ({ }) for all loops, for example for the lines with the error above, it would be better if they had been written as:

```
10          for($myCount=0; $myCount < 5; $myCount++){
11              echo("<td>" . $myCount . "</td>");}
```

Error Types in PHP

As we've seen in the previous section, PHP error messages usually give an adequate description of the error that's occurred, along with the line number of the code with the error. For example:

Parse error: parse error in /home/sites/site17/web/errors/error1.php on line 15

Usually though, this isn't an error that you would want the users of your site to see, as it looks unprofessional, and can make your users lose trust in the site, which could be extremely damaging, for example to an e-commerce web site. PHP comes to the rescue however, and allows you to write your own custom error-handling functions, which can output HTML and show a more user-friendly error message. PHP also provides three custom error types that you can use to handle errors in your code.

We're now going to take a look at the different error types that are available within PHP.

Standard Error Types

There are twelve standard error types, which are shown in the table below. Some errors are warnings, and allow the script to continue running, others require the script to halt.

Constant	Description	Notes
E_ERROR	fatal run-time errors	
E_WARNING	run-time warnings (non fatal-errors)	
E_PARSE	compile-time parse errors	
E_NOTICE	run-time notices (less serious than warnings)	
E_CORE_ERROR	fatal errors that occur during PHP's initial startup	PHP 4 only
E_CORE_WARNING	warnings(non fatal errors) that occur during PHP's initial startup	PHP 4 only
E_COMPILE_ERROR	fatal compile-time errors	PHP 4 only
E_COMPILE_WARNING	compile-time warnings (non-fatal errors)	PHP 4 only

Debugging Your Code

Constant	Description	Notes
`E_USER_ERROR`	user-generated error message	PHP 4 only
`E_USER_WARNING`	user-generated warning message	PHP 4 only
`E_USER_NOTICE`	user-generated notice message	PHP 4 only
`E_ALL`	all of the above	

PHP Standard Error Types

We're now going to look at each of the above error types separately (apart from `E_USER` error types, which we'll be looking at later in this chapter, as these allow you to enter your own error messages unlike the other PHP error types).

E_ERROR –Fatal

`E_ERROR` is a fatal error, which means that if this error is encountered, the PHP script will halt, as the error cannot be recovered from. This error type is displayed by default.

E_WARNING –Non-Fatal

`E_WARNING` is an example of a non-fatal error. A non-fatal error is one that can be recovered from, and the script can continue running. It's normally caused by something that could have been prevented within the code, such as passing a parameter with the wrong data type to a function. Although this error is non-fatal, it is displayed to the user by default.

E_PARSE –Fatal

`E_PARSE` occurs when the PHP parser encounters an error, for example a syntax error. In PHP 4 the script is parsed before it is run, and the script will terminate then if the parsing process finds any errors.

E_NOTICE –Non-Fatal

`E_NOTICE` is another non-fatal error. This error isn't reported by default, because it could be generated during normal execution of a script. It's normally caused by an error in the script, such as trying to reference an undefined variable.

E_CORE_ERROR –Fatal

`E_CORE_ERROR` means that there is a problem with the PHP engine starting up. This is the same type of error as `E_ERROR`.

E_CORE_WARNING –Non Fatal

`E_CORE_WARNING` is similar to the `E_WARNING` type above. It reports non-fatal failures during the startup of the PHP Engine.

E_COMPILE_ERROR –Fatal

`E_COMPILE_ERROR` is generated by the PHP Engine and reports errors in compilation.

E_COMPILE_WARNING –Non-Fatal

`E_COMPILE_WARNING` is similar to the `E_WARNING` type above, but reports non-fatal errors in compilation.

The last four errors (the CORE and COMPILE type errors) will not normally be seen on a day-to-day basis, as they are more to do with the setup of the server, and are not likely to occur when an installation is stable.

Error Reporting Levels

Setting a custom Error Reporting Level, means that you can tell PHP which errors to report, and which to ignore. You can tell PHP for example to show all errors, which gives you extra information when you're writing and debugging your code, and then when the site goes live to only show the important errors, and ignore warnings for example.

The default error reporting level is set with the `error_reporting` option in your `php.ini` file. If you do not have access to the `php.ini` file, because you are on shared hosting for example, you can set the error reporting level on a per script basis, using the `error_reporting()` function.

The error types can be referred to symbolically (by using the constant in the table above), or numerically (by using the error value in the table above). You can select which error types are shown, by using a combination of the error types, and the operators shown below:

Name	Operator	Example
AND	&	E_ERROR & E_WARNING
OR	|	E_ERROR | E_CORE_ERROR
NOT	~	~ E_NOTICE

Error Type Operators

By combining the error values or constants with the operators above, you can create a custom level of error reporting.

In PHP 4, the default error reporting setting is:

```
E_ALL & ~E_NOTICE
```

This can be read as:

```
E_ALL And Not E_NOTICE
```

This means that PHP will display all errors and warnings, except those of type E_NOTICE.

By combining the operators in the table above, and the Error Types in the table earlier in the chapter, you can create different combinations of errors and warnings etc. that are reported. For example to only show fatal error messages, and to ignore all warnings and notices, you could use the combination:

```
E_ERROR & E_CORE_ERROR & E_COMPILE_ERROR & E_PARSE
```

This enables you to easily create a custom level, showing only the information you require.

Changing the Error Reporting Settings

We're now going to discuss changing the error reporting settings to our own custom level, using the information above.

We could then turn on error reporting for all the different error types and warnings, so we can get as much information as possible when code is being tested and debugged. For example, if you take a look at the code below:

```
<?php
   for($myCount=0; $myCount<10; $mycount++){
     echo "$myCount";
   }
?>
```

If you run the above code in a browser (not advisable!), all you would get is a never-ending stream of 0's sent to the browser. Because $myCount is never incremented, due to it being mis-typed (it is typed as $mycount++), the code goes into an endless loop. Because the code is valid however, with the default level of error reporting, the code is executed, and an endless loop occurs.

If however you set the error reporting level to report everything, using the setting E_ALL as in the following code example:

```
<?php
   error_reporting(E_ALL);
   for($myCount=0; $myCount<10; $mycount++){
     echo "$myCount";
   }
?>
```

This would cause an error to be triggered, and PHP would show the following error:

```
Warning: Undefined variable: mycount in
/home/sites/site17/users/phpbook/web/errors/test2.php on line 9
```

You could then intercept this error, and stop the endless loop from occurring.

When your site goes live, you can set the error reporting back to the default level, or choose a custom level of your own, as all the minor errors will have been fixed, and you would not want notices etc. to be shown.

There are two ways of changing the error reporting level, on a global level, or on a per-script basis, and we are going to look at both of these.

Setting the Error Level Globally

If you want to change the error level globally, so it affects all scripts running on that server, you need to edit your `php.ini` file.

If you are not sure of the location of your `php.ini` file, you can use the incredibly useful `phpinfo()` function. We'll look at this in more detail later on, for the time being add the following PHP code to a blank page, upload it to your server, and then view it in your browser.

```
<?php
   phpinfo();
?>
```

At the very top of the information, in the first table, the path to your `php.ini` is displayed.

Edit your `php.ini` file, and under the heading

```
;;;;;;;;;;;;;;;;;;;;;;;;;;;;;;
; Error handling and logging ;
;;;;;;;;;;;;;;;;;;;;;;;;;;;;;;
```

you will find the following four directives.

```
error_reporting = E_ALL & ~E_NOTICE
display_errors  =  On
log_errors      =  Off
track_errors    =  Off
```

The above shows the default settings for a PHP installation.

The meanings of these directives are as follows:

```
error_reporting = E_ALL & ~E_NOTICE
```

This directive allows you to set a custom level of error reporting, as we discussed above, and holds the error types and operators that define your custom error level.

```
display_errors = Off | On
```

This directive specifies whether error messages should be printed as HTML output or not

```
log_errors = Off | On
```

This directive controls whether error messages are logged to the server error logs or not..

```
track_errors = Off | On
```

If this directive is set to `On`, the last error message will be stored in the PHP global variable `$php_errormsg`.

When you have saved the changes, you will need to restart your web server, so that the changes can take effect.

Changing the Error Level On a Per-Script Basis

If you don't have access to the `php.ini` file, or don't want to make global changes, you can set the error reporting level on a per-script basis with the `error_reporting()` function. The format for the `error_reporting()` function is:

```
error_reporting(level)
```

When you call the `error_reporting()` function to set a new level of error reporting, the previous error reporting level is returned. To set the error reporting level you enter a combination of the error types as shown in the previous tables. So if we wanted to set the PHP default of `E_ALL & ~E_NOTICE`, which means `ALL_ERRORS` apart from `E_NOTICE`, we would use:

```
E_ALL - E_NOTICE
```

So the following piece of code:

```
<?php
    $oldSetting = error_reporting(E_ALL - E_NOTICE);
?>
```

would set the error reporting level to the default level, and the previous level would be stored in `$oldSetting`. If desired you can restore back to the old setting later in your script using the code:

```
<?php
    error_reporting($oldSetting);
?>
```

To turn on all error reporting and notices use:

```
<?php
    $oldSetting = error_reporting(E_ALL);
?>
```

Being able to change the error reporting level is extremely useful, as you can turn on all error reporting when you are developing and debugging, and then drop back down to the default level when your site goes live, so that extra information such as notices are not shown.

User-Defined Errors

As well as the standard error types PHP 4 also allows three custom error types. We saw these briefly earlier in the chapter, and they are reprinted below.

Value	Constant	Description	Notes
256	E_USER_ERROR	User-generated error message	PHP 4 only
512	E_USER_WARNING	User-generated warning message	PHP 4 only
1024	E_USER_NOTICE	User-generated notice message	PHP 4 only

We're now going to look at the different user error types, and give examples of how they could be used.

E_USER_ERROR

`E_USER_ERROR` is the most serious of the user-defined error messages allowed by PHP. It is of the same type of error as `E_ERROR`, and should only be triggered when the script is going to process some code that would cause a critical error, and it requires the script to be halted.

An example of its use would be in a routine which checks parameters before a division operation occurs, and the error is triggered if a divide by zero is going to take place.

Chapter 11

E_USER_WARNING

E_USER_WARNING is a user-defined version of the E_WARNING error type, and is used for errors that prevent the script from running as normal.

An example of its use would be in a routine to check the data being sent to a function is the correct type. If a function was expecting an array as one of its parameters and it was passed a string, the error should be triggered, as PHP can't convert a string to an array.

E_USER_NOTICE

E_USER_NOTICE is, as you would expect, of the same type as its E_NOTICE counterpart. Its use is for displaying potential warning messages, which are non-fatal and won't stop the execution of the script.

Now we've looked at the user-defined error types, in the next section we show how to use them in your script.

Custom Error Handling

Custom error handling gives you much more control over the message the user sees should anything happen to go wrong. It looks much more professional to show a customized error message, with your header and footer etc., rather than the standard PHP error message.

Triggering an Error

Using the `trigger_error()` function, you can trigger your own error message or warning, which is either dealt with by the internal PHP error handler, or with your own custom error handler.

For example, the following code:

```php
<?php
    trigger_error("This creates a Fatal Error!", E_USER_ERROR);
?>
```

would trigger a fatal error when it was run, halting the execution of the script, and showing the error message:

Fatal error: This creates a Fatal Error!

The format for the `trigger_error()` function is:

```
trigger_error (error_msg [,error_type])
```

`trigger_error()` is called with a string containing the error message, and optionally, E_USER_NOTICE, E_USER_WARNING, or E_USER_ERROR.

If the error type is not supplied, the error is shown as the default error type E_USER_NOTICE.

The following code shows the results of all 3 error types:

Debugging Your Code

```
 7  <?php
 8    trigger_error("Test error message", E_USER_NOTICE);
 9
10    echo "Recovered from E_USER_NOTICE error type";
11
12    trigger_error("Test error message", E_USER_WARNING);
13
14    echo "Recovered from E_USER_WARNING error type";
15
16    trigger_error("Test error message", E_USER_ERROR);
17
18    echo "Recovered from E_USER_ERROR error type";
19  ?>
```

Here's what the user would see:

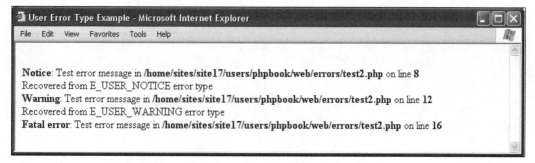

Note that the first two error types E_USER_NOTICE and E_USER_WARNING, do not stop the execution of the code, and it continues running. E_USER_ERROR however, shows the "*Fatal error*" message, and the script is halted, and the text on line 18 is never displayed.

Another function you can use to trigger user errors is user_error(), which is an alias of the trigger_error() function above, and either function can be used.

Handling Errors When They Occur

Now we've looked at the different error types, and how to trigger errors, we're going to look at how to handle errors when they occur. Normally, as we've seen above, the built-in PHP error handler takes over if an error occurs.

The set_error_handler() Function

Using the set_error_handler() function, we can set our own function to handle any errors that occur.

The format for set_error_handler() is:

```
set_error_handler (error_handler)
```

where error_handler is the name of your function, for example:

```
set_error_handler("myErrorHandler")
```

Before we use `set_error_handler()`, we need to have a function to set as the error handler, and we'll create this function now. The custom error handler function needs to be able to accept two parameters, an error number and an error string. By comparing the error number to a list in your script, you can decide which action is necessary for that error. The error string contains the internal description of the error.

From PHP 4.0.2 another three parameters were added, for the filename where the error occurred, the line number where the error occurred, and the context in which the error occurred.

These extra parameters are:

- `$error_file` – The filename of the script that triggered the error.

- `$error_line` – The line number of the code that triggered the error.

- `$error_context` – Contains an array of all variables that were in use at the time of the error.

As an example, look at the code below:

```php
<?php
  function errorHandler($errNumber, $errDetails, $errFile, $errLine, $errContext){
    echo "Error Number: $errNumber <br>";
    echo "Error Details: $errDetails <br>";
    echo "Error File: $errFile <br>";
    echo "Error Line: $errLine <br><br>";
    foreach($errContext as $key=>$value){
      echo "Error Context: $key : $value <br>";
    }
  }
?>
<html>
<head>
<title>Custom</title>
</head>
<body>
<?php
  set_error_handler("errorHandler");
  user_error("This is a test error", E_USER_ERROR);
?>
</body>
</html>
```

This code sets up a simple error handler that prints all the parameters that are sent to it by the PHP engine. Note that as `$errContext` is an array, we have to loop through it, so we can print all its data.

In the body of the code we trigger a test error, so that the `errorHandler` function will be invoked. When the page is viewed in a browser, the following is seen:

Debugging Your Code

```
Error Number: 256
Error Details: This is a test error
Error File: /home/sites/site17/users/phpbook/web/errors/test2.php
Error Line: 20

Error Context: DOCUMENT_ROOT : /home/sites/site17/web
Error Context: HTTP_ACCEPT : */*
Error Context: HTTP_ACCEPT_ENCODING : gzip, deflate
Error Context: HTTP_ACCEPT_LANGUAGE : en-gb
Error Context: HTTP_CLIENT_IP : 86.7.104.102
Error Context: HTTP_HOST : php.myserver.com
Error Context: HTTP_USER_AGENT : Mozilla/4.0 (compatible; MSIE 6.0; Windows NT
5.1; Q356871)
Error Context: HTTP_VIA : HTTP/1.1 (Traffic-Server/4.2.15-M-12744 [uScM])
Error Context: PATH : /sbin:/usr/sbin:/bin:/usr/bin:/usr/X11R6/bin
Error Context: REMOTE_ADDR : 128.152.69.10
Error Context: REMOTE_PORT : 53091
Error Context: SCRIPT_FILENAME :
/home/sites/site17/users/phpbook/web/errors/test2.php
Error Context: SCRIPT_URI : http://php.myserver.com/~phpbook/errors/error2.php
Error Context: SCRIPT_URL : /~phpbook/errors/error2.php
Error Context: SERVER_ADDR : 218.64.212.84
Error Context: SERVER_ADMIN : gareth
Error Context: SERVER_NAME : php.myserver.com
Error Context: SERVER_PORT : 80
Error Context: SERVER_SIGNATURE :
Error Context: SERVER_SOFTWARE : Apache/1.3.20 Sun Cobalt (Unix) mod_ssl/2.8.4
OpenSSL/0.9.6b PHP/4.1.2 mod_auth_pam_external/0.1 FrontPage/4.0.4.3
mod_perl/1.25
Error Context: UNIQUE_ID : PPcCsCRDwx0BNGHVRf4
Error Context: GATEWAY_INTERFACE : CGI/1.1
Error Context: SERVER_PROTOCOL : HTTP/1.1
Error Context: REQUEST_METHOD : GET
Error Context: QUERY_STRING :
Error Context: REQUEST_URI : /~phpbook/errors/error2.php
Error Context: SCRIPT_NAME : /~phpbook/errors/error2.php
Error Context: PATH_TRANSLATED :
/home/sites/site17/users/phpbook/web/errors/error2.php
Error Context: PHP_SELF : /~phpbook/errors/error.php
Error Context: HTTP_POST_VARS : Array
Error Context: _POST : Array
Error Context: HTTP_GET_VARS : Array
Error Context: _GET : Array
Error Context: HTTP_COOKIE_VARS : Array
Error Context: _COOKIE : Array
Error Context: HTTP_SERVER_VARS : Array
Error Context: _SERVER : Array
Error Context: HTTP_ENV_VARS : Array
Error Context: _ENV : Array
Error Context: HTTP_POST_FILES : Array
Error Context: _FILES : Array
Error Context: _REQUEST : Array
```

As you can see, the `errContext` array holds a huge amount of data, about the server and the different types of variables that were present at the time of the error.

Building a Custom Error Handler

Our error handler needs to be able to trap the `E_ERROR` and `E_USER_ERROR` levels of error, and instead of simply displaying the standard error message, it's going to show a more professional-looking error message, which is also more user friendly.

Here is the code for our custom error handler:

```
<?php
function customErrorHandler($error_num, $error_string) {
  // Check error type is either E_ERROR or E_USER_ERROR
  if ($error_num == E_ERROR || $error_num == E_USER_ERROR){
    echo "
      <div align='center'><p>
      <font color='#FF6600' size='3' face='Arial, Helvetica, sans-serif'>
        We're sorry, but an error has occured !
      </font></p><p>
      <font size='2' face='Verdana, Arial, Helvetica, sans-serif'>
      <strong>
      Please try again later.
      </strong></font><br><br>
      <font size='2' face='Verdana, Arial, Helvetica, sans-serif'>
      If you still have an error, please email our
      <a href='mailto:techsupport@thedreamweaverhotel.com'>
      Tech Support
      </a> team, <br>
      quoting the error details below and we'll do our best to help.
      </font><br><br>
      <font size='2' face='Courier New, Courier, mono'>
      ";
    echo ("$error_num : $error_string");
    echo "
      <br></font><br><strong>
      <font size='3' face='Arial, Helvetica, sans-serif'>
      The Dreamweaver Hotel Staff
      </font></strong></p>
      </div>
      ";
    exit;
  }
}
?>
```

First of all, we check to see whether the error type is either `E_ERROR` or `E_USER_ERROR`, by checking `$error_num`, which is passed to the function by the PHP Engine.

If the error is of the `E_ERROR` or `E_USER_ERROR` type, the function displays a block of HTML code, which explains the error in a more professional user-friendly way.

The function then shows the contents of `$error_num` or `$error_string`, and then prints a closing block of HTML.

Debugging Your Code

Lastly, as the `E_ERROR` or `E_USER_ERROR` types are fatal errors, we stop the script executing with the PHP exit command.

Now we have a custom error handling function, we can add the `set_error_handler()` function to our code.

The code below does this job:

```
<?php
    set_error_handler("customErrorHandler");
?>
```

As you can see from the above, we simply have to call the `set_error_handler()` function, giving it the name of our custom error handling function, `customErrorHandler`, as the parameter.

The last bit of code we are going to use is to manually trigger an error, so that we can see our custom error handler in action.

This is achieved by the following code:

```
<?php
    user_error("This is a test error", E_USER_ERROR);
?>
```

Next, we'll look at the results in our browser.

First we'll look at the normal PHP error handler in action, by triggering an `E_USER_ERROR` with the code above. The result is shown below:

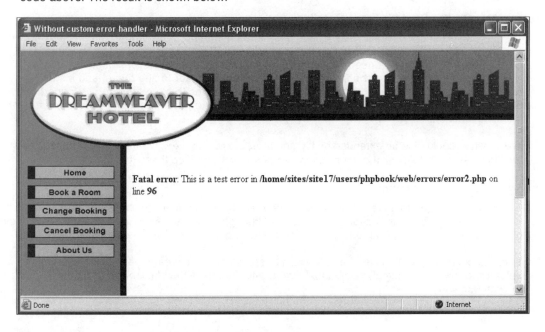

301

Chapter 11

Next, we'll look at the result of our custom error handling function, by triggering the same error.

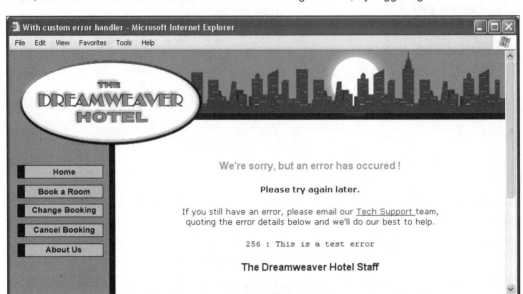

Unfortunately, errors occurring are a fact of life, especially if you rely on external data or servers in your code. Using a custom error handler minimizes the damage, and maintains a professional look for your site.

Expanding On the Custom Error Handler

The previous example was quite simple, and there are a number of ways in which it can be extended.

One important addition that needs to be made is support for the other types of error, such as warnings and notices. It may be the case you don't want the user to see these, and instead they can be logged to a file. You could also set the fatal error types to have their details logged to a file, or even emailed to the developer; all you need to do is to put the relevant code in your error handling function.

The function could also be extended by logging the $error_context variable that is passed to the function, which contains all the variables in use at the time, and log these to a file.

Logging Errors That Occur

Errors can be logged to a file on the server if required, by writing them out as a standard text file. It's best to keep separate log files for each page, as although it's more files to monitor, it makes it easier to track down the cause of the error, if you're only seeing errors for that one particular page.

Because of security settings on the server, it's often easier if you create the log file yourself, and upload it to the server. Simply open a text editor, and then save the blank page as a new file, with the name of your log file.

Debugging Your Code

For example, save an empty text file with the filename `error3.txt`, and upload it to the server. Before you can write to the file, you have to change its permissions level, so that your PHP script can open and add to the file. To do this you need to change the file's permissions to 666, using the `chmod` command for Linux. For Windows, you need to ensure that the file can be opened, read, and written to by the PHP engine.

The following code can be added to our custom error handler function and writes any errors occurring to a log file.

```php
<?php
// Set up variables, such as page name and time and date
$page_errorlog = "error3.txt";
$mytime = date("H:i:s");
$mydate = date("d.m.Y");

//Check file exists
  if (file_exists($page_errorlog))
  {
     //open file for append
     if ($logfile = fopen($page_errorlog,"a"))
     {
        // lock log file during write
        flock($logfile, LOCK_EX);
        // write error number, error string, and the time and date
        fwrite($logfile,"$error_num : $error_string : $mytime : $mydate\n");
        // unlock log file
        flock($logfile, LOCK_UN);
        // close log file
        fclose($logfile);
     }
  }
?>
```

First of all, we put the filename of the log file for the page into the variable `$page_errorlog`. We then use the PHP `date()` function to put the current time and date into the variables `$mytime` and `$mydate`. The parameters for the PHP date function, and the other functions in this section of code can all be found in the PHP manual.

Note however that with functions such as the PHP date function, the case of the parameters matters. For example `date("h")` returns the current hour in 12-hour format (1 – 12), whereas `date("H")` would return the code in 24 hours format (0 – 23). All of the parameters can be found in the online documentation at *http://www.php.net/*, and it's useful to print them out for future reference.

We next check to see if our file exists using the PHP `file_exists()` function, and if it does, open it for appending, using the PHP `fopen()` function, passing the function the filename, and using the "a" mode, to append to the file. We then use the PHP function `flock()` to open an exclusive lock on the file, so that no one else can open it at the same time. We write the error number, error string, time, and date to the file using the PHP `fwrite()` function.

We then unlock the file, using `flock()` and close the file with the PHP function, `fclose()`.

After triggering the test error we created a couple of times, the log file shows:

```
256 : This is a test error : 02:27:27 : 10.05.2002
256 : This is a test error : 02:27:28 : 10.05.2002
256 : This is a test error : 02:27:28 : 10.05.2002
```

This will help you to see any errors that occur in day-to-day use, and track them down and fix them. Obviously the more data that is logged, the easier the process of finding the error is.

E-mailing Errors That Occur

In the first couple of days that your site goes "live", you may want more instant notifications of any errors that occur. In this case, you may prefer to have error information e-mailed direct to you. Be careful, though, to not set errors to be e-mailed to yourself until the site has gone through comprehensive testing, otherwise you could find your mailbox swamped with e-mails!

To send an e-mail we use the PHP `mail()` function, the format for which is shown below:

```
mail (to, subject, message [,additional_headers [,additional_parameters]])
```

`mail()` returns `true` if the e-mail is successfully sent, and `false` if it wasn't.

The piece of code shown below will e-mail the error details to the address specified in the code, and can be added to the error handler, or you could make it into a function which is called by the error handler.

```
<?php
  $errorpage = "error4.php";
  $mytime = date("H:i:s");
  $mydate = date("d.m.Y");
  $to = "error@dreamweaverhotel.com";
  $subject = "Error logged on page: $errorpage";
  $message = "Error logged on page: $errorpage\n\n";
  $message .= "Error Number $error_num, $error_string occurred at $mytime on $mydate\n";
  mail($to, $subject, $message);
?>
```

First of all we set up the variable to hold the page name, `$errorpage`, and variables `$mytime` and `$mydate`, for the time and date. We then set the `$to` with the recipient's e-mail address, `$subject` to the subject line, and `$message` to hold the message which is sent. Finally we send the e-mail with the `mail()` function:

```
mail($to, $subject, $message);
```

When an error is triggered, the following e-mail is sent.

```
Error logged on page: error4.php

Error Number 256, This is a test error occurred at 03:19:17 on 10.05.2002
```

It makes a lot of sense to turn the above code into a function, along with the previous error logging example, and store them in an include file specially for debugging. You can then add the include file to any pages that need debugging, and call the relevant function names from your error handler.

Re-enabling the Default PHP Error Handler

If you have set your own custom error handler using the `set_error_handler()` function, you can switch back to using the default PHP error handler using the function `restore_error_handler()`.

The following code will set the error handler back to the default PHP handler.

```
<?php
  restore_error_handler();
?>
```

Suppressing Error Messages

To hide an error message temporarily if it occurs, you can use the @ directive. For example, look at the following piece of code:

```
<?
  $result = (10 / 0);
?>
```

When the page is opened in the browser, you get the following error message:

Warning: Division by zero in /home/sites/site17/users/phpbook/web/errors/error5.php on line 9

This is expected as the code is attempting to divide 10 by 0. However, if we run the piece of code below:

```
<?
  $result = @(10 / 0);
?>
```

no error message is shown. It's important to remember that the error still occurs, so the remaining code might behave unpredictably.

Note that the @ is placed next to location where the error occurs, rather than at the front of the line. The @ directive cannot be used to ignore parse errors, only run-time errors.

Viewing Your Server Settings

If you're running your own PHP server, you probably have quite an accurate idea of what has been installed, and which settings are being used. If you don't run your own server, you will have less of an idea of the way it is set up. It can be a difficult task trying to find out what has and what hasn't been installed on a server which isn't your own, but help is at hand from the `phpinfo()` function.

phpinfo()

Open up a blank page, and add the following code to the page body, in Code view or using the Code inspector.

```
<?php
  phpinfo();
?>
```

Save the page, upload it to your server, and then open the page in your browser, and you will see a screen similar to the following.

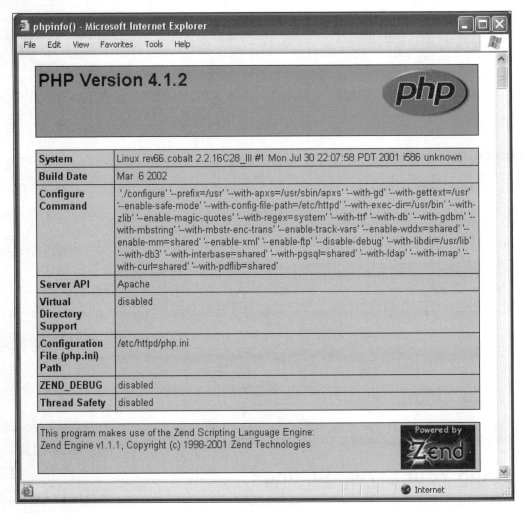

If you scroll downwards, you can see a list of all the PHP settings, and their values.

This information is incredible useful because it is so detailed. You can easily find your path info, whether a certain library is installed or not, as well as showing all the current settings.

Overriding Settings in the php.ini File Locally

It's worth noting that it is possible to change some of the PHP configuration options, on a local basis, if you cannot change `php.ini`. The following functions allow you to set and restore PHP configuration settings.

- `ini_set()`
- `ini_get()`
- `ini_restore()`

You can look these functions up on the PHP or Zend web sites. They explain how to use the functions, and give a table of which configuration settings can be changed, and at which level.

Debugging Techniques

In this section we're going to look at techniques to make debugging quicker and easier, and we demonstrate some functions you can use to give you more information about your script.

Creating a Custom Debugging Function

One of the best debugging techniques, and also one of the simplest, is using the PHP `echo()` function.

Using echo() To Output Useful Information

As `echo()` is not actually a function, but a language construct, it can be used with or without parentheses, although if you want to output more than one parameter, you cannot use the parentheses.

When you're tracking down errors in complicated blocks of code in which a lot of variables are being used, it can be hard to understand what is happening as, although you can see the variables, you cannot see what they will contain while the code is running.

It makes life a lot easier if you add extra statements to your code, which send the contents of the variables to the screen.

It's a good idea to output the line in the following format:

```
echo "\$Stringname: $string <br>";
```

Note the backslash, \, which has to be included to escape the $ character. This means that the PHP engine won't treat it as a variable, and will instead send it to the screen as text.

So for example, for a variable called $testValue, we would use:

```
echo "\$testValue : $testvalue <br>";
```

When the page is opened in the browser, it shows:

$testValue : 25

It is well worth adding a number of these statements, so you can track the value of the variable through the flow of your script. This can be extremely useful, and you will often find that the value of a variable is not what you were expecting.

For instance, if we take the following fragment of code:

```
<?php
  $total = $cartTotal;
  $result = addVAT($total);
  $result = addPackaging($result);
  $result = applyDiscount($result);
?>
```

which could be used to generate a final total for invoice, the variable `$result` is run through a number of different custom functions. If when the code was run, the end total is incorrect, it's difficult to see exactly where in the code the error is occurring.

By adding extra echo statements, as in the following code:

```
<?php
  $total = $cartTotal;
  echo "\$total: $total <br>";

  $result = addPackaging($result);
  echo "addPackaging \$result: $result <br>";

  $result = applyDiscount($result);
  echo "applyDiscount \$result: $result <br>";

  $result = addVAT($total);
  echo "addVAT \$result: $result <br>";

  echo "Total Price: £$result <br>";
?>
```

It would produce output similar to the following:

$total: 100.75
addPackaging $result: 110.75
applyDiscount $result: 0.355
addVAT $result: 0.41
Total Price: £0.41

By displaying the variable `$result` as it moves through the different functions, you can see where the error occurs, in the above case the result from the `addDiscount` function is incorrect, so you would take a closer look at the code in that function.

Adding to the Debug Information with gettype()

We can now expand on this using the PHP `gettype()` function. This function is passed a variable as a parameter, and returns the variable's type: integer, string, etc.

So we can modify our statement to include the `gettype()` function:

```
echo "\$testValue : $testvalue : " . gettype($testValue) . " <br> ";
```

Now when the page is opened in a browser, it shows:

$testValue : 25 : integer

which is more useful.

Creating a Debugging Function

Although using the above `echo()` statement does what we want, it's a chore if you have to keep typing:

```
echo "\$testValue : $testvalue : " . gettype($testValue) . " <br> ";
```

at various points in your code to check the value of variables. To make things easier, we're going to create a function, into which we'll add our code:

```
<?php
  function debuginfo($param1, $param2)
  {
    echo "\$$param2 : $param1 : " . gettype($param1) . "<br>";
  }
?>
```

We can now call this function in our code using:

```
debuginfo($string, "stringname");
```

So if we have a variable called `$teststring`, you can call the function as follows:

```
debuginfo($teststring,"teststring");
```

This is much easier and quicker to type. The output for `$teststring` is:

$teststring : Hello World : string

Next, we'll start adding to the function to make it more useful.

Creating a Global Debug Option

It's useful to be able to leave your debug function calls in your code on a permanent basis, and it's even worth going so far as to add them as you're creating the page.

However, we don't want the debug functions to show when the page is normal use, so we are going to add a switch so we can turn the function on and off, as appropriate. We are going to use the variable `$debug` as our switch, and it can be set to `true` or `false`.

Adding this to our function gives the following code:

```
<?php
  function debuginfo($param1, $param2)
  {
    global $debug;
    if ($debug == true)
      echo "\$$param2 : $param1 : " . gettype($param1) . "<br>";
  }
?>
```

We can now set `$debug` on our page once, and it will apply to every use of the `debuginfo` function. Normally, variables in the main script cannot be used inside functions. Declaring `$debug` as global means that it can be seen from within the function, even though it is declared outside of the function.

309

To turn our function on, we use:

```
$debug = true;
```

To turn it off, we use:

```
$debug = false;
```

We can now activate or de-activate the `debuginfo()` function by setting the one variable. If you don't declare or set the variable `$debug` in your main script, then by default the `debuginfo()` function is turned off.

To set up the script so that you can quickly turn on the `debuginfo()` function using the page URL, add the following code:

```
$debug = $HTTP_GET_VARS['debug'];
```

if your normal page URL is:

http://www.mywebsite.com/testpage.php

You can turn on the `debuginfo()` function by using the URL:

http://www.mywebsite.com/testpage.php?debug=true

This only works if `$debug` is not set to `false` in your main script. It's very useful however, as it allows you to turn on debugging and check the status of your page, without having to make a change to the code and uploading the page again.

Adding Array Support Into the debuginfo() Function

Next we're going to add to the `debuginfo()` function, so that it can handle arrays which are passed to it.

The new code is shown below:

```
<?php
function debuginfo($param1, $param2, $param3){
  global $debug;
  if ($debug == true){
    if (gettype($param1) == "array") {
      if (count($param1) > 0 ) {
        echo "
          <table width='200' border='1' cellspacing='0' cellpadding='0'>
          <tr>
          <td>
          <table width='100%' border='0' cellspacing='2' cellpadding='2'>
          <tr>
          <td><b> \$$param2 </b></td>
          <td><b> line: $param3 </b></td>
```

```
            </tr>
           ";
       foreach($param1 as $key => $value){
         echo "
           <tr>
           <td> $key </td>
           <td> $value </td>
           </tr>
            ";
       }
       echo "
         </table>
         </td>
         </tr>
         </table>
            ";
     }
   } else {
     echo "\$$param2 : $param1 : " . gettype($param1) . " line number: $param3<br>";
     }
   }
 }
?>
```

First of all, we've added an extra parameter, `$param3`, which is going to hold the line number that the variable occurs on. We can now access the `debuginfo()` function with:

```
debuginfo($variable, "variable name", line number);
```

We've also added a test to see if the variable that is passed to the function is an array, using the PHP `gettype()` function. We next check that the array isn't empty, in which case we ignore it by using the PHP `count()` function, which counts the number of elements in an array. We then send out some HTML code to create a table in which we can show the element keys and values. Look at the block of code that writes out the array's element details:

```
foreach($param1 as $key => $value){
   echo "
       <tr>
       <td>$key</td>
       <td>$value</td>
       </tr>";
```

We use `foreach` to loop through each element of the array, creating a new table row for each line. This means that the code creates as many table rows as necessary to show the array's elements.

Creating a Debugging Include File

To tidy our code further, we are going to move our debugging function into a separate include file. Open a blank page, and cut and paste the `debuginfo()` function (including the PHP tags `<?php` and `?>`), into the new page. Save the new page as `include/debug_helper.php`.

311

So now we have the `debuginfo()` function in an include file, all we need is the following code to load our include file, and then set the debug status:

```php
<?php include_once("../include/debug_helper.php"); ?>
<?php $debug = true; ?>
```

This code can be inserted onto any page to make the `debuginfo()` function available. We've used the PHP function `include_once()` as it's a good habit to get into. Errors can be caused by loading in an include file more than once, which could happen on a page with a lot of code and a lot of include files. As its name suggests, `include_once()` ensures this doesn't happen and makes sure each include file is opened once by the page, so should be used in preference to the ordinary PHP `include()` function.

debuginfo() in Action

Next we're going to show `debuginfo()` in action, by creating a simple form consisting of 3 fields: `name`, `age`, and `level`. The code for the whole page is shown below:

```php
<?php include_once("../include/debug_helper.php"); ?>
<?php $debug = true; ?>
<html>
  <head>
    <title>Using the debuginfo function</title>
  </head>
  <body>
    <form name="form1" method="post" action="<?php echo "$PHP_SELF" ?>">
    <table width="25%" border="0">
      <tr>
        <td>name:</td>
        <td>
          <input name="name" type="text" id="name"></td>
      </tr>
      <tr>
        <td>age:</td>
        <td>
          <input name="age" type="text" id="age"></td>
      </tr>
      <tr>
        <td>level:</td>
        <td>
          <select name="select">
              <option value="1" selected>Level 1</option>
              <option value="2">Level 2</option>
              <option value="3">Level 3</option>
              <option value="4">Level 4</option>
          </select>
        </td>
      </tr>
      <tr>
        <td> </td>
        <td>
          <input type="submit" name="Submit" value="Submit"></td>
      </tr>
    </table>
   </form>
<?php
```

```
   debuginfo($HTTP_POST_VARS, "formdata", 42);
?>

</body>
</html>
```

First we start with a blank HTML page. Add the following code above the `<HTML>` tag:

```
<?php include_once("../include/debug_helper.php"); ?>
<?php $debug = true; ?>
```

We then create a simple form with the three fields above, and set it to submit back to itself using:

```
<?php echo "$PHP_SELF"; ?>
```

for the form action. This automatically inserts the name and path of the current page when the script is run. Below the form we added the following PHP code:

```
<?php
   debuginfo($HTTP_POST_VARS, "formdata", 42);
?>
```

`$HTTP_POST_VARS` is the array we're sending to the `debuginfo()` function, `formdata` is the reference name we're giving the data and `42` is the line number the `debuginfo()` function is on.

Next we upload the new page to the server and load it in a browser. We then enter some test data, and submit the form, which gives the following result.

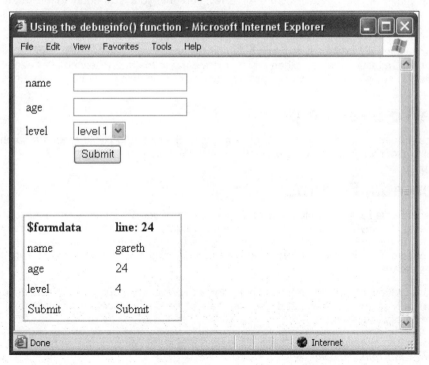

As you can see the `debuginfo()` function prints the form field names and values in a nicely formatted table.

Expanding debuginfo() Further

Although we used a very simple example to show `debuginfo()` in action, it can be extremely useful, and can help you see the variables during the script execution, so you can quickly spot errors.

`debuginfo()` is still quite simple, and there are many ways it could be expanded further, such as adding code to log the variables to a text file, instead of printing them to the screen, or only showing certain variable types, etc.

After a while, you'll soon have an ever-expanding debugging facility, to help keep your pages error free.

Two Brains Are Better Than One

It's often harder to spot errors in your own code, as opposed to another programmer's, as you know how the code is supposed to function, and it can be hard to see past this, and to see what the code is actually doing.

If you have a friend or colleague who also programs in PHP, it can be a good idea to swap code with errors. Not only can someone else probably spot the errors quicker than you can, but they can also give their opinion and suggest ideas you may not have thought of.

SQL Errors

Errors in your SQL can be resolved more easily if you print your SQL query to the screen, again by using the `echo()` function. This way ensures you can see the actual query that's being sent to the MySQL server, including the parts of the query that are dynamic and change at runtime.

If you're building a complex SQL query, it can be best to build it in segments, starting with a basic query and then testing that, and then adding extra parts to the query, testing after each part, until the final query is completed. This way is quicker and easier than trying to debug a complex query.

Where To Seek Help

If you get totally stuck with an error, or have any questions about PHP, there are a number of excellent resources available on the Internet which can help you.

Macromedia Forums

The Macromedia forums should really be your first port of call, if you have any questions or problems when using Dreamweaver MX. They contain a large number of friendly, helpful people, who are more than likely to be able to help you. Just searching through the appropriate groups can give you quick answers to your questions. The forums are available through your browser on the web, or through your newsreader.

There are groups for each Macromedia program, as well as subgroups in some cases, and they are "staffed" by Macromedia users, and also members of the Team Macromedia program, so you're sure to find the help you need.

Full details and addresses for the forums can be found at the Macromedia web site at *http://www.macromedia.com/*.

Web Sites

There are a large number of PHP-related web sites on the Internet, with new ones frequently appearing:

- *http://www.php.net/*

    This as the address suggests, is the home of PHP, and is an excellent resource for everything related to PHP. You can download the manual, latest build version, as well as patches and security fixes.

- *http://www.mysql.com/*

    This is the home of MySQL, and has the MySQL manual available for download, as well as the latest news and developments, and the latest versions.

- *http://www.zend.com/*

    Zend is the other home of PHP, and it is the Zend Engine that powers PHP 4. Again you'll find a copy of the PHP manual, searchable by function name, as well as a huge number of helpful articles and tutorials.

- *http://www.macromedia.com/*

    The Macromedia site contains all the latest news from Macromedia, as well as a large support section containing articles and tech notes for Dreamweaver MX. You should also take a look at the Macromedia Exchange, which hosts a large number of free extensions to expand the abilities of Dreamweaver MX, including a number of PHP extensions.

- *http://php.faqts.com/*

    This site contains a constantly growing database of PHP questions and answers, which are sure to help answer your questions.

- *http://www.phpbuilder.com/*

    PHP Builder is another excellent PHP resource, with articles, code libraries, forums, and other helpful items that can help with your PHP problems.

Newsgroups

There are also a number of newsgroups dedicated to PHP. Newsgroups are a lot faster moving, and messages are posted 24 hours a day. As a result, posting your question to one of the PHP groups can get you a much quicker response, and faster answers to your questions.

- *alt.php*

    Newsgroup for discussion of anything PHP-related.

- *alt.php.sql*

    A newsgroup for discussion of PHP and SQL.

- *alt.comp.lang.php*

    Another PHP-related newsgroup.

Another useful resource is the experimental front end for all of the PHP mailing lists, which can be found at: *http://news.php.net/*.

Summary

In this chapter we've looked at the different error types that occur in PHP, and discussed the default PHP error handler.

We then went on to look at how to handle errors with our own error handling function, which can show more professional and helpful messages, should an error occur.

Next, we looked at creating our own custom debugging function, which can be used to quickly see information about the variables and arrays in your script as it's running.

In the last section, we looked at various debugging techniques, and showed ways of getting help online, from web sites, newsgroups, and Macromedia's own forums.

Debugging Your Code

Index

A Guide to the Index

The index is arranged hierarchically, in alphabetical order, with symbols preceding the letter A. Most second-level entries and many third-level entries also occur as first-level entries. This is to ensure that users will find the information they require however they choose to search for it.

Symbols

 # (hash marks) comments, PHP, 242
/* */ (multi-line) comments, PHP, 243
// (double forward slashes) comments, PHP, 243
@ directive, PHP, 305
    error messages, example suppressing, 305
{} tags/braces, Dreamweaver MX
    Balance Braces, 244

A

ADD expression, ALTER TABLE
    column, adding to table, 190
        create_definition, 191
    indexes, creating, 194
advanced recordsets
    hotel booking system, 141, 149
        reasons for using, 142
    search engines, building queries, 207
        parameters, adding, 208
Advanced section, New Optional Region, 114
    see also Basic option.
aliasing recordset columns, 171
ALTER expression, ALTER TABLE
    column default value, altering, 191
ALTER TABLE command, SQL, 190
    indexes, handling on existing tables, 194
        altering NOT possible, 195
        creating, ADD, 194
        deleting, DROP, 195
    syntax, altering table structure, 190
        ADD, adding column, 190
        ALTER, altering column default value, 191
        CHANGE, modifying field definition, 191
        DROP, removing column, 191
        IGNORE, handling unique key duplicates, 190
        RENAME, renaming table, 191
Answers panel, Dreamweaver MX, 18
Apache web server
    configuring, PHP Linux installation, 25
    configuring, PHP Windows installation, 23
        PHP as Apache module, 23

Application panel, Dreamweaver MX, 16
    Databases/Bindings/Server Behaviors/Components sub-panels, 16
arrays, PHP, 221
    debugging, custom function example, 310
ASP (Active Server Pages)/ASP.NET, 9
    as PHP alternatives, 8, 9
Assets panel, Files, 17
auto_increment attribute, primary keys, 193
avg(expr) function, MySQL, 186
    GROUP BY using, 186

B

Balance Braces option, Dreamweaver MX, 244
    errors, handling, 288
    example, 244
Basic section, New Optional Region, 114
    see also Advanced option.
Behaviors tab, Design, 15
behaviors, Dreamweaver, 11
    server behaviors, PHP support, 11
        SBB (Server Behavior Builder), 265
Bindings panel, Application, 17
book overview, 1
    startup requirements, 2
    style conventions, 2
        code formatting, 3
    support/feedback, online, 3
    target audience, 2
Browser Specific options, tag editor, 230

C

CFML (Cold Fusion Markup Language), 9
    as PHP alternative, 8, 9
CGI (Common Gateway Interface)
    configuring PHP as CGI process, 23
CHANGE expression, ALTER TABLE
    field definition, modifying, 191
check boxes, dynamic
    hotel booking system, 132, 144, 151

Checkbox control, SBB UI, 279
check-in/~-out, Dreamweaver files
  site definition, Basic Configuration Wizard, 62, 64
Cloaking category, Advanced Site Definition
  specifying file types NOT uploadable to server, 68
Code * options, Preferences, 226
code blocks, SBB, 271, 272
  behavior/selection, UI, 272
  inserting into document, example, 270
    positioning/selecting code block, 275
  inserting parameters into, 273
  list/area, UI, 271
Code Hints system, Dreamweaver MX, 227
  functionality, overview, 227
    built-in PHP tag/function/variable references, 228
    inserting tag/seeing its attributes, example, 227
Code panel, Dreamweaver MX, 16
  Snippets/Reference panels, 16
Code view/inspector, Dreamweaver MX, 224
  functionality, options, 224
coding by hand, Dreamweaver MX, 217, 224
  Code view/inspector, 224
  good practices, 240
    Balance Braces, using, 244
    commenting code, 242
    indenting code, 241
    naming variables, 243
    View Options, code options contained, 241
  login system example, hotel booking, 246
  new features, 227
    Code Hints, 227
    Insert panel, 229
    quick tag editor, 231
    Snippets panel, Code, 237
    tag editor, 229
    Tag inspector, 232
    Tag Library editor, 233
  PHP code syntax, 217
  Preferences window options, 225
    Code Coloring, 226
    Code Format, 226
    Code Hints, 226
    Code Rewriting, 226
    Fonts, 227
  reasons for, 224
ColdFusion Data Source menu, SBB UI, 277
ColdFusion MX, Macromedia
  automatically detected, site definition, 58
columns, MySQL tables/recordsets
  selecting, SELECT, 169
    all columns at once, selecting, 171
    concat(), using, 170
    recordset columns, aliasing, 171
    table columns, selecting, 169
columns_priv table, MySQL, 42
comments, PHP, 242
  types, 242
    # (hash marks), 242
    /* */ (multi-line), 243
    // (double forward slashes), 243
comparison operators, 179
Components panel, Application, 17
concat() function, MySQL
  columns example, 170
conditional operators, PHP, 222
configuring MySQL/PHP, see installing/configuring.
Connection/~ Table/~ Column menus, SBB UI, 277

control structures, PHP, 221
  foreach, 222
  if, 222
count() functions, MySQL, 186
  versions, GROUP BY using, 186
CREATE DATABASE command, SQL, 38
  hotel booking system, 100
CREATE TABLE command, SQL, 39
  example, 39
  hotel booking system, 91, 92, 93, 94, 100, 118
crypt() function, PHP, 258
  login system example, hotel booking, 258
CSS (Cascading Style Sheets)
  Style Sheet/Accessibility options, tag editor, 230

D

Databases panel, Application, 16
  connecting to database, site definition, 71
databases, MySQL, 32, 37
  connecting to, site definition, 70
  creating, CREATE DATABASE, 38
  database-enabled sites, hotel booking system, 6, 117
  database servers, 31
  displaying, SHOW DATABASES, 38
  hotel booking system, 91
  overview, 35
    company employees/departments example, 36
    example, diagram, 35
  using, USE, 38
date() function, PHP
  custom error handling using, 303
db table, MySQL, 41
DBMS (DataBase Management Systems)
  Dreamweaver MX PHP support, 20
debugging, 307
  debuginfo() custom example, creating, 309
    array support, adding, 310
    expanding function, 314
    global debug option, adding, 309
    include file, creating, 311
    running, HTML form & output, 312
    turning function ON/OFF, 310
  echo(), outputting useful info, 307
  gettype(), returning variable type, 308
Default Images Folder option, Local Info, 66
Default menu, Editable Tag Attributes, 112
Default/Runtime Value options, Add Parameter
  search engines, building queries, 208
Delete Record server behavior, Dreamweaver MX
  hotel booking system, 160
DESC command, SQL, 40
  example, 40
Design Notes category, Advanced Site
  Definition, 68
Design panel, Dreamweaver MX, 15
  Behaviors tab, 15
Display Record Count pre-defined behavior, Server
  Behaviors, 267
display_errors directive, php.ini
  global error reporting level change, 294
DISTINCT/~ROW keywords, SELECT
  NOT selecting same row twice, 168

Dreamweaver MX, Macromedia, 12
    as WYSIWYG web page editor, 56
    coding by hand, 224
        Code view/inspector, 224
        good practices, 240
        new features, 227
        Preferences window options, 225
    functionality, panels overview, 12
        Answers, 18
        Application, 16
        Code, 16
        Design, 15
        Files, 17
        Insert, 14
        New Document wizard, 19
        Properties Inspector, 18
        tabbed document windows, 18
        UI, choosing, 13
    PHP support, 20
        DBMS supported, 20
        web servers compatible, 21
        Windows/Linux PHP installation, comparing, 20
    site definition, creating, 55
Dreamweaver UltraDev, Macromedia, 11
    PHP support, 11
        limitations, 11
        PHAkT/ImpAKT projects, Interakt, 11
        server behaviors, using, 11
DROP expression, ALTER TABLE
    column, removing, 191
    indexes, deleting, 195
DROP TABLE command, SQL, 39
DSO (Dynamic Shared Object), Linux
    installing PHP as DSO module, 24
dynamic check boxes/radio groups
    hotel booking system, 144, 151
Dynamic text field, SBB UI, see Text Field/ Dynamic ~/ URL ~/Numeric ~.
Dynamic Text/~ Form Elements pre-defined behaviors, Server Behaviors, 267
dynamic web pages, 5
    client-/server-side scripting, comparing, 6
    PHP creating, 5
dynamic web sites, 75
    architecture, 76
        flowcharts, using, 80
        hierarchical structure, 76
        hotel booking system, 76
        latency, using, 78
        site features, determining, 77
    database structure, planning, 78
    designing, principles, 86
        hotel booking system, 86
        layout, defining, 86
        navigation, 87
        site purpose & goal, defining, 86
        target audience, defining, 86
        tools required, 88
    site functionality/features, determining, 80

E

E_* errors, PHP, 290
    standard types, 290
        E_CORE_ERROR/E_COMPILE_~, fatal, 291
        E_CORE_WARNING/E_COMPILE_~, non-fatal, 291
        E_ERROR, fatal, 291
        E_NOTICE, non-fatal, 291
        E_PARSE, fatal, 291
        E_WARNING, non-fatal, 291
        listing, 290
    user-defined types, 295
        E_USER_ERROR, 295
        E_USER_NOTICE, 296
        E_USER_WARNING, 296
E_ALL/~_NOTICE error reporting levels, PHP, 292
    changing, example, 293
    default setting, 292
    error type operators, listing, 292
    globally changing, 293
        php.ini directives, using, 294
    per-script changing, 294
        error_reporting(), using, 294
echo() function, PHP, 307
    outputting useful info, 307
        debugging example, 307
Edit Tag mode, quick tag editor, 232
Editable Recordset/~ Field menus, SBB UI, 277
editable tag attributes, templates, 112
    creating, 112
    Type/Default menus, 112
Element Name option, Insert Navigation Bar, 107
Enable Cache option, Local Info, 66
error_reporting directive, php.ini
    global error reporting level change, 294
error_reporting() function, PHP
    per-script error reporting level change, 294
errors, handling, 285
    another person checking, advantages, 314
    custom error handling, 296
        @, suppressing error messages, 305
        customErrorHandler() example, building, 300
            expanding handler, 302
            output, 301
            set_error_handler(), adding, 301
            user_error(), adding, 301
        logging errors, example, 302
        mail(), e-mailing errors, 304
        restore_error_handler(), re-enabling default, 305
        set_error_handler(), 297
        trigger_error(), 296
    debugging techniques, 307
    E_* errors, PHP, 290
        error reporting levels, changing, 292
        standard, 290
        user-defined, 295
    installing/configuring PHP, 26
    logic errors, 289
        ; added unnecessarily, example, 289
    phpinfo(), viewing server settings, 305
        ini_*(), overriding configuration settings, 306
    resources, 314
        Macromedia forums, 314
        newsgroups, 315
        web sites, 315
    runtime errors, 288
        text into numerical input box, 288
    site definition, database connection, 71
    SQL errors, 314
    syntax errors, 286
        ; missing, example, 286
        } missing, example, 287
        Balance Braces, using, 288
        Line Numbers turned ON, advantages, 286
        variable name/type change, 288
escaping characters, PHP, 220
    escaped characters, list of, 221
Events options, tag editor, 231

F

fclose() function, PHP
  custom error handling using, 303
file_exists() function, PHP
  custom error handling using, 303
Files panel, Dreamweaver MX, 17
  Site/Assets panels, 17
filtering rows
  SELECT...HAVING, filtering recordset rows, 187
  SELECT...WHERE, filtering table rows, 178
    logical expressions, example building, 178
Fireworks MX, Macromedia
  hotel booking system, creating layout, 102
    slicing, using, 102
flock() function, PHP
  custom error handling using, 303
flow control operators, 181
flowcharts, 80
  hotel booking system, 83, 85
  overview, 80
    symbols used, 80
Fonts option, Preferences, 227
fopen() function, PHP
  custom error handling using, 303
foreach statement, PHP, 222
  debugging, custom function example, 311
foreign keys
  linking tables example, 174
  MySQL NOT enforcing, 174
Forms tab, Insert panel
  UI design tools, search engines, 201
FROM keyword, MySQL
  SELECT FROM statement, 172
FTP (File Definition Protocol)
  site definition, Basic Configuration Wizard, 61, 63
    editing/testing files remotely using FTP, 63
full-text indexes, MySQL, 194
functions, PHP, 223
  writing own & calling anywhere, 223
fwrite() function, PHP
  custom error handling using, 303

G

General options, tag editor, 230
gettype() function, PHP
  debugging example, 308
GRANT * commands, SQL, 44
  ~ ALL PRIVILEGES, example, 44, 45
  ~ SELECT, example, 44
  privilege names accepted, listing, 45
  syntax, analyzing, 45
GROUP BY keyword, grouping rows, 182
  functionality, example, 182
    implicit grouping, 184
  functions used, 185
    avg/min/max/sum(), 186
    count(), 186
  syntax, 184
    arguments, examples, 185

H

hand coding, see coding by hand.
HAVING clause, SELECT, 187
  filtering recordset rows, 187
header() function, PHP
  login system example, hotel booking, 259
HomeSite code editing tool, Dreamweaver, 13
  integrated in Dreamweaver MX, 13
host table, MySQL, 41
hotel booking system, case study, 6, 91, 117
  add_user_record.php, 118, 121
    adding Insert Record behavior, 127
      adding parameters to page redirection URL, 128
    connecting to database, 126
    creating page, 121
      name/address details, 123
      title/country, 124
    displaying, 128
    validating form, 125
  architecture, 77
    diagram, 78
  book_a_room.php, 118, 129
    creating page, 129
    displaying, 130
  booking system, 82
    planning, flowchart, 83
    SSL for credit card transactions, 83
  booking_cancelled.php, 120, 161
    creating page, 161
      URL variable selection, 161
    displaying, 162
  booking_details.php, 118, 131
    creating database recordsets, 134
      inserting name/surname recordset values, 135
    creating form, 132
      adult/children no. selection, 132
      dates/room type seelction, 132
      smoking/non-~ room selection, 133
      special requirements input, 133
    displaying, 138
    hiding/displaying text, 136
    inserting record into database, 137
  booking_updated.php, 120, 156
    creating page, 156
    creating recordsets, 157
      booking/client ID recordsets, 157
    displaying, 158
  cancel_booking.php, 120, 159
    creating form, 159
    Delete Record behavior, adding, 160
      adding parameter, 160
    displaying, 160
  canceling booking, 159
    booking_cancelled.php, 120, 161
    cancel_booking.php, 120, 159
  change_booking.php, 120, 146
    creating form, 146
    displaying, 147
  change_booking_details.php, 120, 147
    creating form, 147
    creating recordsets
      user details retrieval, advanced recordset, 149
    displaying, 156
    dynamic list/menu/check box/radio group, adding, 150
    Update Record behavior, adding, 154
      adding parameters, 155
  changing booking, 119, 146
    booking_updated.php, 120, 156
    change_booking.php, 120, 146
    change_booking_details.php, 120, 147

JSP (Java Server Pages)

hotel booking system, case study (continued)
  confirm_booking.php, 119, 140
    advanced recordset, adding, 141
      adding variable parameter, 142
      adding variable to WHERE clause, 143
    creating page, 140
    creating recordsets, 141
    displaying, 145
    dynamic check boxes/radio buttons, adding, 144
      adding link to change_booking_details, 145
  database structure, planning, 78
    info types stored, 79
    table layout/relationships, building, 79
  database tables, creating, 91, 94
    bookings table, 91
    clients table, 92
    layout, standardizing using templates, 102
    MySQL Monitor, using, 98
    phpMyAdmin, using, 94
      table wizard, creating table, 96
    room table, 93
    users table, 94
  editing template & updating page links, 162
    page links, listing, 163
    updating links, 163
  layout, designing, 86
  layout, standardizing using templates, 102
    accessing templates, 110
    creating layout, Fireworks MX, 102
      exporting sliced images into Dreamweaver, 104
      saving layout as template, 104
    defining content placement area, 109
    Navigation Bar, creating/adding to template, 105
      adding layer to page, 105
      Insert Navigation Bar dialogue, 106
      saving bar as Library Item, 109
  login system, administration, 85, 246
    create users PHP page, 247, 252, 261
    database users table, 247
    include PHP page, 249
    login PHP page, 256
    menu PHP page, 260
    overview, PHP pages, 246
    planning, flowchart, 85
  making a booking, 118, 121
    add_user_record.php, 118, 121
    book_a_room.php, 118, 129
    booking_details.php, 118, 131
    confirm_booking.php, 119
    confirm_booking.php, 140
  overview, 6
  requirements, 76
  search engine, building, 201
    building base query, 205
    building dynamic query, 206
    displaying results, 212
    UI design, 201
  site functionality/features, determining, 80
    booking system, 82
    flowcharts, symbols, 80
    login system, administration, 85
  $HTTP_POST_VARS/~_GET_~ arrays, PHP, 203
    search engines, building query, 211
    search engines, UI design, 203

I

if statement, PHP, 222
IGNORE expression, ALTER TABLE
  unique key duplicates, handling, 190
IIS (Internet Information Server), Microsoft
  configuring PHP as CGI process, 23

* Image options, Insert Navigation Bar, 107
ImpAKT project, Interakt
  as PHAkT enhanced version, 12
include_once() function, PHP, 312
  debugging, custom function example, 311
indenting code, 241
indexes, MySQL, 192
  functionality, overview, 192
    limitations, 195
  handling on existing tables, ALTER TABLE, 194
    altering NOT possible, 195
    creating, ADD, 194
    deleting, DROP, 195
  optimization using, 192
  types, 192
    full-text, 194
    multiple, 194
    primary keys, 193
    UNIQUE, 193
ini_get/~_set/~_restore() functions, PHP
  PHP configuration settings, overriding, 306
Insert HTML mode, quick tag editor, 232
Insert Navigation Bar dialogue, see Navigation Bar.
Insert panel, Dreamweaver MX, 14, 229
  inserting PHP tags, example, 229
Insert Record server behavior, Dreamweaver MX
  hotel booking system, 127, 137
installing/configuring MySQL, 33
  configuring database, 41
    tables, listing/describing, 41
  configuring privileges system, 42
    granting privileges, GRANT *, 44
    immediate effect of, 46
  installing on Windows, 33
    winMySQLadmin.exe, functionality, 34
installing/configuring PHP, 21
  comparing Windows/Linux installation, 20
    Mac OSX as UNIX-like OS, 21
  errors, handling, 26
    500 error returned when testing, 27
    blank page returned when testing, 27
    other errors, 27
  installation shortcuts, 21
  installing on Linux, 24
    activating PHP module in Mac OSX, 25
    compiling PHP as DSO module, 24
  installing on Windows, 22
    configuring PHP as CGI process, IIS v4+, 23
      NTFS users, additional configuration, 24
    configuring PHP as module, Apache 1.3.x, 23
  testing installation, 26

J

JOIN SQL statements, joining tables, 176
  aliasing tables, 178
  [CROSS] JOIN, simple joining, 176
  INNER JOIN, condition always true, 177
  JOIN syntaxes, 176
  LEFT JOIN, linking tables, 175
    example, 174
    USING keyword, 177
  NATURAL JOIN, listing all existing columns, 177
JSP (Java Server Pages), 10
  as PHP alternative, 8, 10

323

L

LAN (Local Area Network)
   site definition, Basic Configuration Wizard, 63
Language options, tag editor, 230
latency, 78
   dynamic web sites architecture, 78
Library Item, Dreamweaver MX
   hotel booking system, standardizing layout, 109
LIKE operators, PHP, 181
LIMIT clause, SELECT, 188
   limiting rows no., 188
      lottery example, 189
      simple example, 188
Line Numbers option, Code view/inspector
   errors, handling, 286
linking tables, 173
   SELECT...LEFT JOIN example, 173
      foreign keys & LEFT JOIN, using, 174
      query mechanism, overview, 175
      table relationship, diagrams, 173, 174
Linux
   installing/configuring PHP on, 24
List menu, SBB UI, 279
Local Info category, Advanced Site Definition, 66
   Default Images Folder/Enable Cache options, 66
log_errors directive, php.ini
   global error reporting level change, 294
logical expressions, 178
   filtering example building, 178
      comparison operators, 179
      LIKE operators, 181
      logical operators, 180
      parenthesis, 178
         flow control operators, 181
logical operators, 180
login system example, hotel booking, 246
   create users PHP page, 247
      displaying form, 248
      insert_data(), 252
      session_start(), security settings, 261
      using functions, main code, 255
      using page, 255
      verify_data(), 253
   database users table, creating, 247
   include PHP page, 249
      check_form(), 250
      check_password_length(), 250
      check_unique(), 251
      confirm_password(), 250
      trim_data(), 249
   login PHP page, 256
      check_login(), 257
      displaying form, 256
      using function, main code, 259
   menu PHP page, 260
      displaying form, options, 260
      session_start(), login/logout redirection, 261
   overview, PHP pages, 246
   requirements, 246

M

Mac OSX
   installing/configuring PHP on, 21, 25
mail() function, PHP, 304
   errors, example e-mailing, 304

manual input symbol, 82
min(expr)/max(~) functions, MySQL, 186
   GROUP BY using, 186
Monitor, MySQL, 98
   configuring, switches, 99
   creating tables, hotel booking system, 100
   syntax, commands, 99
multiple indexes, MySQL, 194
MyCC administration tool, MySQL, 46
   connecting to database, 46
   displaying tables list/structure, 48
   downloading/installing, 46
   executing SQL statement, 48
MySQL, 31
   as SQL database server, overview, 31
      advantages & disadvantages, 32
      database, 32
      downloading, sources, 33
      server, 31
      SQL, 32
   database tables, configuring, 41, 91
      listing/describing tables, 41
   databases, 35, 37
      creating, CREATE DATABASE, 38
      displaying, SHOW DATABASES, 38
      overview, examples, 35
      using, USE, 38
   foreign keys, NOT enforcing, 174
   hotel booking system, 91
   installation, Windows, 33
      winMySQLadmin.exe, functionality, 34
   Monitor, 35, 98
   MyCC administration tool, 46
      functionality, 48
      installing & connecting to database, 46
   PHPMyAdmin administration tool, 49
      functionality, 51
      installing & connecting to database, 49
   privileges system, configuring, 42
      granting privileges, GRANT *, 44
      user table privileges, listing, 42
   tables, 38
      creating, CREATE TABLE, 39
      deleting, DROP TABLE, 39
      retrieving table definition, DESC, 40

N

Navigation Bar, Dreamweaver MX, 105
   hotel booking system, adding to template layout, 105
   Insert Navigation Bar dialogue, options, 107
      Element Name, 107
      * Image, 107
      Insert, 108
      Show 'Down Image' Initially, 108
      Use Tables, 108
      When Clicked, Go To URL:, 108
nested templates, Dreamweaver MX, 111
New Document wizard, Dreamweaver MX, 19
New Optional Region dialogue, see optional regions.
NTFS (NT File System)
   configuring PHP as CGI process, IIS v4+, 24
Numeric text field, SBB UI, see Text Field/Dynamic ~/URL ~/Numeric ~.

O

operators, logical expressions, 178
   comparison, 179
   flow control, 181
   LIKE, 181
   logical, 180
   parenthesis, 178
optimization, SELECT, 192
   indexes, using, 192
optional regions, templates, 113
   inserting into template, New Optional Region, 113
      Basic/Advanced sections, 114
   usability, example, 113
ORDER BY clause, SELECT, 187
   sorting recordset rows, 187

P

parenthesis, 178
PHAkT project, Interakt, 11
   Dreamweaver UltraDev, PHP support, 11
PHP (PHP: Hypertext Preprocessor), 5
   alternatives to, 7
      ASP, 8, 9
      ASP.NET, 8, 9
      CFML, 8, 9
      JSP, 8, 10
   coding, syntax, 217
      arrays, 221
      conditional operators, 222
      escaping characters, 220
      functions, 223
      if/foreach control structures, 221
      opening/closing tags, 218
      statements, 218
      variables, 218
   Dreamweaver MX support for, 20
   Dreamweaver UltraDev support for, 11
   functionality, overview, 5
      dynamic web pages, creating, 5
      hotel booking system, 6
      server-side scripting, using, 6
   history, 7
      PHP 3 breakthrough in 1997, 7
   installing/configuring, 21
   resources, 223
phpinfo() function, PHP, 305
   error reporting levels, changing, 293
   server settings, example viewing, 305
PHPMyAdmin administration tool, MySQL, 49
   connecting to database, 50
   displaying tables list/structure, 51, 96
   downloading/installing, 49
   executing SQL statement, 52
   hotel booking system, 94
   running, 50
   table wizard, creating table, 96
   zero default value columns, creating, 97
Preferences window, Dreamweaver MX
   coding options, 225

primary keys, SQL, 193
   auto_increment attribute, 193
   definition, 193
privileges system, MySQL, 42
   diagram, 42
   granting privileges, GRANT *, 44
      ALL PRIVILEGES to boss account, example, 44
      ALL PRIVILEGES to employee account, example, 45
      ALL PRIVILEGES/SELECT to employee account, example, 44
      immediate effect of, 46
      privilege names accepted, listing, 45
   user table privileges, listing, 42
process symbol
   named/standard types, comparing, 81
Properties Inspector panel, Dreamweaver MX, 18

Q

quick tag editor, Dreamweaver MX, 231
   invoking, Design view, 232
   modes, 231
      Edit Tag, 232
      Insert HTML, 232
      Wrap Tag, 232

R

Radio Group control, SBB UI, 279
radio groups, dynamic
   hotel booking system, 133, 144, 151
RDS (Remote Development Service)
   site definition, Basic Configuration Wizard, 61
Recordset Fields ordered list, SBB UI, 278
Recordset/~ Field menus, SBB UI, 277
Recordset/~ Paging pre-defined behaviors, Server Behaviors, 266
recordsets, SQL
   columns, aliasing, 171
   hotel booking system, 134, 141, 157
   search engines, building queries, 205
Reference panel, Code, 16
Remote Info category, Advanced Site Definition
   Automatically upload files to server on save, option, 67
RENAME expression, ALTER TABLE
   table, renaming, 191
Repeat Region pre-defined behavior, Server Behaviors, 266
   search engines, displaying results, 213
repeating regions, templates, 114
restore_error_handler() function, PHP
   default error handler, re-enabling, 305
rows, MySQL tables/recordsets
   filtering recordset rows, SELECT...HAVING, 187
   filtering table rows, SELECT...WHERE, 178
      logical expressions, example building, 178
      operators used, 178
   grouping, SELECT...GROUP BY, 182
   limiting no., SELECT...LIMIT, 188
   sorting, SELECT...ORDER BY, 187

S

SBB (Server Behavior Builder), Dreamweaver MX, 265
  building server behavior, example, 268
    building UI controls for parameters, 279
    finalizing, 280
    inserting code block into document, 270
      positioning/selecting code block, 275
    inserting parameters into code block, 273
      parameters, listing, 274
    setting server behavior title, 275
    steps, 268
  building UI, Generate Behavior Dialog Box, 276
  code blocks, UI, 271
    behavior/selection, 272
    inserting parameters into, 273
    list/area, 271
  controls, UI, 277
    ColdFusion Data Source menu, 277
    Connection/~ Table/~ Column menus, 277
    Editable Recordset/~ Field menus, 277
    List Menu/Checkbox/Radio Group, 279
    Recordset Fields ordered list, 278
    Recordset/~ Field menus, 277
    Text Field comma-separated list, 278
    Text Field/Dynamic ~/URL ~/Numeric ~, 278
  copying server behaviors, example, 281
  overview, 265
    main window, 269
    pre-defined server behaviors, 266
  starting, 269
scripting
  client-/server-side, comparing, 6
search engines, SQL, 199
  building query dynamically, 200, 204
    base query, 205
      creating recordset, 205
    dynamic query, 206
      advanced recordset, creating, 207
    parameters, adding to recordset, 208
      Default/Runtime Value options, 208
      modifying query for price range, 210
      PHP source code, updating, 210, 211
  displaying results, 200, 212
    inserting dynamic values into page, 213
    repeating region, 213
  executing query, 200
  functionality, overview, 199
    diagram, 200
  hotel booking system, building for, 201
    base query, building, 205
    displaying results, 212
    dynamic query, building, 206
      beds no./price range options, selecting, 206
    UI design, 201
  UI design, 200, 201
    example designing, 201
      elements, listing, 202
    retrieving user input values, 203
      $HTTP_POST_VARS/~_GET_~, using, 203
      example, 203
    tools contained in Forms tab, Insert, 201
security
  login system example, hotel booking, 261
SELECT statement, SQL, 167
  columns, selecting, 169
  filtering recordset rows, SELECT...HAVING, 187
  filtering table rows, SELECT...WHERE, 178
  grouping rows, GROUP BY, 182
  hotel booking system, 92
  limiting rows no., SELECT...LIMIT, 188
    lottery example, 189
    simple example, 188
  linking/joining tables, SELECT...JOIN, 172
    FROM, using, 172
  optimization using indexes, 191
  retrieving rows without table reference, 167
  sorting recordset rows, SELECT...ORDER BY, 187
  syntax, 168
    DISTINCT/~ROW, NOT selecting same row twice, 168
    USING keyword, 177
server behaviors
  PHP support, Dreamweaver UltraDev, 11
  pre-defined, 266
  SBB (Server Behavior Builder), 265
    building server behavior, 268
    copying server behavior, 281
Server Behaviors panel, Application, 17
  pre-defined behaviors, 266
    Display Record Count, 267
    Dynamic Text/~ Form Elements, 267
    Insert/Update/Delete Record, 267
    Recordset/~ Paging, 266
    Repeat Region/Show ~, 266
servers, 31
session_start() function, PHP
  login system example, hotel booking, 259
set_error_handler() function, PHP, 297
  additional parameters, PHP 4.0.2, 298
  customErrorHandler() example, 301
  example, 298
  output, 298
SHOW COLUMNS FROM query, SQL, 101
  hotel booking system, 101
SHOW DATABASES query, SQL, 38
Show 'Down Image' Initially option, Insert Navigation Bar, 108
Show Region pre-defined behavior, Server Behaviors, 267
site definition, Advanced
  Cloaking file types NOT uploadable to server, 68
  Design Notes, usefulness, 68
  Local Info, local machine settings, 66
    Default Images Folder/Enable Cache options, 66
  Remote Info, remote machine settings, 67
  Site Map Layout, options specifying, 69
  Testing Server, configuring testing server, 67
site definition, Basic Configuration Wizard, 56
  editing files locally/testing remotely, 60
    checking files in/out, 62
    communicating with testing server, 62
    connecting to testing server, 60
      FTP option, 61
      Local/Network option, 61
      RDS option NOT available for PHP, 61
    copying edited file to remote server, 60
  editing files, overview, 58
  editing/testing files locally, 59
    communicating with testing server, 60
  editing/testing files remotely using FTP, 63
    checking files in/out, 64
    communicating with testing server, 64
  editing/testing files remotely using LAN, 63
    communicating with testing server, 63
  naming site, 57
  overview, 56
    configuration, ways of, 56
  server technology, choosing, 58
    ColdFusion MX automatically detected, 58
  summary, reviewing all entered values, 65

site definition, Dreamweaver MX, 55
   connecting to database, 70
      creating connection, 71
      errors, handling, 71
      naming convention, connections, 71
      testing connection, 71
   creating, overview, 56
      Basic Configuration Wizard, using, 56
      pre-requisites, 55
Site Map Layout category, Advanced Site Definition, 69
Site panel, Files, 17
slicing, 102
   hotel booking system, creating layout, 102
Snippets panel, Code, 16, 237
   adding function snippet, example, 238
      wrapping snippet around code block, 239
   editing/deleting snippet, 240
   inserting snippet into code block, 240
   sharing snippet, 240
SQL (Structured Query Language), 32
   ALTER TABLE functionality, 190, 194
      indexes, creating/deleting, 194
   errors, handling, 314
   MySQL, 32
   queries/commands, 37
      data access, 37
      databases, 37
      granting privileges, 44
      tables, 38
   SELECT functionality, 167
      columns, choosing, 169
      filtering recordset rows, 187
      filtering table rows, 178
      grouping rows, 182
      limiting rows no., 188
      linking/joining tables, 172
      optimization using indexes, 191
      retrieving rows without table reference, 167
      sorting recordset rows, 187
   statements, executing
      MyCC, 48
      PHPMyAdmin, 52
SSL (secure Sockets Layer)
   hotel booking system, 83
statements, PHP, 218
   see also control structures.
strings
   appending to strings, 220
   assigning to variables, 219
Style Sheet/Accessibility options, tag editor, 230
sum(expr) function, MySQL
   GROUP BY using, 187
symbols, flowcharts, 80
   manual input, 82

T

tabbed document windows, Dreamweaver MX, 18
table wizard, phpMyAdmin
   creating table, hotel booking system, 96
tables, MySQL, 38
   altering structure, ALTER TABLE, 190
   choosing columns, SELECT, 169
   creating, CREATE TABLE, 39
   database tables, listing, 41
   deleting, DROP TABLE, 39

   hotel booking system, 91
      creating tables, 94
   joining, SELECT...JOIN, 176
      aliasing tables, 178
   linking, SELECT...LEFT JOIN, 173
   multiple table references, SELECT, 172
   retrieving table definition, DESC, 40
tables_priv table, MySQL, 41
tag editor, Dreamweaver MX, 229
   Tag Info feature, 231
   tag options, displaying, 230
      General/Browser Specific, 230
      Language/Events, 230
      Style Sheet/Accessibility, 230
Tag inspector, Dreamweaver MX, 232
Tag Library editor, Dreamweaver MX, 233
   adding new tags, 233
      adding tag attributes, 235
      output, 236
   editing/deleting tags, 237
tags, PHP
   opening/closing PHP code, 218
templates, Dreamweaver MX, 102
   editable tag attributes, 112
   hotel booking system, standardizing table layout, 102
      accessing templates, 110
      creating layout, 102
      Navigation Bar, creating/adding to template, 105
   nested, 111
   optional regions, 113
   repeating regions, 114
Testing Server category, Advanced Site Definition, 67
Text Field comma-separated list, SBB UI, 278
Text Field/Dynamic ~/URL ~/Numeric ~ controls, SBB UI, 278
   building server behavior, example, 279
text fields
   hotel booking system, 123, 132, 133
track_errors directive, php.ini
   global error reporting level change, 294
trigger_error() function, PHP, 296
   examples, 296
   user_error() as alias of, 297
Type menu, Editable Tag Attributes, 112

U

UI (user interface)
   choosing, Dreamweaver MX, 13
      UI changes, HomeSite integration, 13
   SBB (Server Behavior Builder), 271
      building UI, Generate Behavior Dialog Box, 276
      code blocks, 271
      controls, 277
   search engines, SQL, 200
      hotel booking system, 201
UNIQUE indexes, MySQL, 193
Update Record server behavior, Dreamweaver MX
   hotel booking system, 154, 155
URL text field, SBB UI, see Text Field/Dynamic ~/URL ~/Numeric ~.
USE command, SQL, 38
   hotel booking system, 100
Use Tables option, Insert Navigation Bar, 108
user table, MySQL, 41
   privileges, listing, 42

user_error() function, PHP, 297
  customErrorHandler() example, 301
USING keyword, MySQL
  SELECT FROM LEFT JOIN USING statement, 177

V

variables, PHP, 218
  appending strings to strings, 220
  assigning strings to variables, 219
  naming, 218, 243
    str/val/rs prefixes, using, 243
  values, 219
View Options menu, Code, 241

W

When Clicked, Go To URL: option, Insert Navigation Bar, 108
WHERE clause, SELECT, 178
  filtering table rows, 178
  hotel booking system, 142
    adding variable to WHERE, 143
Windows, Microsoft
  installing/configuring MySQL on, 33
  installing/configuring PHP on, 22
Wrap Tag mode, quick tag editor, 232
WYSIWYG (What You See Is What You Get)
  Dreamweaver MX as WYSIWYG web page editor, 56

Notes

Notes

Notes

Notes

Notes

Notes

Notes

Notes

Notes

Notes

Also from glasshaus:

web professional to web professional

Usable Web Menus

Andy Beaumont, Dave Gibbons, Jody Kerr, Jon Stephens

1-904151-02-7

March 2002

US: $19.99
C: $ 29.95
UK: £15.99

When developing a web site, one of the most important things to consider is the navigation menu, to allow your users to find their way around it. It needs to be usable, informative, and well implemented, but this can take time.

This book will take all the hassle out of implementing web menus, in whatever style and technology you wish, by providing full code samples, along with walkthrough tutorials on how they work to allow easy customisation for your own needs.

Includes

Guidelines on designing usable web menus, with 12 common-sense rules to follow
Information Architecture for menus (including identifying your target user), and user testing
Easy to Follow tutorials on building menus with HTML, JavaScript, CSS and Flash
Advanced tutorials on dynamically populating menus from XML and databases with server-side scripting, including PHP and ASP
Extensive Web support including fully adaptable downloadable code for your own use and a gallery of working menu examples

Practical JavaScript for the Usable Web

Paul Wilton, Stephen Williams, Sing Li

1-904151-05-1

March 2002

US $ 39.99
C $ 52.95
£ 28.99

This is a new kind of JavaScript book. It's not cut'n'paste, it's not a reference, and it's not an exhaustive investigation of the JavaScript language. It is about client-side, web focused, and task-oriented JavaScript.

JavaScript is a core skill for web professionals, and as every web professional knows, client-side JavaScript can produce all sorts of glitches and bugs. 'Practical JavaScript for the Usable Web' takes a two pronged approach to learning the JavaScript that you need to get your work done: teaching the core client-side JavaScript that you need to incorporate usable interactivity into your web applications, including many short functional scripts, and building up a complete application with shopping cart functionality.

When you have finished working with this book, you'll have a thorough grounding in client-side JavaScript, and be able to construct your own client-side functionality quickly, easily, and without falling into any of the usability traps that this technology leaves wide open.

Also from glasshaus:

web professional to web professional

Usability: The Site Speaks for Itself

Kelly Braun, Max Gadney, Matt Haughey, Adrian Roselli, Don Synstelien, Tom Walter, David Wertheimer

1-904151-03-5

May 2002

US: $49.99
C: $77.99
UK: £36.99

This book features case studies in usability and information architecture from the makers of **eBay**, **SynFonts** (a Flash-driven font foundry e-commerce site), the **BBC News Online** site, **Economist.com** web site, **evolt.org** (a peer-to-peer web professional site), and **MetaFilter**.

There are no hard-and-fast rules for usability on the Web, which is why this book steers away from the rigid prescriptions of gurus. Instead, it looks at six very different, but highly usable sites. The web professionals behind these sites discuss the design of each from their inception to today, how they solicited and responded to feedback, how they identified and dealt with problems, and how they met the audience's needs and expectations.

This book is edited by Molly E. Holzschlag, a member of Web Standards Project (WaSP) and author of a dozen books on web technologies, and Bruce Lawson, glasshaus brand manager.

Cascading Style Sheets: Separating Content from Presentation

Owen Briggs, Steven Champeon, Eric Costello, Matt Patterson

1-904151-04-3

May 2002

US $ 34.99
C: $54.99
UK: £25.99

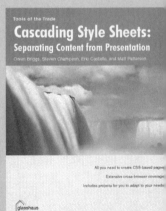

This is a focused guide to using Cascading Style Sheets (CSS) for the visual design of web pages. It's practical, there's no fluff, and the core CSS skills are balanced by techniques for using the technology in today's browsers.

With CSS, we can lay out HTML data on a web page without either misusing tags or using hacks to get the page looking right. The complete separation of content from presentation enables web professionals to change the entire design of a site by modifying one stylesheet, rather than updating every document that the web site contains.

CSS is one of the trio of core client-side web professional skills: HTML for markup, JavaScript for dynamism, and CSS for style. All web professionals who want to take their page design to the next level, with all the advantages that CSS brings, will need this book.

web professional to web professional

glasshaus writes books for you. Any suggestions, or ideas about how you want information given in your ideal book will be studied by our team. Your comments are always valued at glasshaus.

Free phone in USA 800-873 9769
Fax (312) 893 8001

UK Tel.: (0121) 687 4100   Fax: (0121) 687 4101

Dreamweaver MX: PHP Web Development – Registration Card

Name _____
Address _____
_____
_____
City _____ State/Region _____
Country _____ Postcode/Zip _____
E-Mail _____
Occupation _____
How did you hear about this book?
☐ Book review (name) _____
☐ Advertisement (name) _____
☐ Recommendation _____
☐ Catalog _____
☐ Other _____
Where did you buy this book?
☐ Bookstore (name) _____ City _____
☐ Computer store (name) _____
☐ Mail order _____
☐ Other _____

What influenced you in the purchase of this book?
☐ Cover Design   ☐ Contents   ☐ Other (please specify):
_____
How did you rate the overall content of this book?
☐ Excellent   ☐ Good   ☐ Average   ☐ Poor
What did you find most useful about this book? _____
_____
What did you find least useful about this book? _____
_____
Please add any additional comments. _____
_____
What other subjects will you buy a computer book on soon?
_____
What is the best computer book you have used this year?
_____

Note: This information will only be used to keep you updated about new glasshaus titles and will not be used for any other purpose or passed to any other third party.

Check here if you DO NOT want to receive support for this book ☐

web professional to web professional

Note: If you post the bounce back card below in the UK, please send it to:

glasshaus, Arden House, 1102 Warwick Road,
Acocks Green, Birmingham B27 6HB. UK.

Computer Book Publishers

NO POSTAGE
NECESSARY
IF MAILED
IN THE
UNITED STATES

BUSINESS REPLY MAIL
FIRST CLASS MAIL   PERMIT#64   CHICAGO, IL

POSTAGE WILL BE PAID BY ADDRESSEE

glasshaus
29 S. LA SALLE ST.,
SUITE 520
CHICAGO IL 60603-USA